Family Matters

Family Matters

Puerto Rican Women Authors on the Island and the Mainland

Marisel C. Moreno

University of Virginia Press

Charlottesville and London

University of Virginia Press
© 2012 by the Rector and Visitors of the University of Virginia
All rights reserved
Printed in the United States of America on acid-free paper
First published 2012

9 8 7 6 5 4 3 2 1

Library of Congress Cataloging-in-Publication Data
Moreno, Marisel C., 1973–
    Family matters : Puerto Rican women authors on the island and the mainland
/ Marisel C. Moreno.
        p.   cm. — (New World studies)
    Includes bibliographical references and index.
    ISBN 978-0-8139-3331-3 (cloth : alk. paper)
    ISBN 978-0-8139-3332-0 (pbk. : alk. paper)
    ISBN 978-0-8139-3333-7 (e-book)
    1. American literature—Puerto Rican authors—History and criticism.
2. Puerto Rican literature—Women authors—History and criticism. 3. Families
in literature. 4. Feminism and literature—United States—History—20th
century. 5. American literature—Women authors—History and criticism.
6. Puerto Rican women—United States—Intellectual life. I. Title.
PS153.P83M67   2012
810.9'9287'097295—dc23

2012012746

THE AMERICAN LITERATURES INITIATIVE

A book in the American Literatures Initiative (ALI), a collaborative
publishing project of NYU Press, Fordham University Press, Rutgers
University Press, Temple University Press, and the University of Virginia
Press. The Initiative is supported by The Andrew W. Mellon Foundation.
For more information, please visit www.americanliteratures.org.

For my husband Tom,
and our beautiful children, Gabriel and Mariana

In memory of my two abuelas,
Mama Sonia and Abuela Neya

All Puerto Ricans are today, in one way or another, inhabitants of *some other* island of Puerto Rico.

—Rubén Ríos Ávila

Contents

Acknowledgments

THIS BOOK REPRESENTS the culmination of a great deal of effort, and like everything else in my life it isn't something that I accomplished alone. A lot of people supported me along the way: family, friends, colleagues, and mentors put their trust in me and in this project. I can hardly imagine having succeeded in this endeavor without the crucial support of the American Association of University Women, which awarded me an American Fellowship for the year 2009–10 that allowed me to dedicate all my energy to the completion of the manuscript. It is difficult to overstate the role that this organization has had in my career as a scholar, and I hope that it can continue its mission of "breaking through barriers so that all women have a fair chance." I also need to thank my home institution, the University of Notre Dame, for all the support it has provided me during the preparation of this book.

Although many years have passed since I began to work on the foundation of this book, I am indebted to all those who provided me with their comments during those early, yet critical stages. I want to thank Verónica Salles-Reese, Ricardo Ortíz, and Ivette Hernández-Torres for their comments and suggestions but especially for believing from the beginning that this was a worthwhile project. Other friends and colleagues also provided me with their priceless support as my book project moved forward. My deepest gratitude goes to Rubén Ríos Ávila, Yolanda Martínez-San Miguel, Colleen Ryan, and Julia Douthwaite, and to my two anonymous readers from the University of Virginia Press, your insightful comments and suggestions have been invaluable. I am also grateful to Cathie Brettschneider, humanities editor at the University of Virginia Press, for her assistance throughout this process and for having been one of my greatest supporters all along.

Thanks also to my mother, Lourdes Lugo, and my siblings, Luli, Cristina, and Bilso, for their emotional support during these years; to my father, William Moreno, and my grandfather Papa. To all those friends who are practically like family, thanks for being there when I most needed you.

And finally, the publication of my book could not have been possible without the unwavering support of my dear husband, colleague, and friend, Tom Anderson. I thank him for giving me the strength to continue and for reminding me not to take life too seriously. Even though writing this book has been an emotional *del tingo al tango*, his humor has always been uplifting. I cannot end without expressing my deepest gratitude to our two children, Gabriel and Mariana, who have been amazing little companions during my academic journey. They helped me keep life in perspective and provided me with healthy doses of sanity when I most needed it. I know that we all had to make sacrifices to see my book published, but I trust that someday they will grow to appreciate its message and that it will help bring them closer to their Puerto Rican roots.

Sections of chapters 1 and 2 were originally published in *CENTRO: Journal of the Center for Puerto Rican Studies* under the title "Family Matters: Revisiting *la gran familia puertorriqueña* in the Works of Rosario Ferré and Judith Ortíz Cofer," vol. 22, no. 2 (Fall 2010). Reprinted by permission.

A section of chapter 4 was originally published in *Latino(a) Research Review* under the title "The Tyranny of Silence: *Marianismo* as Violence in the Works of Alba Ambert and Annécy Báez," vol. 7, no. 3 (2009–10). Reprinted by permission.

Introduction

Family Matters

ON SEPTEMBER 23, 2009, a group of Puerto Ricans in Hartford, Connecticut, participated in a historic occasion: the unveiling of the first Monumento a la Familia Puertorriqueña (Monument to the Puerto Rican Family).[1] As trivial as this event may seem, its significance in the historical context of Puerto Rican migration to the United States should not be overlooked. Prominently displayed between the Greater Hartford Academic Arts and Performing Arts buildings on Vernon and Washington Streets, José Buscaglia's sculpture stands as a reminder of the presence of Puerto Ricans in this country and of how they have contributed to shaping U.S. society. Its inscription, "Honoring the contribution of the Puerto Rican families to the development of the United States of America," also evokes the blood, sweat, and tears that millions of Puerto Ricans have shed as they have struggled to improve the living conditions of their families and communities in this country.

That this monument stands as a reminder of the Puerto Rican presence in the United States might not strike one as particularly noticeable; after all, the assertion of Puerto Rican identity on the mainland has been a predominant concern reflected in the literature, music, visual arts, and political and civic participation of Puerto Ricans in the United States. What is most remarkable about this monument, especially in light of this study, is that it not only revitalizes a cultural icon that has been predominantly associated with the island's past, but it reaffirms the patriarchal and racial mores that define that past. The implications of symbolically transplanting *la gran familia puertorriqueña* to the East Coast are many, not the least of which is the reassertion of familial ties between the island and its diaspora.

To those familiar with Puerto Rican history, the irony of two details of the monument's unveiling, namely, its date and place, adds another layer of symbolism to the already charged metaphor of *la familia* that this monument embodies. First, the date chosen for the event, September 23, marks the anniversary of the Grito de Lares, the so-called first nationalist revolt against Spanish colonialism, symbolic of the Puerto Rican struggle for liberation. The significance of this date thus allows for the interpretation of the unveiling as another, albeit harmonious manifestation of resistance against colonialism—in this case by inserting the greatest icon of Puerto Rican identity in the belly of the beast. Second, the place where the monument has been erected, Hartford, Connecticut, has emblematized colonial U.S.–Puerto Rico tensions since 1983.[2] In that year, the nationalist revolutionary organization Ejército Popular Boricua (Boricua Popular Army), better known as Los Macheteros, robbed a Wells Fargo facility in West Hartford and allegedly distributed the money among the poor. Hailed as an act of social justice by many but condemned as an act of terrorism by the government, this incident has survived in the Puerto Rican imaginary as a reminder of the conflictive relationship between both sides.

Puerto Ricans in Hartford have striven to efface the negative stereotypes that intensified after 1983. The election of Eddie Pérez as mayor of Hartford in 2001 was celebrated as a major achievement given that he became "the first Puerto Rican mayor in New England and the first nationwide to become mayor of a state capital" (Glasser 174). Unfortunately, in September 2011 Pérez was convicted on corruption charges and sentenced to eight years in prison, of which he will serve three. Although Pérez's predicament does not bode well for the image of Puerto Ricans in that state once again, there is faith that his successor, Pedro E. Segarra, will be able to restore that community's reputation.[3] For the hundreds of thousands of Puerto Ricans who did, or continue to, sacrifice for their community, the monument in the heart of Hartford constitutes both a celebration and a statement about the crucial role that Puerto Ricans have played in the construction of that society. However, at the same time, I find that the nationalist symbolism associated with the location and the unveiling of the monument undermines the image of Puerto Ricans as an integral part of that community. In this sense, the statue reflects the ambiguity and complexity associated with Puerto Rican-U.S. colonial relations. Yet, regardless of how one chooses to interpret its message, one thing is certain: the monument claims not only a symbolic space for Puerto Ricans in the U.S. mainland but also, and equally important, a space signifying that Puerto Ricans are members of a broader family that transcends geopolitical borders.

I have chosen to begin with this anecdote because I find that it encapsulates and brings to life some of the main arguments I put forth in this book, namely, that *la gran familia* continues to inform notions of Puerto Rican identity both in and outside the island and that the diaspora community has invoked this myth as a strategy to reclaim its kinship ties to the greater Puerto Rican family. Unfortunately, this desire to be recognized and embraced as members of the *family* has not always been reciprocated by communities on the island, which for decades have excluded migrants from the national imaginary. And here precisely lies one of the greatest ironies of their exclusion from the national family, given that post–World War II Puerto Rican migration to the United States "began essentially as a process of 'expulsion,'" as Edna Acosta-Belén and Carlos E. Santiago remind us (128).

A lack of knowledge about Puerto Rican history, on both sides of *el charco* (the pond, a common reference to the Atlantic Ocean), has definitely taken a toll on the way that each side imagines the other. As a young girl born and raised on the island, sometimes I also regarded with suspicion some of my second cousins who came back to Puerto Rico for Christmas speaking almost no Spanish. Yet at the same time, I found myself mesmerized by their effortless English, a language that I yearned to master but would not feel comfortable in until much later. Back then, I could not understand why so many of my grandparents' brothers, sisters, cousins, and friends lived *afuera*, outside the island (i.e., in the United States), and it didn't help that the subject of Puerto Rican migration to the United States was not openly addressed in school. It was not until I experienced living *afuera*, where I attended college and graduate school, and where I have been teaching for more than a decade, that I actively began to search for answers. In the process, I learned of a rich and complex history, and became aware of the negative stereotypes that I had internalized as a child. I also understood the disservice we have done to our communities by glossing over the history of half the Puerto Rican population. Luckily, there are scholars who have dedicated their lives to fighting for the preservation of that history and the memories that tie both sides together. Presently, an interest in understanding that history has been rekindled, to the point that "never before have the communities of the island and diaspora been so interested in discovering the issues and conditions that both separate and bring them together" (Acosta-Belén and Santiago 187). This study was born precisely out of that same desire to understand their continuities and discontinuities, albeit through an in-depth study of their literary traditions.

Family Matters reflects the spirit of a new dawn for Puerto Rican island-diaspora studies, achieved through a comparative, yet not exhaustive, analysis of narrative texts by some of the most influential Puerto Rican female authors from the island and the diaspora, including Rosario Ferré, Magali García Ramis, Ana Lydia Vega, Olga Nolla, Judith Ortíz Cofer, Esmeralda Santiago, Nicholasa Mohr, and Alba Ambert. I seek to demonstrate that the metaphor of *la gran familia* constitutes an overlooked link or "literary contact zone," a variant on the term coined by Mary Louise Pratt, as I explain below. In other words, my comparative approach emphasizes some of the connections that exist between these two literary corpuses but that have not received enough critical attention to date. In doing so, my study goes against the grain by juxtaposing key narratives produced in and outside the island, defying the tendency to examine these literary bodies independently of one another. While there are certain advantages to analyzing them separately, such as precluding the "colonization" of diaspora literature by insular intellectuals, completely rejecting a comparative approach can have an even more detrimental consequence: it can hinder a holistic understanding of Puerto Rican literature.[4]

The tendency to study these two bodies independently continues unabated, as is reflected in the recently published critical anthology, *Writing Off the Hyphen: New Perspectives on the Literature of the Puerto Rican Diaspora*. A polarized conception of Puerto Rican literatures becomes evident in statements such as the following: "From these earlier writers, and their texts, we begin to appreciate how the stark differences between the populations residing here and on the island grow more glaringly apparent with the consequent creative production of each generation. These are differences that will eventually necessitate resisting the nationalistic impulse to unite all writings created by all authors of Puerto Rican descent and establishing a space for literature written by Puerto Ricans born and residing in the United States" (Torres-Padilla 88). Torres-Padilla is correct to point out that there are significant differences between Puerto Ricans on the island and the U.S. mainland and that, consequently, there are disparities in the literary production of both sides. However, these distinctions do not preclude the possibility of regarding these two literary branches as elements of a more ample Puerto Rican corpus, if we are willing to conceive of it as an heterogeneous body of works that is united not just by a "nationalistic impulse" but also by the acknowledgment of a shared history and social memory.

Family Matters is the first book-length study to juxtapose narratives by Puerto Rican women authors on the island and its diaspora. While some critics have paved the way for the comparative frame I develop here, my book expands the limited scope that thus far has characterized this previous production. A recent and noteworthy analog of the present study, albeit conceived within a different discipline, is César Ayala and Rafael Bernabé's *Puerto Rico in the American Century: A History since 1898* (2007), in which the authors "have tried to move toward a history of both the island and its diaspora as facets of a single historical process" in order to avoid presenting diaspora history as "an appendix to an otherwise island-centered text" (11). This bold, fresh, and integrated look at Puerto Rican history finds a parallel in *Family Matters,* where island and diaspora production are examined in light of each other.

The focus of the present study also sets it apart from previous critical works published in either field, whether in insular or diaspora literary studies. In terms of the former, most previous book-length studies have focused primarily on the narratives of the 1970s, typically combining male and female authors. For instance, Juan Gelpí's *Literatura y paternalismo en Puerto Rico* (Literature and paternalism in Puerto Rico, 1998), Marie Ramos Rosado's *La mujer negra en la literatura puertorriqueña: Cuentística de los setenta* (The black woman in Puerto Rican literature: Short stories of the seventies, 1999), and Víctor Federico Torres's *Narradores puertorriqueños del 70: Guía bibliográfica* (Puerto Rican narrators of the 1970s: Bibliographic guide, 2001) exemplify the tendency to highlight the 1970s production. Mario Cancel's recently published *Literatura y narrativa puertorriqueña: La escritura de entre siglos* (Puerto Rican literature and narrative: Between-centuries writings, 2007) focuses on post-1980s narratives by male and female authors alike. All of these studies and anthologies have greatly enriched the development of Puerto Rican literary studies, particularly Gelpí's groundbreaking *Literatura y paternalismo*, with which I establish an active dialogue throughout my study. *Family Matters,* in contrast to the texts mentioned above, fixes its critical gaze on the 1980s and early 1990s in terms of insular literature, when the most salient female prose writers on the island published their first novels or novellas. Rosario Ferré's *Maldito amor* (1986; *Sweet Diamond Dust,* 1996), Magali García Ramis's *Felices días, Tío Sergio* (1986; *Happy Days, Uncle Sergio,* 1995), Ana Lydia Vega's *El baúl de Miss Florence: Fragmentos para un novelón romántico* (1991; *Miss Florence's Trunk,* 1994), and Olga Nolla's *La segunda hija* (The second daughter, 1992) are for the first time grouped together and analyzed as representative texts from the island.

My book also expands on the scholarship produced on the topic of U.S. Puerto Rican women's literature, which tends to focus on the 1990s and beyond, and either compares their production to that of other U.S. Latinas, as Ellen McCracken's *New Latina Narrative: The Feminine Space of Postmodern Ethnicity* (1999) and Juanita Heredia's *Transnational Latina Narratives in the Twenty-First Century* (2009) illustrate, or simply examines it in conjunction with that of male authors, as in Lisa Sánchez González's *Boricua Literature: A Literary History of the Puerto Rican Diaspora* (2001) and the critical anthology *Writing Off the Hyphen* (2008). Carmen S. Rivera's *Kissing the Mango Tree: Puerto Rican Women Rewriting American Literature* (2002), a compendium of critical essays focusing on the literature of women in the diaspora, is perhaps the book that most approaches what the present study sets out to achieve in terms of its exclusive focus on U.S. Puerto Rican female writers.

Family Matters, therefore, goes beyond the scope of previous studies by conducting an in-depth analysis of insular and U.S. Puerto Rican women's narratives. Perhaps even more important, it offers an opportunity to examine the dynamics between so-called First and Third World feminisms.[5] As M. Jacqui Alexander and Chandra Talpade Mohanty put it, First World feminism "often obscures relationships of colonial domination and, thus, potentially precludes the formation of alliances between Third World women within colonizing nations or between women in colonizing and colonized/postcolonial nations" (xxxi). I see the gap between women's literatures produced on the island and in the diaspora—and the perceived general lack of solidarity between authors on both sides—as a reflection of the division that exists between First and Third World feminisms.

However, the notion of First and Third Worlds in the context of Puerto Rico must be teased out given that they are not as apparent as they might be in other contexts. The complexity lies in the fact that in Puerto Rico's case, First and Third Worlds coexist as a result of the island's history and status as U.S. unincorporated territory. Clearly, Puerto Rico's development has given the island a significant economic advantage over many Caribbean and Latin American nations, which consider it part of the First World due to its close ties to the United States. At the same time, the island's colonial condition and the still recent memory of rampant poverty and deprivation are elements that are more in alignment with the predicaments of Third World societies.

Puerto Rico's unique condition as the "longest existing colony in the world," the island's transformation from impoverished colony to "miracle of the Caribbean" through an intense industrialization campaign in the 1940s and 1950s, and the massive exodus of working-class Puerto Ricans searching for opportunities on the U.S. mainland—in many instances only to see their hardships replicated in "foreign" soil—have all been crucial to defining the Puerto Rican experience not only at home but also in the diaspora.[6] The history of migration from periphery to center (i.e., from developing to developed countries)—or from Third to First Worlds—is not unique to the Puerto Rican case but has become part and parcel of the modern transnational world we inhabit. The presence of 50.5 million Latinos/as in the United States, a significant number of whom hail from developing countries in Latin America, and the transnational links they tend to retain with their countries of origin, often creates a situation in which the dynamics between home and diaspora are reflective of those between First and Third Worlds.[7]

In Puerto Rico's case, the paradox lies in the island's ambiguity; sometimes it is seen as an extension of the First World, and sometimes it is considered Third World. A similar ambiguity characterizes the experience of many Puerto Ricans in the diaspora; while the United States is indisputably considered a First World country, the experience of *internal colonialism* of ethnic minorities, such as Chicanos/Mexican Americans, is more in tandem with that of the so-called Third World.[8] For this reason, critics such as Talpade Mohanty use the term *Third World women* to refer to both "women from the geographical Third World and immigrant and indigenous women of color in the U.S. and Western Europe" ("Women Workers" 7). An examination of the cultural and literary production of Puerto Ricans at home and in the continental United States reveals a correlation between island/First World and diaspora/Third World, as contradictory as this may sound. In the case of female authors in Puerto Rico, many of the concerns present in their literary works—class, politics, sexuality, and gender equality—are more typically associated with First World feminisms. On the other hand, the issues present in the production of their counterparts in the diaspora—such as survival, violence, prejudice, marginalization—seem more in alignment with those of Third World feminisms. Yet, despite the significant differences that exist between these two bodies of literature, we are able to find strong links between them. In this sense, a study of insular and diaspora Puerto Rican literatures can help unveil some of the potential connections that exist between First and Third World feminisms, which have yet to be adequately explored in numerous other contexts.

In addition to exploring links between First and Third World feminisms, the present study contributes to the advancement of Puerto Rican studies in being the first to examine the foundational myth of *la gran familia puertorriqueña* from a literary perspective. Despite the central role that this metaphor occupies in Puerto Rican cultural, political, and literary discourses, no book-length study has been published exclusively on this topic. Gelpí's *Literatura y paternalismo* is one of the few critical works that highlights and examines the use of this metaphor in insular literature, raising provocative questions that I have taken on in *Family Matters*; for instance, does this metaphor appear in the novels of female authors, or how do their narratives enter into dialogue with this myth?

An examination of the trope of the family in Puerto Rican literary and cultural discourses also serves to underscore the affinities that link Puerto Rican literature to the broader landscape of Latin American letters. Twenty-five years ago, Djelal Kadir observed, "The literary family romance is inextricably enmeshed in the broader family history, the history of the histories of Latin America" (4). Doris Sommer's oft-cited study, *Foundational Fictions: The National Romances of Latin America*, expanded the inquiry on the family metaphor by examining the "mutual dependence of family and state in Latin America" (20). Focusing on pre-Boom, in fact, nineteenth-century canonical narratives, Sommer locates an "erotics of politics, to show how a variety of novel national ideals are all ostensibly grounded in 'natural' heterosexual love and in marriages that provided a figure for apparently nonviolent consolidation during internecine conflicts at midcentury" (6).

Of course, the role that the national romance played in Latin America during the period of consolidation of the new republics was not exactly replicated in the Puerto Rican context given that the island never achieved independence or state consolidation (Gelpí 64). However, despite political differences, the case of Puerto Rico, like those of other countries in Latin America, reveals the "inextricability of politics from fiction" (Sommer 5). Canonical works of Puerto Rican letters—Manuel Zeno Gandía's *La charca* (1894; *The Pond*, 1983) and Enrique Laguerre's *La llamarada* (The blaze, 1935), among others—also relied on the family trope to convey an image of national unity, especially in periods of crisis (Magnarelli 12). This is why the myth of *la gran familia puertorriqueña* reemerged with such vitality in the 1930s and mid-twentieth century, as I discuss in chapter 1.

My concern regarding the use of the family metaphor in post-1970s Puerto Rican women's narratives arose on the realization that female authors were questioning, challenging, and sometimes invalidating the inherited paradigm of *la gran familia*. Yet, despite their shared impulse to defy this model, there are noteworthy distinctions among writers, especially between island- and U.S.-based authors. Therefore, we must ask ourselves, is the myth present in diaspora works, and if so, how does it differ from island-based representations?

Clearly, the metaphor of the family is very much present in the production of women authors in and outside the island. Although this book argues that *family* encompasses a link between both literary bodies, it is possible that U.S. Puerto Rican female authors are engaging with a different conception of the term. For instance, as we know, the traditional nuclear family comprises father, mother, and child(ren).[9] However, the (virtual) absence of a father figure in many U.S. Puerto Rican narratives—including *Silent Dancing, When I Was Puerto Rican,* and *A Perfect Silence*—suggests that the fatherless model is more reflective of prevailing family structures in the diaspora. Possibly, this image serves to reflect the high proportion of Puerto Rican female-headed households in the United States (Acosta-Belén and Santiago 108). The absence of the father, in addition to the grandmother-mother-daughter paradigm that is emphasized in diaspora narratives (as well as in U.S. Latina and other ethnic literatures in the United States), mirrors the social patterns that have placed women at the center of the family structure. Whether U.S. Puerto Rican authors speak to the traditional or an alternative model of the family, there is no doubt that this metaphor is crucial to their critique and challenge of patriarchy.

As part of my investigation into the origins and development of this myth, my incursions into the disciplines of history, sociology, anthropology, and cultural studies have been indispensable in achieving a more profound understanding of *la gran familia*. Therefore, I have not hesitated to draw from these disciplines in order to enhance our comprehension of this myth. Another unique aspect of the present study is that it draws on archival materials from the Luis Muñoz Marín era that shed light not only on the prevalence of this myth but also on the diffusion strategies used by the government to disseminate its family/nation rhetoric throughout the 1940s, 1950s, and 1960s. Key among these was a series of books, posters, and movies produced by the División de Educación de la Comunidad (DIVEDCO), a "program for civic education piloted in 1947 and subsequently established as an agency within the

Department of Education in 1949," which stressed the importance of the family in the construction of the nation (Goldstein 320). Access to these rare materials has enhanced my own understanding of the central role of the family in the political rhetoric of the 1940s through the 1960s, and it has allowed me to better contextualize the production of post-1970s Puerto Rican women authors on the island and the mainland.

Concepts and Definitions

Before proceeding, let me define and qualify some of the terms that I use throughout the book. For instance, I employ the term *nation* with much trepidation and awareness of the problems that this concept can raise. Not only does a standard definition of the term still elude us due to a lack of consensus among experts, but the very notion of *nation* has been put under scrutiny by postmodern theoretical currents. Contemporary debates on the island regarding the nation have been polarized mainly in two camps: neonationalists (or *puertorriqueñistas*), who continue to defend the idea of a Puerto Rican nation, and *los posmodernos* (U.S. Puerto Rican intellectuals are usually placed in this category), who have questioned and sometimes denied its very existence. For instance, the postmodern intellectual Carlos Pabón claims that the nation does not exist because it is not a thing, but rather a "producción discursiva" (discursive production) (314). While I agree with Pabón to an extent, I also recognize the benefit of utilizing this widely accepted construct because it allows us to understand, and speak with, each other across borders. Understanding the limits of its usage, I have chosen to adopt Nancy Morris's definition of the nation as "a self-defined community of people who share a sense of solidarity based on a belief in a common heritage and who claim political rights that may include self-determination" (12).

I also borrow the concept *frontera intranacional* (intranational frontier), coined by Yolanda Martínez-San Miguel in her study *Caribe Two Ways*, to refer to the various frontiers/borders erected by Puerto Ricans on the island to mark their difference from recent migrants such as Dominicans and Cubans. I find this concept applicable to the emergence of barriers between Puerto Ricans on the basis of language, race, and location. In this study I have therefore stretched the original connotation of the term to encompass marginal Puerto Rican identities such as that of (return) migrants and Afro–Puerto Ricans.

In a similar vein, Mary Louise Pratt's concept of the contact zone has proved useful in shaping my arguments. Originally, Pratt used it to refer to "the space of colonial encounters, the space in which people geographically and historically separated come into contact with each other" (6). Contact zones are also spaces where "disparate cultures meet, clash and grapple with each other, often in highly asymmetrical relations of dominance and subordination," such as under colonialism or the slavery system (Pratt 4). Clearly, Pratt's usage of the term seeks to call attention to the power differentials between groups. My own usage seeks to reflect the power differentials that until now have informed island-diaspora relations. While these power differentials are not reflective of their intrinsic values—in fact, I argue that these must be considered as equivalent—it is undeniable that U.S. Puerto Rican communities and their cultural production have been marginalized in relation to both the island and Anglo-American dominant cultures.

More recently, Martínez-San Miguel has used the term *contact zone* to reflect on the postcolonial and neocolonial cultural exchanges that are taking place among Puerto Ricans, Dominicans, and Cubans throughout the Caribbean region and the continental United States (38). Here, I expand on Martínez-San Miguel's usage to refer to *literary* contact zones as a way to address the continuities that can be observed between the literature of women authors from the island and the diaspora. She seems to diverge from Pratt's original usage of the term by highlighting that in the Hispanic Caribbean, the context that she examines, the cultures that come into contact with each other might be different but not disparate (38). Thus, I follow Martínez-San Miguel's lead by applying the concept to the relationship between Puerto Ricans on the island and in the diaspora, which many view as "different" despite their commonalities.

And last, also aware of the various levels of controversy associated with the term *Latino/a,* I would like to qualify its use here in referring to Puerto Ricans on the U.S. mainland. For decades, scholars in the fields of ethnic, minority, and migration studies have debated the advantages and drawbacks of using *Latino/a, Hispanic,* or similar umbrella terms to refer to an immense and highly heterogeneous group of people whose only common link is their Latin American descent. The problematic nature of any such label will always lead to the risk of stereotyping and of erasing significant differences between and among group members. At the same time, such designations can prove beneficial to underrepresented groups in their political quest to obtain more rights. Amid the dispute, the term *Latino/a* has emerged as the preferred label due to its grassroots origins, while *Hispanic,* although still widely used, has been rejected by many as a label imposed on them by the U.S. government (Oboler 4).

In addition to the confusion that already surrounds these terms, their application to Puerto Ricans on the mainland carries with it further implications that render its usage even more problematic. Although plenty of people from diverse backgrounds reject the "Latino" label, opposition to it has generally been accentuated in the context of the Puerto Rican diaspora given the typically fierce defense of national identity among Puerto Ricans, undoubtedly linked to, and a product of, U.S.-Puerto Rico colonial relations. So, regardless of how individuals choose to define themselves, Puerto Ricans in the diaspora are imagined as members of a broader "Latino" community, because they share with other Latinos/as their minority experience in the United States. *Latinidad* thus emerges as a central experience for many Puerto Ricans in the United States, a phenomenon that has been examined by Mérida Rúa in the context of Puerto Rican–Mexican relations in Chicago. As she explains it, "*latinidad* is a cultural expression that embraces blood and fictive kin, lovers, friends, neighbors, co-workers, and even strangers in an everyday form of community building" (120).[10] The sense of *latinidad* that sometimes characterizes the diaspora experience constitutes a significant distinction between it and the community on the island, which does not identify itself as Latino/a and, some would argue, vehemently rejects such a denomination (except perhaps those who are return migrants) but which is sometimes ironically and erroneously labeled as such from the outside.[11]

Structure of This Book

Before fully embarking on a historical background and trajectory of the foundational myth of *la gran familia puertorriqueña*, chapter 1 addresses a topic that is intricately connected to it, despite not having received enough attention: the issue of canon formation in Puerto Rico. Here I examine the role that this process has had in the construction of the Puerto Rican nation based on Gregory Jusdanis's theories on the interconnection between canon and nation. This, of course, leads to a brief discussion about the *generación del treinta* (Generation of the 1930s), members of the intellectual elite who to this day continue to be regarded as the chief architects of the Puerto Rican nation. For the members of this group, the definition of Puerto Rican identity became the primary issue of their nation-building project. After three decades of American political, economic, and cultural infiltration on the island, these intellectuals hailed Hispanophilia, or the cult of all things Spanish, as a pivotal site of resistance against U.S. colonialism. Ironically, their struggle against one colonial power led to the exaltation of a previous colonizer, Spain.

The majority of works now considered canonical were profoundly shaped by the zeal of *hispanismo* (Hispanism) that shaped the world-view of insular elite intellectuals. Therefore, in order for us to gain a better understanding of Puerto Rican society during the twentieth century, it is imperative to take into consideration not only what lies within the canon but also what has remained outside it. One of the main arguments I put forth in this study is that the myth of *la gran familia puertorriqueña* was instrumental in delineating the contours of the canon because it was used to legitimize its "silences" through three main tenets: social harmony and racial democracy, the glorification of the past, and the cult of patriarchy. Throughout the twentieth century, the Puerto Rican canon was built on these principles and remained virtually uncontested until the 1970s, when voices previously silenced by the canon—women, blacks, homosexuals, and migrants—irrupted into the island's literary scene (Cruz-Malavé 139). How do female writers challenge each one of the principles underlying *la gran familia* and carve a space for "other" voices constitutes the main topic of the following chapters.

This study is firmly grounded in the conviction that the narratives of Puerto Rican female authors are linked by the myth of *la gran familia*. Chapter 2 examines the first tenet of *la gran familia*, that is, its claim of harmony and familial unity, through an analysis of Rosario Ferré's *Maldito amor* and Judith Ortíz Cofer's *Silent Dancing: A Partial Remembrance of a Puerto Rican Childhood* (1990). I discuss how these texts undermine the privileged site of *la casa patriarcal*—the "primal scene of the nation"—by revealing the anachronistic and exclusionary power structure embedded in *la gran familia* (Pabón 344). Race, class, and political divisions are central to my analysis of Ferré's text, while race and migration informs my discussion of Ortíz Cofer's narrative.

An inquiry into how the narratives of Puerto Rican female authors contest *la gran familia*'s principle of a glorified past constitutes chapter 3's focal point. Following a brief discussion of the role that history plays in Ferré's *Maldito amor* and Ana Lydia Vega's *El baúl de Miss Florence*, the chapter contrasts Magali García Ramis's *Felices días, Tío Sergio*, to Esmeralda Santiago's *When I Was Puerto Rican* (1993), in order to show how these semi/autobiographical works engage with questions about the past, history, and cultural identity. Never previously analyzed in light of each other, these two narratives reveal continuities as well as discontinuities that speak to the conditions that have shaped post-1970s Puerto Rican literature.

Last, chapter 4 looks at how the narratives of women writers contest the cult of patriarchy, the third main tenet of *la gran familia* and the strongest literary contact zone between Puerto Rican women's narratives. Their challenges to the system of patriarchal domination are clear evidence of the need to adopt a transnational comparative model. Following a brief discussion of the theoretical concepts that underpin my analysis of the relationship between patriarchy and colonialism, I move on to examine Olga Nolla's *La segunda hija* as a counterpoint to Nicholasa Mohr's "Aunt Rosana's Rocker" (1985) and Alba Ambert's *A Perfect Silence* (1995).

My inquiry into the three main precepts underlying the foundational myth of *la gran familia puertorriqueña* has forced me to reject any single or overarching theoretical paradigm, given that this would compromise the depth of my analysis. Instead, my methodology has required a more eclectic approach. Integrating literary analysis, cultural studies, historical and archival texts, and anthropological and sociological readings, as well as a significant dose of feminist and postcolonial theory, this study seeks to offer a well-rounded and complete analysis of Puerto Rican women's narratives. New readings of works that are now considered "canonical," such as *Maldito amor* and *Felices días, Tío Sergio*, in addition to analyses of texts that have not yet received the critical attention they deserve (Nolla's *La segunda hija*, Ambert's *A Perfect Silence*), contribute to the growth of the field of Puerto Rican studies by breaking with the tradition of separating Puerto Rican letters into two categorically distinct branches. The book's title, *Family Matters*, seeks to capture the need to acknowledge those familial links that unite the Puerto Rican communities on the island and in the diaspora. The comparative approach of this study offers a new paradigm for scholars engaged in international and transnational literary studies, such as that of all U.S. Latino diasporas, and will also prove useful to scholars in the fields of Latin American, Caribbean, migration, gender, race, and cultural studies.

1 The Literary Canon and Puerto Rican National Culture

There are many Puerto Ricos, united by a Möbius strip that enters and leaves our diverse national consciousness. The Puerto Rico of which literature produced on the Island bears testimony is very different from the one produced in the continent. Neither is more or less authentic; the combination of both is the most important thing, because it provides a comprehensive vision of our people.[1]

—Rosario Ferré

"AT ITS INCEPTION national culture is really literary in nature," asserts the critic Gregory Jusdanis, reminding us of the power of literature to create the illusion of unity among the various and disparate groups that constitute any given nation (xi). Literature is often seen as a "mirror" of the nation, to the extent that it succeeds in generating "stories about [the nation's] identity" (46). Yet how, we need to ask, do particular works become central to the construction of the nation while others are discarded and rendered nonessential? What are the criteria for the classification of texts as either dispensable or indispensable to the national project? Or, to put it more simply, how does a work become part of the national literary canon?

Unfortunately, there are no straightforward answers to any of these questions since the criteria for canon formation vary across cultures and fluctuate through time. What is clear, however, is the pivotal role that such canons play in the "survival of societies and traditions," which in turn "depends not only on memory to retain the past but above all on the formation of a hierarchy of prized texts transmitted through time" (Jusdanis 60). The canon, as "a publicly available body of writing, representative of certain national and social interests," primarily seeks to promote the perception of unity among disparate societal elements (Jusdanis 66). In doing so, the power differentials inscribed in the selection process tend to be eclipsed by the canon's success in imagining "unity." Jusdanis foregrounds this problematic caveat when he observes, "The mechanisms of canonicity conceal the classificatory strategies at work to preserve texts by making survival appear natural, self-evident, and deserved. They disguise the struggle waged by social groups over the power to classify" (63). Seen in this light, canon formation constitutes a highly politicized process; while trying to mirror the *nation*, the canon reveals the internal fractures that undermine its own ideal of unification. For this reason, examining a particular canon, as well as the silences created by those texts omitted from it, can reveal much about a particular culture/nation at any given historical juncture.

In the case of Puerto Rican literature, Rubén Ríos-Ávila argues, "the search for identity is without a doubt the organizing paradigm of the Puerto Rican literary canon" (201).[2] Examining the silences and fluctuations of this highly political canon can help us unravel the racial, class, and gender hierarchies that were at play on the island throughout the twentieth century, and which were the result of its complex colonial history. In fact, Puerto Rico's persistent colonial status and the fact that the mainland population presently outnumbers that of the island have contributed to the highly politicized nature of its canon.[3]

The connection between literature and politics underlying national culture is evident since the moment of consolidation of the Puerto Rican canon, which most critics agree took place in the 1930s (Barradas 2003; Gelpí 1993). While a sense of cultural distinctiveness had begun to emerge on this Spanish colony during the nineteenth century, the process was interrupted—and eventually refueled—by the transferring of the island to the United States as a result of Spain's defeat in the Spanish-Cuban-American War of 1898. Through the 1920s, a new generation of intellectuals born under U.S. rule (Antonio S. Pedreira, Luis Muñoz Marín, Pedro Albizu Campos, Luis Palés Matos) came to envisage "Puerto Rico as a national project truncated by the invasion of 1898" (Ayala and Bernabé 90). In the absence of a literary establishment, "the formation of a canon through the identification of classical texts became part of the objectives of the young authors of the 1920s as they matured during the following decade into what came to be known as the *generación del treinta*" (Ayala and Bernabé 91).

Three decades of U.S. colonialism took a toll and "ironically led to the crystallization of a desire for national affirmation among a significant sector of Puerto Rico's rising literary generation" (Ayala and Bernabé 93). The search for the definition of Puerto Rican identity became the primary goal of the *generación del treinta*, albeit conducted from a variety of ideological positions.[4] Deployed mainly against the perceived threat of U.S. influence on the island, the canon's symbolic role as national bulwark was geared to generating a sense of unity among Puerto Ricans. In searching for that common denominator that embodied anti-U.S. resistance, members of the *generación del treinta* turned their gaze backward to the island's Spanish past, which they posited as the true essence of Puerto Rican culture.

Thus Hispanophilia became a privileged site in the consolidation of the canon. In this process, several totalizing metaphors, such as the family and the house, became instrumental in evoking the perception of unity that literary traditions often strive to achieve (Gelpí 5). The patriarchal myth of *la gran familia* reemerged as a foundational narrative that continues to inform Puerto Rican letters even to this day.[5] The myth has been conceptualized along three primary tenets: (1) a unified nation built on racial democracy and harmony; (2) the glorification of the island's agrarian, precapitalist past under Spanish rule; and (3) the cult of patriarchy, embodied by a benevolent father figure. An inquiry into how each of these precepts intersects with Puerto Rican narratives produced by female authors will shed new light on the relevance that *la gran familia* continues to have in contemporary identity discourses. With that purpose in mind, I examine the inherent ambiguities in this myth: its paradoxical impulse to create a semblance of unity and homogeneity while erecting *intrafamilial* borders as it is revealed in Puerto Rican women's narratives.

Contesting the Canon: Female Authors Claiming Their Space in the Family

In *Literatura y paternalismo*, Juan Gelpí decries one of the most blatant omissions in Puerto Rican literary history, that is, the systematic exclusion of women authors from the canon (3). This absence from official literary histories, a fate also shared by black and other minority writers, is firmly cemented on the rhetoric of paternalism that envelops the cult of *la gran familia*. The subordinate position of women and children to a dominant father figure, a hierarchical structure that consolidated sexism as inherent to *puertorriqueñidad* (Puerto Ricanness), has thus been replicated in the terrain of culture. In other words, the silencing of women became pivotal to the defense of the nation among the white male elites, who condemned the more active role that women began to play in twentieth-century Puerto Rican society. For instance, this posture became evident when "the gains of the early-twentieth-century feminists and suffragists alarmed patriarchal writers such as Blanco and Pedreira," whose vision was decidedly antifeminist, according to María Barceló Miller (Matos Rodríguez, "Women's" 11).

While women had been silenced within literary circles, with the exception of those who ascribed to the traditional model of the "poetess" or those who in contrast broke away from such constrictive paradigms—such as Luisa Capetillo—they found ways to make their voices heard in other arenas. The first few decades of the twentieth century witnessed myriad transformations in Puerto Rican society, among them, the emphasis on education and the establishment of co-education as a method of Americanization, despite the fact that women's educational inequality continued to be imposed (Azize-Vargas 175).

At the same time, "women's oppression in the needlework and tobacco industries [had] contributed to the conditions for the emergence of class and feminist consciousness" (Azize-Vargas 177). By 1904 women had begun organizing in unions; by 1920, the Socialist Party organized the Asociación Feminista Popular, which established links with American feminists (Azize-Vargas 180). Such connections would prove pivotal in the struggle for women's voting rights as they paved the way for Puerto Rican suffragists to appeal directly to U.S. colonial authority in their quest for their civil rights (Jiménez-Muñoz 145).

If the strides made by feminists in the first decades of the twentieth century had elicited strong reactions from conservative circles, the reshaping of gender roles brought about by Operation Bootstrap and industrialization during the 1940s and 1950s, explored in more detail below, proved to have an even greater impact among those who defended the patriarchal values that had characterized preindustrial social relations. As Edna Acosta-Belén puts it, "The changes that occur in the traditional role of the Puerto Rican woman and her more visible role in society as a result of industrialization and modernization are simplistically viewed as a direct consequence of a harmful U.S. influence and adoption of an Anglo-Saxon-style matriarchy" ("Ideology" 130). One of the most strident voices to condemn women's advancement as an "ill effect" of Americanization was the prominent Puerto Rican author, essayist, and playwright René Marqués (Acosta-Belén 1986; Solá 1979).

In his essay "El cuento puertorriqueño en la promoción del cuarenta" Marqués states, "It was [with the democratizing gale wind that began] in the forties that Puerto Rican society made a rapid turn toward the Anglo-Saxon–style matriarchy. The cultural and ethical patterns of a social structure based on the tradition of the paterfamilias rapidly deteriorated [and succumbed vertiginously]" (*Docile* 78).[6] As this passage illustrates, Marqués's deep-seated anti-Americanism led him to assert Puerto Rican patriarchal values, which in his view dovetailed with his conceptions of patriotism and *puertorriqueñidad*.[7] Like other male elite figures who viewed certain societal changes as manifestations of U.S.

cultural infiltration, Marqués deployed the myth of *la gran familia puertorriqueña* as a strategy of resistance against U.S. colonialism not only in his creative writings and essays but also in the scores of government-sponsored cultural materials that he produced during his tenure with the División de Educación de la Comunidad, addressed later in this chapter (Acosta-Belén, "Ideology" 94).[8]

In contrast to earlier feminist waves in Puerto Rico, which had emerged out of suffragist (petit bourgeois) and proletariat (working-class) struggles, by the 1970s a number of feminist groups joined forces in the fight for social justice for all women (Vélez Camacho 15). Women's oppression—and the acknowledgment that its roots lay at home—became the pivotal cause that linked and continues to unite diverse feminist groups in the last few decades.

The developments of feminist, racial, and class consciousness propelled the conditions that facilitated the challenging of the myth of *la gran familia puertorriqueña*, which was then placed under scrutiny as marginalized segments of the population, such as feminist writers and critics (including some men) and homosexual authors, began to question its assumptions and to challenge the paternalistic canon (Gelpí 36).[9] Authors such as Rosario Ferré, Ana Lydia Vega, Manuel Ramos Otero, Magali García Ramis, Carmelo Rodríguez Torres, Carmen Lugo Filippi, Luis Rafael Sánchez, Edgardo Rodríguez Juliá, and Olga Nolla were among those who systematically questioned both this foundational myth and the canonical works it inspired. By unveiling the national fictions this myth has produced, their works often propose a more complex and nuanced articulation of the nation-family.

Undeniably, the civil rights and feminist movements were pivotal to the substantial transformations undergone by Puerto Rican letters on the island during the 1970s, which included but were not limited to the emergence of female prose writers, the development of central female characters, an interest in the working class and the use of popular language and musical expressions, the vindication of blackness as a core element of Puerto Rican culture, the questioning of patriarchy and traditional structures of power, and the defiance of stylistic and generic literary norms.[10] In addition to the direct impact of the civil rights movement, Puerto Rican letters were greatly influenced by the development of the *nueva historia* (new history), which promoted the study of marginalized sectors traditionally excluded from official histories. Women, Matos Rodríguez reminds us, "were among the neglected and marginalized groups that the new historians were supposed to incorporate into the mainstream" ("Women's" 13).[11] In 1970 the Centro para el Estudio de la Realidad Puertorriqueña (CEREP), or Center for the Study of Puerto Rican Reality, was organized under the direction of Ángel Quintero Rivera. "As they retrieved the history of forgotten labor struggles and initiatives," Ayala and Bernabé point out, "'new historians' also denounced the antilabor, sexist, and racist views held by some of the most admired figures both of the *independentista* tradition and of the literary canon built by the *generación del treinta*" (252). The revolutionary postures that emerged from the conflation of factors such as the effects of the feminist and civil rights movements and *la nueva historia* led a new generation of writers to openly denounce the androcentrism, racism, classism, and homophobia underlying dominant discourses of national identity.

These factors converged to facilitate the emergence of female prose writers, without a doubt one of the greatest sociocultural and literary achievements taking place in Puerto Rico during the late 1970s. Until then, the presence and recognition of female literary figures had been mainly circumscribed to the genre of poetry, and lyrical poetry at that. For this new generation of budding writers (most were university students) who had been deeply influenced by recent social transformations, the current literary establishment did not offer a forum for development and exposure. Taking the matter into their own hands, and guided by their mentors Ángel Rama and Marta Traba, Rosario Ferré—with the collaboration of Manuel Ramos Otero and her cousin Olga Nolla, among others—founded the antiestablishment literary journal *Zona de carga y descarga*.[12] During its brief run, which lasted from September 1972 until June 1975, *Zona* emerged as a key, and the first, venue of expression for many of the young writers who would later become widely recognized literary figures.

Although a detailed analysis of *Zona* is beyond the scope of the present study, it is imperative to highlight the role that the journal played in the dissemination of works by feminist writers and critics, as well as its commitment to challenging the patriarchal and paternalist establishment that had silenced them (Gelpí 1993; Ramos Rosado 1999). In an interview with Carmen Dolores Hernández, Ferré reflects on the feminist vision of the journal: "A fully achieved goal of *Zona carga y descarga*'s was to allow woman's authentic voice to be known, given that until then its creative expression had been silenced by patriarchal society. In *Zona*, we women, who were the majority from the beginning, broke our silence and achieved full expression" ("Mientras" 104).[13] The journal's pro-feminist, pro-homosexual, and anticolonial stances provoked a backlash from conservative circles and generated a significant amount of debate, ironically one of the main aims behind its publication. The posture of previous generations was crystallized in a letter that René Marqués sent to Ferré, and which *Zona* published in 1975. Marqués's letter, written in a sarcastic and condescending tone (evident beginning with the salutation, "Querida Rosarito," or "Dear Rosarito"), admonishes Ferré for her journal's "pornographic" materials and content, its profanity, and, above all, its feminist (i.e., Americanized) ideology. For example, he writes, "By the way, regarding the so-called Women's Liberation Movement, how should I address you? By Srta., Sra., Mrs., or Ms.? We poor men are somewhat confused regarding this point. . . . Not that I am a 'chauvinistic pig.' I accept any positive changes in society. But you have to enlighten me. So that I know" ("Carta" 26).[14] Ferré never published a response to Marqués's letter, her apparent silence repeatedly broken by each one of her subsequent publications. In fact, we could say that Ferré has been answering Marqués's inflammatory statements for the past thirty-five years (her latest publication is her novel *Lazos de sangre*, 2010) by remaining committed to producing literature focused on women's rights and female empowerment.[15]

Despite its short three-year life span, *Zona* paved the way for an explosion in Puerto Rican women's narratives. The year 1976 marks another milestone in Puerto Rican society and its letters. On the one hand, the Reforma de Familia (Family Reform), better known as Ley 51 (Law 51), which sought to provide more rights to women within marriage, was passed that year (Vélez Camacho 18). On the other hand, the publication of Ferré's *Papeles de Pandora* and Magali García Ramis's *La familia de todos nosotros* signaled not only a definite rupture with the establishment but also the official entrance of female prose writers into the island's literary scene, a trend that would reach unprecedented proportions in the decades to follow.

The female-led literary "boom" that took place in the 1980s—when Ferré, Vega, Nolla, Lugo Filippi, and García Ramis published innovative works—contributed to shaping what has come to be known as *nueva narrativa* (new narrative). The *nueva narrativa* constituted a new direction in Puerto Rican letters that challenged the paternalistic canon.[16] In *Literatura y paternalismo*, Gelpí demonstrates how Ferré's and Vega's counter-canonical stance signaled a rupture with the paternalist tradition, which solidified their location outside the canon (136). While their status as "outsiders" accurately describes their condition at that particular historical juncture, today their status as canonical figures is widely recognized and accepted (Aparicio 1998; Acosta-Belén 1986; Hernández 2007). Their seemingly paradoxical translocation from the periphery to the center, from a counter-canonical position to inclusion in the establishment, is noteworthy given that it attests to the malleable texture of literary canons.

Perhaps no single Puerto Rican female author has tested the boundaries of the canon to the extent that Ferré has done since her writing career was set in motion almost forty years ago. For instance, in *Maldito amor* Ferré challenges and parodies the paternalistic canon through her systematic questioning of the myth of *la gran familia puertorriqueña* (Gelpí 157).[17] The novel's dismantling of most of the core tenets of this foundational myth—familial unity and racial harmony under a white/European benevolent father figure—allows it to be read as a counternarrative to the Puerto Rican canon that challenges the paradigm of the nation-family. Moreover, Ferré's decision to write and publish novels in English beginning in the late 1990s in an effort to reinvent herself "as a transnational writer in order to increase her Anglo audience" refueled the debate surrounding language and identity politics on the island, where Spanish is still considered to embody the "essence" of the nation (Aparicio, "Writing" 86).[18] As a canonical author, Ferré's use of English hints at the possibility of a *bilingual* Puerto Rican canon. While it may be too difficult to fully measure the impact of her decision on Puerto Rican letters, the strong reaction it provoked among critics on both sides—language purists on the island and those who condemn her for trying to pass as a "Latina" author on the U.S. mainland—reminds us of how slippery the terrain of cultural identity can be for canonical and marginalized writers alike.[19]

The last two decades of the twentieth century marked the flourishing of Puerto Rican women's prose narrative, not only on the island, but also in the diaspora, where several female authors gained recognition as key figures in the U.S. Puerto Rican and the U.S. Latina/o canons. Much like their counterparts on the island, the civil rights and feminist movements of the 1960s and 1970s had a profound impact on their works. In fact, this period was so critical to the development of Latina letters that Kevane and Heredia are quick to assert that "if it were not for the social movements of the 1960s, it is doubtful whether U.S. Latina literature would exist today" (3). As they gained a deeper understanding of the multidimensionality of their subordination, U.S. Latinas found themselves excluded by both Anglo middle-class feminism and by a male-oriented

U.S. Latino movement, a situation that led them to assume an oppositional stance toward these discourses. In doing so, they began "to forge
and articulate a feminist consciousness and a collective sense of struggle based on their experiences as members of diverse individual nationalities, as well as on their collective panethnic and cross-border identities as Latinas and women of color" (Acosta-Belén and Bose 1114). Also
critical to the development of U.S. Latina/Puerto Rican feminist studies
was scholarship produced in the field of history by Virginia Sánchez Korrol, Altagracia Ortiz, Ruth Glasser, and Carmen Whalen, among others, who sought to recuperate the history of Puerto Rican women in the
diaspora.

While U.S. Puerto Rican literary production reached a high point
during the 1960s and 1970s as a result of the awareness brought about
by this period's social movements, most of this production remained
male-centered and perpetuated misogynist stereotypes of women.[20]
The Nuyorican corpus was defined by its emphasis on street life in the
urban ghetto, along with the social ills commonly associated with that
space, such as criminality, drugs, prostitution, violence, and disenfranchisement. The predominantly grim portrayal of the barrio put forth
in a great number of these texts was also characterized by one-dimen-
sional depictions of female characters as either virgins or whores. Therefore, when U.S. Latinas began to write and publish, they sought to offer
alternative representations of female characters that broke the virgin/
whore mold as well as more nuanced depictions of life in the barrio that
also explored life inside the home. One of the first women authors to
irrupt into the patriarchal U.S. Puerto Rican literary scene was Nicholasa Mohr, who in 1973 published her first novel, *Nilda*, a semi-autobi-
ographical text that explores the life of a Puerto Rican girl growing up
in the Bronx. Still actively writing, Mohr continues to be recognized as
a pioneer figure not only among U.S. Puerto Rican writers, but, more
important, among U.S. Latinas of all backgrounds given her decisive
role in the development of Latina narrative.

Today most critics agree that the 1980s were a pivotal decade for U.S.
Latina literature, marked by the emergence of Chicana and Puerto Rican
fiction writers as a collective voice (Heredia 1).[21] By the 1990s, however, a true explosion took place as "women authors of Cuban, Dominican, Mexican, and Puerto Rican descent in the United States became
more prominent because they were publishing narratives such as mem-
oirs, novels, and short fiction that became mainstreamed by East Coast
agents who made their works more accessible to a broader, national

audience in the United States" (Heredia 1). It is during this apogee of Latina writings that U.S. Puerto Rican literary production also reached new heights. The works of figures such as Judith Ortíz Cofer, Esmeralda Santiago, Alba Ambert, and Aurora Levins Morales emerged as part of what Ellen McCracken refers to as a "new Latina narrative," which assumed a contestatory posture in relation to the patriarchal U.S. Latino and U.S. Puerto Rican canons. We observe, then, that Puerto Rican women's narrative on the island surges in the 1970s and reaches a climax in the 1980s, while a parallel phenomenon occurs on the mainland beginning in the 1980s and reaching a climax in the 1990s. Despite this slight overlap, these two branches of Puerto Rican women's literature have yet to be explored in depth in order to better understand the links between them.

Thinking Outside the Island: Toward a Transinsular Approach

Situated in the context of the controversy that surrounds Puerto Rican identity politics, this study proposes an alternate approach to the study of Puerto Rican literature inside and outside the island. It seeks to transcend the boundaries that have traditionally defined the Puerto Rican canon in order to reflect the transnational character of this population. This implies a broader understanding of the concept of nation, which renders Nina Glick Schiller, Linda Basch, and Cristina Blanc-Szanton's definition of transnationalism as "the processes by which immigrants build social fields that link together their country of origin and their country of settlement" a key notion in this analysis (1).

Jorge Duany's groundbreaking study, *The Puerto Rican Nation on the Move* (2002), advances this view in stating that "as Puerto Ricans move back and forth between the two countries, territorially grounded definitions of national identity become less relevant, while transnational identities acquire greater prominence" (2). Never before has this statement been more applicable than it is now, two decades into the new millenium. According to the latest 2010 Census figures, there were 4,624,000 Puerto Ricans in the United States and 3,725,789 in Puerto Rico.[22] Needless to say, this unprecedented shift in the population balance will have both material and less tangible implications.[23] In fact, these numbers reveal how urgent it is to reconsider the paradigms that have been implemented historically to define the Puerto Rican nation.

At a time when more than half of the Puerto Rican population resides in the continental United States, it is imperative to recognize the key role of the diaspora in the construction of a Puerto Rican national imaginary (Duany 5). Although not without its own challenges, the recognition of the diasporan population—both by people on the island and by dominant Anglo-American society—has taken place in the realm of popular culture, in large part due to the role that media plays in our lives. From salsa (Aparicio 1998; Flores 2000, 2009) to hip hop (Flores 2000; Rivera 2003) and reggaetón (Rivera 2009; Flores 2009), from Ricky Martin to J.Lo (Negrón-Muntaner 2004; Aparicio 2003) and to the role of music videos produced by Banco Popular de Puerto Rico (Ortíz Márquez 2004; Arroyo 2010), the study of U.S. Puerto Rican/Latino popular culture and its commodification (Dávila 2001, 2008) has shed light on the impact that Puerto Rican cultural production outside the island has had back home and in U.S. society.

The rejection of diaspora literature from national letters contrasts dramatically with the acceptance that other forms of artistic production by Puerto Rican communities in the mainland, such as music (salsa is considered the national music form, although it was originally produced in the United States) and painting, have received on the island. What, one must ask, accounts for the drastic differences in the fates of these various artistic modes? I would like to argue that these can be explained in part on linguistic grounds. The facts that most salsa lyrics are composed in Spanish and that visual art obviously relies on its own language have helped to attenuate the possible "threat" their presence might have posed in their respective insular artistic circles.[24] Although a symbol of national pride today, salsa was originally looked down on as a type of lower-class (black) music and not readily accepted by all strata of the island's population.[25]

The mobile livelihood of a number of Puerto Rican authors has destabilized the traditional criteria, such as language and location, used to distinguish insular from diaspora authors. The fact that a key figure such as the poet Víctor Hernández Cruz has recently published works in Spanish while based on the island "is making Puerto Rican literatures on the island and on the mainland less clearly differentiated, while it also represents a challenge to the traditional homologies between the Puerto Rican literary canon and the Spanish language" (Aparicio, "Writing" 79). Hernández Cruz, a central voice of the diaspora since the 1960s, has published works in Spanish and English and currently commutes between Morocco and Puerto Rico. Expanding the national canon in order to encompass works produced in and outside the island—in Spanish, English, or Spanglish—would therefore serve as a more faithful mirror of the cultural transformations undergone by Puerto Rican society in the past century, as Hernández Cruz's case illustrates.

In examining key narratives by island-based and U.S.-based female writers, this study challenges the tendency to separate these two branches of Puerto Rican literature based on their linguistic, formal, discursive, and thematic divergences and instead seeks to highlight the connections that exist between them.[26] This type of comparative and transnational approach is modeled on what Aparicio deems "a greater need for transnational studies between what is Latin American and what is U.S. Latino" ("Latino" 17).[27] Identifying the links present in the narratives of women authors from both sides allows us to recognize these continuities as *literary contact zones*, such as the presence of shared cultural myths, and thus forces us to rethink the traditional division between insular and diaspora literature. Rather than focus on maintaining monolithic definitions and static boundaries that presumably safeguard the so-called integrity and cohesion of each corpus, it is time to recognize these two bodies of literature as part and parcel of a *transinsular* Puerto Rican literary tradition.

The notion of a transinsular literature, firmly grounded on the acknowledgment of existing literary contact zones, implies a shift away from the island-centered criteria (a vestige of the *insularismo* alluded to by Pedreira) that have traditionally defined Puerto Rican letters. Here I propose the concept of a transinsular literature as encompassing both the literature produced on the island and that produced on the U.S. mainland, departing from the recognition of existing contact zones between them and taking into account the power differentials implicit in Pratt's coinage of the latter. I use the term *transinsular* to emphasize the value of Puerto Rican cultural/literary production outside the island. The use of the prefix *trans-* signals the importance of recognizing works produced "beyond the island," or outside its borders, works that traditionally have been deemed unworthy of inclusion (nonvaluable) in the national corpus.

Unlike Aparicio's notion of *transnational* texts—"those that circulate across national borders, specifically between Puerto Rico and the United States"—the term *transinsular* does not necessarily imply the bidirectional flow of these texts between these localities ("Writing" 83). In other words, the idea of transinsularity does not automatically indicate, although it does not exclude, a conscious literary give-and-take between authors from both sides. Rather, it signals the existence of a broad, complex, and heterogeneous body of literature that is unified, albeit precariously, by the authors' self-identification as Puerto Rican, understanding this term not as a static category but as one that assumes multiple manifestations. Recognizing the advantages of examining the works of diaspora authors through a transinsular optic allows us to transcend some of the anachronistic criteria that have failed to take into account the transnational reality of the Puerto Rican population.

While the concept of a transinsular literature clearly challenges traditional conceptions of this art form on the island, it also questions prevailing views among scholars of U.S. Puerto Rican letters regarding the positionality of insular vis-à-vis diaspora literature. On the one hand, the argument in favor of viewing diaspora literature as part and parcel of the Puerto Rican literary tradition has been put forth by critics such as Edna Acosta-Belén who have argued for the need to revise the Puerto Rican canon ("Beyond" 984). Similarly, the critics Arcadio Díaz Quiñones, Juan Flores, and Efraín Barradas have proposed expanding the concept of nation to include the diaspora. Barradas stresses this point in *Partes de un todo* (1998): "The literature of Puerto Ricans in the United States is an integral part, I emphasize, of Puerto Rican literature" (27).[28] On the island, this posture has been challenged not only by *neonacionalista* sectors, but, and perhaps more surprisingly, by some of the so-called *posmodernos*. Carlos Pabón, a leading figure among the latter, denounces this move, albeit on different grounds from those of the *neonacionalistas:* "Isn't this perhaps a sort of colonization, a sort of coloniality of power? If 'Nuyoricans' are now viewed as part of the nation it is because this is how it's been legislated by the authorized voices of the island's intellectual elite in agreement with U.S.-based intellectual elite" (93).[29] And while the inclusion of the diaspora as part of *lo nacional* could be seen as an instance of *coloniality of power*, a plethora of sociological studies would confirm that this posture is in consonance with prevailing attitudes and sentiments among diasporan Puerto Ricans, who in many cases continue to see themselves as members of the nation.

Historically, resistance to linking diaspora production to that of the island has also been common among U.S.-based writers and critics as a gesture of cultural affirmation. A telling example is the reappropriation of the pejorative label *Nuyorican* by diaspora writers in the 1970s, which was grounded in their "shared working-class realities and experiences of poverty and racism" and was "meant to differentiate those Puerto Ricans born or raised in the United States from those living in Puerto Rico" (Acosta-Belén and Santiago 192). This sense of distance between writers from both sides has also been echoed by the pioneer female author Nicholasa Mohr, who in her essay "Puerto Rican Writers in the U.S., Puerto Rican Writers in Puerto Rico: A Separation Beyond Language" (1989), speaks against the rejection experienced by diaspora writers on the island. Mohr's piece, considered a key text in U.S. Puerto Rican literature, cites language, thematic concerns, and the working-class diaspora experience as some of the irreconcilable differences that mark a rupture between insular and diaspora literary production. Her essay in part constitutes a reaction to Ana Lydia Vega's story "Pollito Chicken," which offers a negative portrayal of its main character, "Nuyorican" Suzie Bermiúdez, but the piece was also informed by Mohr's personal experiences with prejudice in Puerto Rico.[30] In an interview with Carmen Dolores Hernández, Mohr says, "However, after I started writing, I had a difficult time in Puerto Rico. Many intellectuals on the island could not accept who I was and what I was doing. . . . Island Puerto Ricans often postulated that I was not an authentic island Puerto Rican, but I've never pretended to write as an island Puerto Rican" (*Puerto Rican Voices* 89). One must wonder if this essay would have been written had she felt more welcome and embraced by island critics and intellectuals, as appears to have been the experience of the poet Víctor Hernández Cruz.[31]

In addition to the rejection experienced by a number of diaspora writers at either a personal or professional level on the island—and here Miguel Piñero's poem "This Is not the Place Where I Was Born" and Tato Laviera's "nuyorican" come to mind—some U.S.-based critics and intellectuals have openly proclaimed the irreconcilable rupture between these two branches of Puerto Rican literatures. Recently, the literary critic Lisa Sánchez González's *Boricua Literature: A Literary History of the Puerto Rican Diaspora* (2001) has dismissed the idea of "tethering Boricua literature to either 'Puerto Rico' or 'America' as acts of 'nationalist signification'" because this position fails to account for the *in-betweenness* that characterizes this corpus (20). Sánchez González convincingly states that forcing diaspora literature to fit within the parameters and ideological frameworks of either of these two canons potentially hinders our understanding of their hybrid nature.

However, as the comparative approach of this study illustrates, acknowledging the in-betweenness of diaspora literature *and* its continuity to both the island and the U.S. literary traditions need not be mutually exclusive. It is possible to be cognizant of the ties that bind these two branches of Puerto Rican literature while recognizing their specificities. The ideological compromise that this posture may entail for each camp—neonationalists on the island versus advocates of a distinct and culturally independent diaspora identity on the U.S. mainland—by no means implies that diaspora literature ought to be subsumed under the insular canon. Rather than debate whether or not it should be considered an "extension" of the insular corpus, the concept of a Puerto Rican transinsular literature implies the level and equal positionality of insular and diaspora letters. In proposing transinsularity as a theoretical frame in the study of Puerto Rican literatures, this book seeks to chip away at the *frontera intranacional* that has been erected between Puerto Ricans on the island and their diasporan counterparts. Before embarking on the rest of my analysis, I want to begin by tracing the origins and development of the foundational myth of *la gran familia puertorriqueña*.

Puerto Rican Identity and the Foundational Myth of *la gran familia puertorriqueña*

The foundational myth of *la gran familia puertorriqueña*, deployed by the *generación del treinta* as a weapon against the perceived threat of Americanization, had actually emerged on the island in the late nineteenth century. In *Conflictos de clase y política en Puerto Rico*, A. G. Quintero Rivera traces the origins of *la gran familia* back to the hacienda system of production that dominated the island's economy under Spanish rule, which was based on an ethos of deference and paternalism. As he explains, "The exploitation (expropriation of productive labor) was necessary to the hacendado's economic dominance and to satisfy the consumerist needs associated with the power and prestige of this class. But also important to his position, his lifestyle, was to be respected, admired and loved by the hacienda workers."[32] He later reiterated this point in *Ponce: La capital alterna* (2003): "The seignorial means of production upon which this ideology was based facilitated the paternalist notion of the motherland as a great family: a socially stratified family, headed by a surrogate father—the hacendado—, yet nevertheless a family, based on a shared citizenship."[33]

When this entire system, based on the social hegemony of the *hacendados*, was jeopardized by the increasing power of other sectors (i.e., Spanish-born traders), they organized politically along party lines and established the Partido Liberal Reformista (Liberal Reformist Party) in 1870 (*Conflictos* 23).[34] The party's anticolonial stance, reflected in its struggle for the constitution of a Puerto Rican state, contributed to the emergence of a "national sentiment" (24). The centering of these politics on the conflict between "puertorriqueños y 'peninsulares'" eventually led to the *hacendados*'s deployment of *la gran familia puertorriqueña*, a revolutionary (anticolonial) concept at the time, stemming from the paternalist ideology of the *hacendados* (*Conflictos* 24, 30). According to Quintero Rivera, by 1895 "the hacendado class had managed to convince others that their interests were representative of those of the entire country through the concept of 'the great Puerto Rican family,' which stood against the arbitrary and foreign colonial power."[35] The conflation of nationalist sentiment and the *hacendados*'s struggle for political empowerment that are embedded in the concept of *la gran familia* proved to have an ironic twist in the future, as the descendants of this class embraced the old colonial metropolis as a strategy of resistance to the new American colonial power.

The North American invasion of 1898 took place at a time when the *hacendado* class was making significant advances toward achieving political hegemony.[36] However, this event also took place at a time when the cohesiveness of *la gran familia* was deteriorating and the image of Puerto Rican society was fraught with lack of unity and discord (*Conflictos* 43). Rapid changes were taking place, most important the transformation of the island's semifeudal hacienda economy to a capitalist plantation economy (117). This process had already begun under Spanish rule, but now the balance of power was shifting from the *hacendados* to absentee U.S. corporate interests (141). Eroding the power of the *hacendados*, who represented a significant obstacle to U.S. domination, became a primary goal of the new colonial power. The centralization of education—along with the institutionalization of English in the classroom—and the introduction of Protestantism became the primary instruments used to maim the long-standing *hacendado* power structure (54).

One of the most significant blows to the hacienda system was in fact a direct repercussion of Protestantism: the substitution of the *hacendado* by the North American minister as the primary figure of authority (*Conflictos* 66). Faced by their imminent lack of power, *hacendados* revitalized the concept of *la gran familia*, only this time imbuing it with patriotic rhetoric that sought to expand their political base by attracting other sectors of the population to their party Unión de Puerto Rico (68–69). Blacks and *mulatos*, previously excluded from the definition of the nation, came to be considered part of the Puerto Rican family as the *criollo* elite realized "that a lack of cohesion among the laboring classes undermined their attempts to promote and maintain national solidarity" (Torres, "La gran familia" 295).[37]

Having significantly expanded their political base by the inclusion of previously marginalized social sectors, the *criollo* elite's agenda included the demand for independence and the defense of Spanish as the national language. As they saw it, two decades of U.S. colonialism had taken a serious toll on the island's cultural makeup. In addition to the imposition of American citizenship in 1917 through the Jones Act, some of "the most controversial Americanization policies," according to Acosta-Belén and Santiago, were "the implementation of English as the official language of Puerto Rico and of its school system, the use of island schools to inculcate US values and accelerate the adoption of English, the undermining of Puerto Rican history, culture, and the Spanish language, and the religious proselytizing by Protestant missionaries among a population that was primarily Catholic" (40). The defense of Spanish and Puerto Rican culture remained a priority among the intellectual elites—mostly descendants of the *hacendados*—for decades to come. Despite the fact that by the 1930s the hacienda-based structure represented by the Unión party had collapsed—undoubtedly accelerated by the catastrophic effects of the Great Depression on the island—the myth of *la gran familia* continued to represent a symbol of resistance to North American colonialism.

La gran familia in the 1930s

Quintero Rivera affirms that the eradication of the hacienda system, coupled with the increasing visibility of the professional sector, led many *hacendado* families to sell their lands in order to provide an education for their children. This is how the second-generation *hacendado* bourgeoisie distanced itself from agriculture and became associated with the liberal professions (*Conflictos* 153). As he puts it:

> This second generation, born at a time when the social structure of the haciendas was beginning to collapse, and politically-born when their class had lost its political and economic hegemony, therefore occupying a secondary position in the social hierarchy, developed a more radical and change-driven ideology. . . . With strong roots in the traditions and its hacienda culture, it maintained, nevertheless, the support of hacienda workers and small independent farmers, but its more radical ideology and its secondary social position allowed for an alignment with an important sector of the proletariat.[38]

Some, though not all, of the most important intellectual and public figures to emerge during the crucial 1930s—the *generación del treinta*—were members of this second-generation *hacendado* bourgeoisie. The revitalization of *la gran familia* by the *generación del treinta* illustrates the sense of historical continuity that compelled members of this group, in Pedreira's words, to participate in what amounted to "the completion of the agenda interrupted in 1898" (Ayala and Bernabé 119). Determined to define the Puerto Rican nation vis-à-vis the U.S. colonial metropolis, the redeployment of *la gran familia* by the bourgeois writers of the 1930s "invoked an ideal past that never truly materialized, by locating social harmony and *convivencia* within a specific historical time and space (Ponce, the haciendas, and pre-1898)" (Aparicio, *Listening* 6). The pivotal role this myth has played in the nation-building project of island intellectuals is evidenced in the degree to which it recurs in the works of the canonical authors Tomás Blanco, Antonio S. Pedreira, René Marqués, Emilio Belaval, and Enrique Laguerre, to name a few.

In *Literatura y paternalismo*, Gelpí examines the rhetoric of paternalism that imbues the literary production of the 1930s, which "often harks back to familial relationships, and whose fundamental metaphor consists of comparing the nation to a great family."[39] Pedreira's *Insularismo* (1934), perhaps the most important text of the *generación del treinta*, constitutes an interpretation of Puerto Rican history and culture that became the foundational narrative on which the rest of the Puerto Rican paternalistic discourse was later built.[40] As Gelpí points out, "For those who read it in the decades of the forties, fifties, and sixties, *Insularismo* is a *logos*, a sort of founding voice through which the truth about Puerto Rican nationality emanates."[41] Yet the truth to which the text aspires is thwarted by its open debasement of blackness.

Pedreira begins his first chapter by stating that the present "confusion" regarding Puerto Rican identity is due to the "fusion" that took place among indigenous, Spanish, and African populations, which in his view produced an "imperfect" Puerto Rican subject: "At moments of historical transcendence when the martial rhythms of our European blood surface in our gestures, we are capable of the most celebrated undertakings and the most concerted heroism. But when our gesture is engulfed by a wave of African blood we remain indecisive, spellbound by color beads or terrified by cinematic images of witches and ghosts."[42] The laudatory attitude Pedreira assumes regarding European heritage contrasts sharply with the disdain he shows toward Puerto Rican African roots. The renowned historian Tomás Blanco, another central figure of the *generación del treinta*, displays a similar posture in his *Prontuario histórico de Puerto Rico* (Puerto Rico historical guide, 1935) and *El prejuicio racial en Puerto Rico* (Racial prejudice in Puerto Rico, 1938).

In his preface to *El prejuicio racial en Puerto Rico*, Arcadio Díaz Quiñones calls attention to the paternalist rhetoric that informs Blanco's
essay. As he puts it, "His historical narrative articulates an identity in
relation to a *generous father figure* who defends the unity of the family
against 'foreign' elements, at the same time that he reaffirms the legiti-
mating hierarchy of his own authority. It is, in many ways, a patriarchal and paternalist discourse. It constructs a history of paternal, white,
Hispanic, Catholic, and Western kindness, with which he announces
a future program for unity, once the 'disturbing' elements have been
acknowledged and eliminated."[43] Blanco's paternalist stance becomes
especially evident in the tone that his diatribe assumes in *Prontuario
histórico*, where he openly condemns U.S. colonialism. In the last chapter, "Siglo XX, Ocupación norteamericana: Desorientación" (Twentieth century, North American occupation: Disorientation), when Blanco
states that U.S. intervention in Puerto Rico "hindered the possibility of
forming truly cultured men," he asserts his own authority over less educated individuals, whom he sees as victims of Americanizing educational
policies.[44] This paternalist posture is also palpable when he describes
the people's initial reaction to the U.S. occupation: "and the disorientation of the common people continued its course, going from candid
dazzlement to despondency and disorganization, planting hesitation and
doubt, giving rise to paradoxical and negative attitudes such as dissent-
ing resignation, scholarly-optimist desperation, Yankee-lover or chau-
vinist *jaibería*, et cetera."[45] Again, in describing "las masas," Blanco
establishes a distinction between them and himself as a member of the
generación del treinta that seeks to cement his authority. The use of
terms such as *desorientación, deslumbramiento,* and *desorganización*
hints at the conception of *las masas* as confused children in desperate
need of his parental tutelage. Ironically, one of Blanco's main critiques
of U.S. colonialism is precisely what he sees as their paternalist stance
vis-à-vis Puerto Rico. He decries the impossibility of a dignified U.S.–
Puerto Rico relationship "when the colonial people is considered inferior, primitive, backwards, immature or unprepared."[46] While he might
not describe *las masas* in these exact terms, his discourse in *Prontuario
histórico*, and in *El prejuicio racial*, seeks to cement his authority as
intellectual father figure.

In addition to Pedreira and Blanco, other members of the *generación
del treinta*, such as Emilio S. Belaval and Enrique Laguerre, also evoked
the icon of *la gran familia* in their works. A case in point is Belaval's
Los problemas de la cultura puertorriqueña (Problems of Puerto Rican

culture) (1933), which exalts not only the hacienda but also the white *hacendado,* "who, he argued, ruled over women and slaves with a loving but strict hand" (Ayala and Bernabé 121). Belaval's glorification of the hacienda as the primary locus of Puerto Rican culture is reflected in the following excerpt: "The genesis of our rural psychology is found in the bygone Puerto Rican hacienda, the unit that simultaneously functioned as fortress, town hall, town council, stock room, warehouse, chapel, concubinage quarter, family estate, hurricane shelter, watchtower of European-ness, relay point for the civil guard and the wandering hardware dealer. Inside it, our white European man lived, the structure of our rural life emerged, and the creole type we call the Puerto Rican was created."[47] In this description of the hacienda as a multifunctional space, Belaval emphasizes its role as pillar of patriarchal European culture, a discursive strategy that asserts the power of the *hacendado* while undermining and sometimes erasing the presence of subaltern sectors. He is, as Belaval puts it, a "pequeño señor feudal," a "small feudal lord, arbiter of life and the hacienda. . . . [A]round him congregate the indigenous, black, creole, mulatto, and mestizo men who he forces to coexist."[48] The use of the term *señor,* from the Latin *senior* (originally used to refer to elders and those who commanded respect), speaks to the authority of this figure (Segura Munguía 664). Perhaps more interestingly, the fact that etymologically the term became synonymous with *dominus* ("dueño," lord) during the Middle Ages reveals the power differentials embedded in the term (Segura Munguía 227).[49] He is, according to Belaval, the source of life, a father figure who has the power to confer survival to his subordinates.

Belaval's glorification of the *hacendado* goes even further: "Each peon feels attachment to the hacienda as if it were a miniature fatherland and worships his master as long as he satisfies his fundamental needs: sustenance, dance, and alcohol."[50] This deceptively straightforward remark conflates a series of associations that speak to the power differentials between the ruling *hacendado* and those who depended on him. Once again, this description evokes the *hacendado*'s godlike role by repeating the term *señor,* which is also etymologically related to God (el Señor, Dios), and by describing the peon's gratitude as one of "adoration" (Segura Munguía 227). The *hacendado*'s ostensible power to provide his peons with their "basic" needs also foregrounds this analogy. In addition, by limiting the peon's needs to nourishment, dance, and alcohol, Belaval's discourse renders the subaltern powerless through their evocation as dependent, juvenile, and uncontrollable beings (characteristics reminiscent of depictions of persons of African descent in the racist narratives of the period). As this example illustrates, the hacienda power structure replicates the exclusionary antics that underlie *la gran familia*; hidden under the veil of paternalism, strong racist and androcentric undercurrents rendered women and blacks (slaves) powerless in order to preserve the power structure that placed the white/Spanish man at the top of the hierarchy.

A similar posture is found in Enrique Laguerre's novel *La llamarada* (1935), another foundational text of Puerto Rican literature that has been hailed for exploring issues beyond national identity such as the social inequality fomented by the U.S. sugar plantation economy (Ayala and Bernabé 128). However, its "nostalgic-romantic recovery of the coffee *hacienda*" at the end of the novel remits us again to the myth of *la gran familia* (Ayala and Bernabé 128). The recycling of this metanarrative, now in a work of literature, speaks to the potential of this type of narrative to promote a sense of unity and cohesiveness. This point is underscored by the fact that *La Democracia*, the newspaper affiliated with Luis Muñoz Marín's party, "serialized *La llamarada* beginning in January 1938 during the initial campaign of the PPD" (Ayala and Bernabé 128).[51] The incorporation of this narrative into one of the PPD's primary diffusion mechanisms attests to the fact that literature, as an expression of culture, "plays an indispensable role in modernization because it promotes national cohesion" and "permits an imaginary perception of unity before it is achieved politically" (Jusdanis xiv).

While many more examples could be added to the list of authors and works discussed above, those briefly examined here seek to unveil how the conflation of political and cultural discourses on the island ultimately crystallized in the metanarrative of *la gran familia*. For decades to come, the Puerto Rican family would remain a pivotal discourse permeating multiple facets of Puerto Rican life, including literature, visual arts, and politics.

The Myth Revitalized: 1940s–1960s

By the 1930s some significant changes were taking place in the island's political landscape. On the one hand, the Partido Nacionalista Puertorriqueño (PN; Puerto Rican Nationalist Party) had been founded under the leadership of Pedro Albizu Campos, a pivotal political figure who fought for the liberation of Puerto Rico from U.S. colonialism. On the other hand, as Acosta-Belén and Santiago point out, "a populist political movement was also taking shape; it presented itself as a new and more viable political option for change, offering the poverty-stricken peasantry and other working-class Puerto Ricans the dream of '*pan, tierra y libertad*' (bread, land, and liberty)" (61). In 1938 the PPD was founded under the leadership of Luis Muñoz Marín, son of the autonomist leader Luis Muñoz Rivera.

The PPD came to dominate island politics during the 1940s and 1950s. Its "hegemony also included an institutional attempt to construct a distinct conception of Puerto Rican identity," given that "for many PPD intellectuals, the party's efforts were a continuation of the work of the *generación del treinta*" (Ayala and Bernabé 208). This sense of historical continuity is evident in the fact that several members of this generation became strong supporters of the PPD (Ayala and Bernabé 211). The PPD's link to the *generación del treinta* is also evident in the paternalist posture that characterized the rhetoric of Puerto Rican governor, Luis Muñoz Marín, a member of the second-generation *hacendado* bourgeoisie. In re-creating the *hacendado*-peon power dialectic, Muñoz Marín often emphasized the submission of the proletariat to the government as a prerequisite for success (Quintero, *Conflictos* 163).[52] This posture, in fact, is linked to the myth of *la gran familia* propounded by the *generación del treinta*. Gelpí's observation attests to this connection: "From its emergence to its most recent avatar—the developmental populism of the forties, fifties, and sixties—that discourse has had a privileged metaphor: the likening of Puerto Rico to a great family. What we have, in essence, is a conciliatory discourse based on respect toward the authority of a symbolic paternal figure."[53]

While the discourse of *la gran familia* was successfully deployed by the PPD to build its political base—leading up to Muñoz Marín's governorship from 1948 to 1964—it was also used strategically to attenuate opposition to his modernization campaign, a key component of which was its Operación Manos a la Obra, or Operation Bootstrap, a "government campaign to attract investment and special tax breaks designed to encourage commercial development [that] propelled rapid industrialization," which was launched in 1947 (Morris 41). The success of the program, whose aim was to foster development by transforming the agrarian Puerto Rican economy into an industrial one, was contingent on the influx of U.S. corporate capital and the stimulation of consumerist patterns.

The initial success of Operation Bootstrap bolstered Puerto Rico's reputation as the "showcase of the Americas," a "model for democratic and capitalist development" (Sánchez Korrol 216). However, as Sánchez

Korrol points out, "in the early seventies it became clear that the Bootstrap industrialization plan also had its darker side: It never fully incorporated the island's growing population into the workforce; it displaced thousands from agrarian production and reinforced the island's dependency on the United States; and the radical decline of the island's agrarian sector had caused higher unemployment and an escalation in the importation of basic food staples" (217). One of the aspects of the "darker side" of Operation Bootstrap, referred to by Sánchez Korrol, was the initial displacement of thousands of people from rural areas to urban centers, where many were forced to peripheral slums and shantytowns (El Fanguito, La Perla, Caño Martín Peña) that had sprouted on the island in the early twentieth century and swelled in the 1930s as a result of the Great Depression.[54]

Also intricately tied to the eventual failure of Operation Bootstrap was the implementation of policies to control "overpopulation," which according to the government was one of the most significant obstacles to achieving "the increases in per capita income that the massive industrialization process of Operation Bootstrap was intended to produce" (Acosta-Belén and Santiago 76). It is for this reason that Muñoz Marín's government simultaneously launched initiatives to control the population growth rate—including massive sterilization campaigns—while also encouraging migration to the U.S. mainland, for instance, through the promotion of contract labor programs (Whalen 29).[55] In the end, "much of the unprecedented emigration that followed on the heels of Operation Bootstrap was composed of individuals displaced from declining production sectors and those newly unemployed as a consequence of industrial technology" (Sánchez Korrol 217).

It is important to remember that the destitution confronted by the agrarian and working-class sectors of Puerto Rican society, and which also propelled migration to the U.S. mainland, was informed by the context of the island's colonial ties to the United States. The same can be said about the condition of disenfranchisement that characterizes the lives of working-class migrants and their descendants to this day. While most Puerto Ricans in the diaspora have faced obstacles similar to those faced by other U.S. Latino minorities, the case of Puerto Ricans is unique. For instance, despite their U.S. citizenship, as colonial citizens they cannot benefit from the support typically offered by the home country's state apparatus, which is not the case for other U.S. Latinos. As Flores states, "This paradoxical and 'exceptional' orphan state of the Puerto Ricans among the many Latino groups is directly attributable to its colonial condition and the ramification of that status in the diaspora in the form of internal colonialism" (*Diaspora* 65–66).[56] While Flores's use of the term *exceptional* hints at the unique (i.e., colonial) status of Puerto Rico, the quotation marks suggest otherwise. It is therefore important to recognize that Puerto Ricans are not the only group living under conditions of colonialism in the United States. When Rodolfo Acuña states, "I have attempted to underscore my thesis that Chicanos are a colonized people in the United States," he reminds us of the links between Mexicans, Puerto Ricans, and many other marginalized groups that live under conditions of internal colonialism in this country (1).

The island's official change of status in 1952 added another layer of complexity to the rapid transformations that Puerto Rico was undergoing at the time. Through the establishment of the Estado Libre Asociado (ELA), officially translated as Commonwealth of Puerto Rico, "Puerto Rico was to be granted the right to enact its own constitution but would remain a territory 'in permanent union with the United States'" (Acosta-Belén and Santiago 66). Under this political formula, Puerto Ricans' U.S. citizenship would not carry the same degree of privilege typically associated with it. Among its stipulations, Puerto Ricans living on the island do not have the right to vote in presidential elections and have no voting representation in the U.S. Congress, and, while they are exempt from federal income taxes, Puerto Rican men can be drafted by the U.S. military.

Keenly aware of the general discontent surrounding his government's emphasis on modernization and conscious of the need to counterbalance the effects of Americanization, Muñoz Marín announced the launch of Operación Serenidad (Operation Serenity) during a speech at Harvard in 1955 (Maldonado 347). In what would amount to one of the most important speeches of his entire career, Muñoz Marín declared, "Serenity may perhaps be defined as the habit of seeing your world whole, instead of just economically. . . . To see it whole you must see it simply. . . . A society in which Operation Serenity had been successful would use its economic power increasingly for the extension of freedom, of knowledge, and of the understanding imagination rather than for a rapid multiplication of goods, in hot pursuit of a still more vertiginous multiplication of wants" (Maldonado 346). This was clearly an attack on consumerism, which had rapidly escalated as a result of industrialization and modernization. His words emphasized the imperative to cultivate the "spiritual character" of the nation, which Muñoz Marín set out to accomplish through a range of initiatives promoted through Operación Serenidad.

Underscoring the distinction between these two programs, Ayala and Bernabé observe, "While Operation Bootstrap promoted the growth of production and the advance of 'civilization,' Operación Serenidad insisted they had to be subordinated to the enrichment of human culture. While Operation Bootstrap relied on incentives to U.S. capital, the ICP [Instituto de Cultura Puertorriqueña] insisted on the affirmation of a distinct Puerto Rican culture, all of this within the shell of the ELA, a regime that was portrayed as resolving the tension between the contradictory impulses toward annexation and independence" (210). Operations Bootstrap and Serenity thus emerged as counterparts of each other, yet the latter has received limited attention despite the critical role it played in shaping the Puerto Rican cultural landscapes on both the island and the mainland.

Operation Serenity's impulse to salvage the nation's "essence" from the threat of modernization and progress brought with it the reactivation of certain metaphors and discourses meant to strengthen a sense of cultural nationalism. The ICP, created in 1956, was instrumental in this process through its "official task of defining and disseminating the constituent elements of Puerto Rico's national identity" (Dávila, *Sponsored* 4). However, the way this mission was carried out speaks to the highly politicized nature of the cultural terrain at that juncture. As Ayala and Bernabé put it, "The official conception of the ICP not only avoided the question of colonialism but also attempted to reconcile past and present class and racial conflicts. A history of conquest, enslavement, and exploitation became the history of the emergence of a Puerto Rican culture through the mixing, in harmonious synthesis, of the Taíno, Spanish, and African traditions. Affirmations of a Puerto Rican identity. . . . have also sought to neutralize tensions within Puerto Rican society, glossing over or seeking to harmonize persistent class and racial hierarchies" (210). The articulation of a romanticized and harmonious past came to rely on the degree of success attained by certain icons to project a convincing image of harmony and unity. Once again, *la gran familia* was strategically deployed against U.S. cultural infiltration. Paradoxically, the insular government simultaneously encouraged migration and the eventual assimilation of Puerto Ricans who migrated in the post–World War II years.

This apparently contradictory effort on the part of the Puerto Rican government was crystallized in the series *Libros para el pueblo* (Books for the People), published by the División de Educación de la Comunidad (DIVEDCO), a branch of the Departamento de Instrucción Pública in Puerto Rico. DIVEDCO launched an educational program, mainly directed at the rural population, built on a threefold structure: the production of documentary films, booklets that delved into the same topics as the films (i.e., *Libros para el pueblo*), and *carteles* (posters) to advertise the films. The wide distribution of these booklets, which addressed a broad range of topics (arts, literature, the family, migration, health, human rights, slavery, Christmas), responded to the government's goal of bolstering national pride among the Puerto Rican people, and although some of these materials predated the launch of Operation Serenity, they remained a cornerstone of that initiative. The series' emphasis on literature and the arts speaks to the crucial role that these play in the construction of any national imaginary (Anderson 1983; Jusdanis 1991). As the back cover of the second booklet in the series reads, "These brochures will introduce the reader to the best Puerto Rican literary works and will help him/her to learn about history, the arts, and sciences."[57] In addition to the publication of poems and stories by distinguished literary figures, a large percentage of the booklets were written and edited by the renowned playwright René Marqués and illustrated by celebrated Puerto Rican artists such as Lorenzo Homar, Rafael Tufiño, Carlos Raquel Rivera, J. A. Torres Martinó, Antonio Maldonado, Carlos Marichal, and Eduardo Vera Cortés, to name a few.

Although an in-depth examination of *Libros para el pueblo* is beyond the scope of the present study, it is important to point out that the frequency with which references to Puerto Rico as a family appear throughout the series attests to the key role that *la gran familia puertorriqueña* continued to play in official national discourses throughout the 1950s and 1960s. The centrality of this image as a leitmotif in DIVEDCO's production must be understood in relation to Marqués's ideology, given his role as author of most of the works (films and narratives) produced by this entity. Marqués, the "last 'pure' representative figure of Puerto Rican paternalist literature," as Gelpí describes him, was a fervent defender of those patriarchal values that he, and others, considered concomitant to *puertorriqueñidad* (121). His leading role in DIVEDCO's programs afforded him an additional opportunity and venue to promote his patriarchal ideology, presumably reaching a significantly wider audience than at any other point during his career.[58]

The allegory of the nation-family is the main focus of the booklet titled *La familia* (c. 1955), which opens with the statement, "The family is the smallest group or unit within society. It is the basis or foundation of a nation."[59] This equivalence between family and nation is emphasized throughout the narrative and culminates in the last paragraph, where Marqués states: "Whatever the individuals are like, so will be the family to which they belong. Whatever the families are like, so will be the fatherland to which they belong. Whatever Puerto Rico is, will depend on Puerto Rican individuals and on their relationships within the Puerto Rican family. Whatever we are as a people, as a nation, depends to a great extent on how you are and on how your family is."[60] Individual, family, and nation, become intertwined in this discourse, which relies on a guilt-ridden rhetoric to instill a sense of responsibility among parents. The emphasis on family values and cultural traditions was considered necessary to solidify a sense of *puertorriqueñidad*.

In contrast to the ideal of familial/national unity that is present in most of the *Libros para el pueblo*, the government's official rhetoric on migration suggests that expectations regarding the defense of culture varied according to place of residence. In the booklet *Emigración* (c. 1954)—the longest in the series—those who "freely choose" to migrate to the United States are encouraged to "assimilate" to Anglo-American culture: "The Puerto Rican who decides to be a part of an American community must know that he/she is part of that community and that he/she is responsible for collective improvement and welfare."[61] This marks a stark contrast to what is expected of Puerto Ricans on the island: "For those who stay here, it is different. Those who stay here must assert and exalt their Puerto Rican identity. They must preserve their customs and habits given that these are good and desirable. They must preserve their language and their culture. They must be proud of their history and their tradition. . . . Those who remain here have, therefore, the responsibility to contribute to Puerto Rico's ennoblement."[62] In emphasizing prevailing notions about diaspora versus island, these excerpts reveal some of the misconceptions about migration that were common at the time. To begin with, the narrative's emphasis on the migrant's freedom to "choose" between leaving or staying in Puerto Rico clearly glosses over the complexity of post–World War II Puerto Rican migration. While it is true that personal agency is involved in this decision—not all Puerto Ricans chose to migrate—the combination of economic necessity and a relentless government campaign to promote migration are considered today as factors that "pushed" or "forced" most migrants to leave their homeland. For this reason, it is telling that in the section titled "¿Por qué emigra la gente?" (Why do people migrate?), the first two reasons cited are economic depression and overpopulation, the two main targets of Muñoz Marín's government. Not coincidentally, the succeeding section,

"¿Por qué es fácil la emigración para los puertorriqueños?" (Why is migration easy for Puerto Ricans?), lists five main reasons why Puerto Ricans have an advantage over other migrants, which can be interpreted as a tacit promotion of this practice.

Even more remarkable—particularly in light of the present study—is how the booklet *Emigración* suggests a distinction between Puerto Ricans who stay and those who migrate, where the former are held responsible for preserving the Spanish language and cultural traditions associated with the island while the latter are encouraged to integrate, or assimilate, into Anglo-American society (including linguistically) in order to contribute to its advancement. In other words, the narrative hints at the exclusion of the migrant by "excusing" him or her of the responsibility to safeguard the *nation*. Considering the central role that DIVEDCO's cultural products played as instruments of government-sponsored education for the masses, their power to foment a division between Puerto Ricans at home and abroad should not be underestimated.

The initial "artificial" separation between communities on both sides certainly had an impact on the discourse of cultural nationalism that operated during Muñoz Marín's government. Key to this discourse was the myth of *la gran familia*. Another cultural icon that became revitalized during this time was the figure of the *jíbaro,* or highland peasant, examined in greater detail in chapter 3, which shared with *la gran familia* what were considered to be the core values of Puerto Rican culture (Hispanophilia, whiteness, Catholicism, patriarchy).[63] Thus, the myth of *la gran familia* and the iconic *jíbaro* (re)emerged as privileged images that embodied the much sought after sense of identity that was claimed to define the Puerto Rican nation.

In addition to the institutions, organizations, and educational programs designed to carry out the PPD's cultural project, the 1950s and 1960s witnessed the revamping of a Puerto Rican official canon that reflected the values associated with *la gran familia*. The correspondence between this myth and the Puerto Rican canon supports Jusdanis's postulate about the formation of canons within "discourses that value tradition and possess a strong consciousness of the past" (59). The publication of Francisco Manrique Cabrera's *Historia de la literatura puertorriqueña* (History of Puerto Rican Literature) in 1956, one year after the launch of Operation Serenity, serves to underscore the intricate relationship among politics, cultural nationalism, and canon formation in Puerto Rico. As an anthology, Manrique Cabrera's *Historia* represents "a valuable source for an inquiry into the canon," given that anthologies typically reflect "the canonical texts of a particular period" (Jusdanis 66). In fact, the privileged status that for years the *Historia* enjoyed as the island's official canon led to its symbolic role as national constitution for this stateless nation, according to the critic Efraín Barradas ("Silencios" 30). In his illuminating study of *Historia*, Barradas suggests that Manrique Cabrera's strong sense of *hispanismo*, which he shared with many of his contemporaries, ultimately led to "unjust" silences and exclusions from his text (30). This sense of *hispanismo* that had been present since the early twentieth century and continued throughout Puerto Rican literary history was inextricably linked to the metanarrative of *la gran familia puertorriqueña* and became a strong mechanism of exclusion along the axes of gender, race, and language.

Contemporary Debates: Neonacionalistas and Posmodernos

The definition of the nation continues to be a source of heated debate even among island intellectuals today. Francisco Vivoni traces the origin of most current debates to the 1995 publication of Arturo Torrecilla's *El espectro posmoderno* (The postmodern specter), a key text that exposes the crisis of the role of the intellectual generated by the collapse, or the exhaustion, of foundational metanarratives (73). During the 1990s, the emergence of various postmodern-leaning intellectual figures rendered the island's intellectual landscape more complex; it led to the questioning of the "carácter absoluto de la categoría nación" (the absolute character of the category of the nation) and to heated debates on the repercussions of globalization and cultural hybridity in Puerto Rico (73).

Another important debate took place between Juan Duchesne-Winter and Carlos Gil in the early 1990s regarding the crisis of *independentismo*, which led to the intersection of postmodern theory and the issue of the national question in Puerto Rico (Vivoni 78). While Duchesne-Winter and Gil agreed that the crisis of discursive strategies used by the pro-independence sector was due to the breakdown of foundational metanarratives, they assumed different positions vis-à-vis the political implications of postmodern thought in the Puerto Rican context (80). Whereas Duchesne-Winter argued for "un independentismo *lite*"—a reference to marketing strategies used to seduce the consumer—Gil argued that *independentismo* and postmodernism are intrinsically incompatible (Vivoni 81).

The debate initiated by Torrecilla, Gil, and Duchesne-Winter has not only evolved, but has been rendered even more complex over the past decade due to significant discursive and social shifts in the island's intellectual panorama.[64] A key protagonist to emerge as part of the discussion is Juan Manuel García Passalacqua, who rejected the application of postmodern theories to discussions about Puerto Rico's culture and politics (Vivoni 82). García Passalacqua's repudiation of postmodern thought led to the crystallization of two contemporary opposing intellectual camps: the *puertorriqueñistas* and the *posmodernos*—the latter a label typically ascribed to U.S. Puerto Rican scholars (Vivoni 83). García Passalacqua's criticism of postmodern intellectuals is also based on what he perceives to be the elitism of the opposing camp, whose highly theoretical discourse circumscribes their debates to the realm of academia. He, on the other hand, subscribes to the notion of the *intelectual mediático*—one who assumes an anti-intellectual posture and uses media outlets to voice his populist ideas (Vivoni 85). The discourse of the *intelectual mediático* is firmly grounded in cultural nationalism and a *puertorriqueñista* discourse that actually intersects with Duchesne-Winter's "independentismo lite" proposal, in the sense that it favors the emergence of a lighter and more festive understanding of nationalism (Vivoni 86).

According to Vivoni, the publication of Carlos Pabón's highly polemic essay, "De Albizu a Madonna: Para armar y desarmar la nacionalidad," in the academic journal *bordes* provoked an upsurge of debates on national identity, globalization, and postmodernism in Puerto Rico (87). In this piece, Pabón proclaims the disintegration of *neonacionalista* and *puertorriqueñista* discourses (87). As Vivoni puts it:

> For this author [Pabón], *puertorriqueñismo* is a reductionist and essentialist discourse given that it reduces Puerto Rican nationality to an ethno-linguistic essence that is centered in Hispanism and the Spanish language. Pabón does not deny the existence of a Puerto Rican nationality, but rather criticizes the exclusionist and homogenizing character of neo-nationalism. . . . Definitions of 'lo puertorriqueño' centered on the Spanish language and Hispanism, maintains Pabón, exclude populations that consider themselves Puerto Ricans, but which do not meet these requirements, for example, those who live in the United States and don't speak Spanish or who reside in Puerto Rico, but do not ascribe to the ethnic category of Hispanic.[65]

This rejection of the traditional conception of Puerto Rican identity has led other critics and intellectuals to espouse the controversial notion of *radical statehood,* known as the *radical democratic movement* proposed by Frances Negrón-Muntaner and Ramón Grosfoguel (1997). Their posture departs from the recognition that "the statehood alternative is not inherently reactionary" and that it is possible to imagine an "anti-militarist and a radical-democratic pro-statehood movement in Puerto Rico that makes alliances with and defends the democratic struggles of other oppressed groups (e.g., Latinos, African Americans, women, gays and lesbians) in the United States" (73).

Taking into consideration the ideological postures that have driven contemporary discussions, *Family Matters* launches its intervention in the current cultural debate on the national question from a literary perspective. While this study acknowledges the existence of a Puerto Rican nationality, it rejects the notion of a static and hegemonic Puerto Rican identity solely grounded in, and/or contingent on, *hispanismo* and the Spanish language. In fact, I would like to suggest that the *hispanismo-*, Spanish-language-, and island-centered discourse of the *puertorriqueñistas* constitutes a sort of *ideological recycling* that originated in the 1930s. Tracing the history and evolution of the role that *hispanismo* has played in the construction of Puerto Rican identities—from the myth of *la gran familia* to its centrality in today's *puertorriqueñista* or neonationalist discourses—is an indispensable step to understanding perceptions of the diaspora on the island and the logic, albeit flawed, behind their exclusion from the island's national imaginary.

At the same time, I share Luis Fernando Coss's posture regarding the need to take into consideration "objective factors" such as language, territory, and ethnicity, which evince the "real" existence of a tangible nation (98). In *La nación en la orilla: respuesta a los posmodernos pesimistas* (The nation on the shore: response to postmodern pessimists), Coss argues that for Puerto Ricans the island is the "original," while New York is just a "copy" (97). And while historically the island is the origin (the Puerto Rican nationality took shape from within this space), the dispersal of its population and the emergence of alternative Puerto Rican identities—not necessarily territorially or linguistically linked to the island—speak to the blurring of distinctions between what could be seen as the symbolic origin, and the copies, of *lo puertorriqueño*. Expanding these ideas to frame a discussion about the diaspora can be a useful step given that, as Duany has observed, these two camps (*puertorriqueñistas* and *posmodernos*) "have probably overstated their opposition in the heat of the discussion, and neither has systematically considered the diaspora in their reflections on the Puerto Rican nation" (*Puerto Rican* 14).

Canon and Diaspora: The Other Side of the Family

Although Puerto Rican migration to the United States had its beginnings in the nineteenth century, it was not until the mid-twentieth century that the demographic profiles of both the island and the mainland societies were significantly transformed as a result of this phenomenon. While the impact of Operation Bootstrap—the driving force behind the massive exodus of job-seeking working-class Puerto Ricans during the 1940s and 1950s—has been examined from various disciplinary perspectives, the repercussions of Operation Serenity on migrant communities has been virtually ignored. Very few scholars have even addressed the impact that the "other side" of Operation Bootstrap might have had in the forma-tion of the Puerto Rican migrant imaginary. Two exceptions are Acosta-Belén and Santiago, who remind us that "cultural activities within the diaspora were influenced by the cultural and intellectual environment that began to be promoted in Puerto Rico during the 1950s. . . . Some of the government-sponsored initiatives under Operación Serenidad included incentives in the form of scholarships, travel grants, perfor-mances, exhibits, films, and publications that often brought Puerto Ricans from the island to the United States to work on joint creative projects with their fellow artists in the metropolis" (208). In addition to the palpable effects that Operation Serenity had through the imple-mentation of cultural exchange programs, such as the ones mentioned above, it is important to take into consideration the less tangible impact that this program might have had on those who migrated. Clearly, the discourse of cultural nationalism that prevailed on the island, which intensified in the 1950s but had been central to the PPD's platform since its foundation, did not remain artificially circumscribed to the island but was also part of the "cultural baggage" (i.e., social memory) that Puerto Rican migrants carried with them. As this study demonstrates, especially in the case of first-generation migrants who came of age on the U.S. mainland, claims of a distinct ethnic identity—presumably discon-nected from the island—fail to reflect the reality of "cultural indoctrina-tion" to which Puerto Rican migrants had been exposed before leaving their homeland and which became apparent in daily cultural practices and various modes of artistic expression.

Despite the strong sense of cultural nationalism that many migrants share with those in the home society—and some would argue that this sentiment is even stronger within diasporic communities (Flores, *Dias-pora* 4)—Puerto Ricans on the U.S. mainland continue to be excluded from the island's national imaginary. The "Hispanophilia, anti-Americanism, racism, androcentrism, homophobia, and more recently xenophobia" that inform the myth of *la gran familia* and identity discourses on the island, have made it increasingly difficult for second- and third-generation U.S. Puerto Ricans to be imagined as members of the national fold (Duany, *Puerto Rican* 24). In fact, I would argue that *la gran familia* has been revitalized once again in the past few decades and that this has led to what many see as the systematic exclusion of diaspora communities from the island's imaginary (Aparicio 1998; Duany 2002; Pabón 2003; Negrón-Muntaner 2004; Ortíz Márquez 2004).

One significant factor in the shaping of contemporary nationalist discourses on the island has been the rate of return, whether in the form of circular, temporary, or permanent return migration. The increasing contact between "those who left" and "those who stayed" has unveiled the symbolic distance, or *frontera intranacional*, that has emerged between these groups. As Flores points out, "Returning home has been a sobering moment for many Nuyoricans, causing them to feel like 'strangers in the ethnic homeland.' . . . They are outsiders and 'others' whose presence all too often spurs resentment, ridicule and fear, and even disdain and social discrimination with clear racial and class undertones" (*Diaspora* 5). Paradoxically, as is the case with the quintessential "other," return migrants also elicit "fascination, engagement, and change" (Flores 5). It can be said that despite the ambiguous attitude that nonmigrants might display toward their counterparts, the former's prevailing posture is to stress distinctions between *us* and *them*.[66]

Overall, there are certain negative views about U.S. Puerto Ricans that are shared by certain segments of the population, especially the elites. "These views," affirms Dávila, "are based on the belief that island Puerto Ricans speak a 'purer' Spanish, or are less crime-ridden, more knowledgeable about their culture, and more conscious of 'proper gender roles' than their New York, Philadelphia, or Chicago counterparts" (*Sponsored* 194). Language, which works as a gauge of cultural "authenticity" par excellence, has been a key bone of contention for conservative intellectuals, whose "eagerness to guard 'Puerto Rican-ness,'" as Pabón puts it, "is manifested with special intensity in the issue of language and literature."[67] The obsession with establishing and defending linguistic "purity" has remained a source of debate among *neonacionalistas*, precisely at a time when the borders of the Puerto Rican nation have become increasingly difficult to define. Spanish itself has surfaced as a border, a sort of *frontera intranacional*, erected by some to mark a division between "authentic" and "inauthentic" Puerto Ricans.

Jusdanis's assertion that "language [is] considered the deepest expression of a nation's individuality" is reflected in Puerto Rico, whose colonial status has led some to see an equivalence between Spanish and *puertorriqueñidad* (46). Of course, the defense of Spanish as a marker of Puerto Rican identity has its roots in the history of colonization and the intense Americanization campaigns to which the Puerto Rican population was subjected, especially in the early decades of the twentieth century—which included the imposition of English as the official language on the island. Thus, the *hispanofilia* associated with *la gran familia* has also led to the exclusion of Puerto Rican literature written in English in the United States from the island's canon.[68] Frances Aparicio explains the role that *hispanismo* has played in Puerto Rican cultural politics: "The conflicting views currently voiced concerning Puerto Rican literature in the United States written in English and about the diasporic community that produces it are excellent examples of how this hispanophilia informs controversies around Puerto Rican identity. The discourse of resistance against U.S. colonialism that has emerged on the island has led, ironically, to a static, fixed, and preterite construct of puertorricanness that excludes and silences those 'other' Puerto Ricans of the diaspora" (*Listening* 6). The exclusion of diaspora literature, mainly written in English or a combination of Spanish and English, is a product of the strong association that exists between language, literature, and nation.

The criteria behind canon formation on the island has systematically guaranteed that only works in Spanish are recognized as "high" literature, whereas works written in English or Spanglish—often viewed as culturally contaminated—are typically dismissed or minimized as "low" culture by the literary establishment. Of course, class and race play a decisive role in dictating how a work of art is perceived. As Flores puts it, "The creative subject of popular culture is the 'popular classes,' and its content the traditions and everyday life of communities and their resistance to social domination. It is typically referred to as 'low' culture, or 'subculture,' and marked off from the 'high' culture of the elite" (*Bomba* 17). The need to assert a distinction between these two artistic dimensions is explained by Frances Negrón-Muntaner as one that stems from a fear of "cultural impurity." As she puts it, "The possibility that the elite's destiny will be explicitly tied to the U.S. diasporas (the *hampa*) or be displaced by the 'lower classes' partly fuels these groups' writing off of two-thirds of the Puerto Rican population" ("English" 279). What one must not lose sight of is the fact that these are constructions and not static or inherent categories. In fact, "several popular manifestations of the twentieth century that have been described as the pillars of national culture [i.e., *plena* music] were considered vulgar and expressions of the lumpen in their time" (R. Rivera, "Rapping" 246).

The very existence of "high" art is contingent on the production of "low"/"popular" art, as Jusdanis points out (63). In this sense, the devaluation of works produced in English in the United States as "lesser than" insular works written in Spanish has perpetuated the vision of the U.S. Puerto Rican as "other." In fact, the relative invisibility of U.S. Puerto Rican literary production on the island, at least until recently, suggests that *la gran familia* has partly succeeded in delineating the boundaries of the nation based on territorial, linguistic, and cultural grounds.

Because *hispanofilia* has defined the linguistic and geographic contours of the national canon, the literature produced by Puerto Ricans on the U.S. mainland has often remained outside the boundaries of "the national."[69] However, the emergence of a solid literary and artistic tradition by Puerto Ricans in the United States, especially during the second half of the twentieth century, has prompted the questioning and reconsideration of the official criteria of canon formation. While Manrique Cabrera's *Historia* has been supplanted by more recent official literary histories, these tend to abide by, and to perpetuate, the canonical principles (i.e., *hispanismo*) delineated therein (Barradas, "Los silencios" 24).[70] For this reason, U.S. Puerto Rican literature—a corpus that falls squarely within two literary traditions—remains marginal to both the Puerto Rican and the U.S. canons. On the one hand, the decades-old production of the diaspora is not typically viewed as part of the island's national canon (Flores 2000; Duany 2002; Aparicio 2006; Acosta-Belén 2006);[71] on the other, its classification as *minority* or *ethnic* literature has precluded its full incorporation in Anglo-American letters. This "uneven integration" in Anglo-American literature is evinced in the fact that, as Aparicio points out, it has "not achieved the visibility and recognition comparable to that of African-American or even Chicano/a literature in the US context" ("Writing" 80).

Nevertheless, U.S. Latino/a writers and critics have recognized the pioneering role that U.S. Puerto Rican literature has played in the development of Latino/a literature. Foundational texts such as Piri Thomas's *Down These Mean Streets* (1967) and Miguel Algarín and Miguel Piñero's *Nuyorican Poetry: An Anthology of Puerto Rican Words and Feelings* (1975) are considered milestones not only of U.S. Puerto Rican but of U.S. Latino/a literature as well (Kanellos 327). Moreover, the inclusion of U.S. Puerto Rican authors alongside U.S. canonical figures in anthologies signals an increasing, albeit limited, aperture in the recognition of minority authors as part of the U.S. literary landscape. Gestures such as the increasing incorporation of U.S. Puerto Ricans in American literary anthologies should not be undermined due to "their potential for transforming the literary canon," as Aparicio reminds us ("Writing" 81).[72]

Nations are fluid, and so are the canons that mirror them. This is becoming more evident in the case of Puerto Rican literature. Recently some scholars on the island and in the diaspora seem interested in lessening the distance between the two camps. On the island, the emergence of a post-1980s generation of writers, some of whom either write in English or emulate Nuyorican writers/poets—such as the case of Urayoán Noel illustrates—indicates a greater degree of acceptance of the diaspora literary tradition, especially among younger generations (Pérez Ortiz 34). In addition, the inclusion of Miguel Algarín, Judith Ortíz Cofer, Víctor Hernández Cruz, Tato Laviera, Pedro Pietri, and Esmeralda Santiago in Víctor Federico Torres's *Diccionario de autores puertorriqueños contemporáneos* (Dictionary of Contemporary Puerto Rican Authors) (2009) signals a breakthrough in its unorthodox gesture of including diaspora authors.[73] In a similarly unconventional move, the inclusion of a chapter on Rosario Ferré's *The House on the Lagoon* in the critical anthology *Writing Off the Hyphen* (2008), the only island-based author examined in the anthology, suggests an increased awareness of the convergences between Puerto Rican authors in and outside the island.[74] As these examples demonstrate, a certain degree of progress has been made toward the recognition of the links between these literary bodies.[75] Despite these advances, significant hurdles still remain to be overcome, because, as Jusdanis reminds us, "literary canons [usually] can be revised, though not without a struggle" (60).

2 Our Family, Our Nation

Revisiting *la gran familia puertorriqueña*

> It is that in front of every peasant dwelling, no matter how humble, there is a seigniorial batey, a reminiscence of the batey of the Puerto Rican hacienda.[1]
>
> —Emilio Belaval

SPEAKING TO A PUBLIC AUDIENCE at the University of Puerto Rico in 1934, Emilio Belaval, one of the key figures of the *generación del treinta*, remarked, "In my opinion the great problem affecting Puerto Rico at the moment is that we are going through a truly messy period, mainly caused by the fact that we are still in a process of segregation from an extensive ethnic, religious, linguistic fabric, created by the homogeneous Spanish-ness that characterized the splendorous Empire of the Indies."[2] The so-called *desorden* (mess), according to him, was partly the result of the identity crisis brought about by three decades of U.S. colonialism and the state's campaign to Americanize the Puerto Rican population, which in Belaval's opinion was still Spanish in its essence. His statement, however, reveals a discursive strategy implemented by several elite intellectuals during the 1930s to promote the perception of a bygone unity under Spanish domination, one in direct opposition to the *desorden* created by U.S. control. His reference to a former period of *españolidad homogénea* (homogeneous Spanishness) not only glosses over the violence that underlies colonialism but also misrepresents the scope and uniformity of Spanish cultural infiltration in the Americas. By invoking *Spanishness* as a unifying influence that stretches across the "esplendoroso Imperio de las Indias," Belaval inserts Puerto Rico in a broader hemispheric colonial history and even declares Puerto Rico's pivotal role as the "cáscara de reunión de la gran familia panamericana" (nutshell of the great Pan-American family) (66).

Thus far I have emphasized that the image of the family as a metaphor for unity was central to the canon's articulation of the nation throughout most of the twentieth century. However, the so-called unity of *la gran familia* proved to be nothing more than a fiction, a mere projection of the elite's desire to recuperate their fleeting hegemony. In reality, the

Puerto Rican family was dysfunctional and highly divided across racial, class, and gender lines. Nevertheless, this image remained in use well into the period of Luis Muñoz Marín's governorship, better known as *la era muñocista*, a time during which "the rhetoric of the nation as family is built upon social, racial, and gender hierarchies that guarantee the hegemony of the creole sector."[3] As Eleuterio Santiago-Díaz reminds us, by the 1970s it was clear that the paradigm of social and racial democracy that had reemerged in the 1930s and became institutionalized under Muñoz Marín's government in the 1950s relied on the family metaphor to conceal deep societal fissures. A thin veil of harmony and unity had been used to mask social, racial, and gender disparities that otherwise would have compromised the hegemonic position of the island's elite.

As *la gran familia* became increasingly scrutinized in post-1970s literature, it became evident that the ideal of *hispanismo* paradoxically served to undermine the image of unity that the myth sought to create. In other words, the myth was built on an internal contradiction: a semblance of homogeneity predicated on a segregationist discourse. While originally it had served to justify racism against blacks and *mulatos*, more recently it had been recycled and used to instigate linguistic prejudice and other forms of discrimination against Puerto Rican (re) migrants. *Hispanismo*, therefore, can be seen as an instrument of "symbolic" and "hard" violence against various marginalized sectors of society throughout Puerto Rico's history.

The perception of homogeneity and racial democracy underlying *la gran familia* has been contingent on the acceptance of *mestizaje*, defined by the anthropologist Arlene Torres as "the ideology of racial mixture, [which] is an integral part of national discourse and practice throughout Latin America and the Spanish-speaking Caribbean" (296). While racial mixture has been deemed a positive notion, Torres is correct to point out that "in Puerto Rico, the ideology of 'mestizaje' acknowledges the contributions of people of African, indigenous, and Spanish descent in the formation of the nation, but it also maintains and promotes racialist ideas and practices" (296). It is also important to remember that despite the mainly positive connotation that is presently ascribed to concepts such as *mestizaje* and hybridity, these concepts conceal the use of violence, in many instances a violence as brutal as that effected by the leash and the *carimbo*, the branding iron used by the Spaniards to mark the African slaves on their heads and/or shoulders (Santiago-Díaz 46). Today, claims of *mestizaje* and racial democracy in Puerto Rico still dominate racial discourses and continue to conceal the desire for the *blanqueamiento* (whitening) of its highly intermixed population. For this reason, it can be argued that *mestizaje* has served to perpetuate both external and internal racism, despite claims to the contrary (Torres 1998; Rivero 2005; Santiago-Díaz 2007).

The ideology of *mestizaje* underlying *la gran familia* has also had a crucial impact as a mechanism of self-censorship among Afro–Puerto Ricans, who have generally been more cautious in their denouncement of racism than their Anglo and/or French Afro-Caribbean counterparts. In Santiago-Díaz's view, this explains why "to Afro–Puerto Ricans, the discussion of racism represents an uncomfortable trap, because they understand that making any claims from their position as blacks is equivalent to casting doubt upon their citizenship and the place that has been 'so generously' granted to them within the heart of 'the great Puerto Rican family.'"[4] In other words, this critic suggests that the ideology of racial democracy has in fact been used as a discursive weapon to silence the denunciation of racism by Afro–Puerto Rican sectors. Even today the perception of national unity promoted through this foundational myth is grounded in an ironic fiction; it apparently signals inclusion while in reality it has been used by dominant (i.e., white) sectors to erect *intrafamilial borders* in an effort to safeguard their hegemony.

The paradoxical coexistence of the discourse of racial democracy—embedded in *la gran familia*—and an abiding quest for *blanqueamiento* has stifled the development of an Afro–Puerto Rican political consciousness.[5] In contrast to other Caribbean nations, Puerto Rico's colonial status has made possible the incongruous coexistence of the ideals of racial democracy and *blanqueamiento*. This is evident in the fact that the attainment of *blanqueamiento,* as contradictory as it may seem, became a paramount preoccupation among the members of the *generación del treinta* in their search to achieve national unity amid the threat of Americanization.

A case in point is Tomás Blanco's *El prejuicio racial en Puerto Rico*, where in an effort to draw a distinction between Puerto Rican and U.S. racial discourses/attitudes as a strategy to strengthen nationalism the author misrepresents the conditions of blacks and *mulatos* on the island. His essay opens with the statement, "In Puerto Rico we still don't know very well what racial prejudice means."[6] According to him, race relations in Puerto Rico offer a sharp contrast to those of the southern United States given the lack of deep-seated hatred and violence found in the former. His denial of racial prejudice on the island leads him to brush aside expressions of discord as simple *ñoñerías* (whining), ridiculous gestures by certain segments of the population—especially women, who in his opinion have no qualms about displaying intense prejudices (129). Throughout his essay, Blanco emphasizes *convivencia* between Puerto Ricans of all colors—also a recurrent concept in his *Prontuario histórico*—as evidence of the lack of racial prejudice that he sees as plaguing U.S. society. He also underscores this point by contrasting the process of abolition of slavery on the island to that in the United States, which leads him to conclude that on the island this process culminates in the pacific and total abolition of slavery (117).

Blanco's portrayal of a conflict-free abolition of slavery had already entered his race relations discourse when in *Prontuario histórico* he claimed, "The initiation, development, and triumph of the abolitionist sentiment in our country is the clearest chapter in island history."[7] Perhaps it was his absolute conviction of a predominant antislavery sentiment on the island that led him to summarize, in just one sentence, this important chapter in Puerto Rican history.[8] His tendency to gloss over certain issues is not only evident in his rendition of the island's history; it also surfaces with respect to African contributions to Puerto Rican culture. For instance, on more than one occasion he makes claims such as "our culture in general is white, 'occidental', with very few and insignificant non-Spanish influences," or even more controversially, that "the African element has had a minimal influence on our cultural traits."[9] Statements such as these—which openly reveal his Hispanophilia— serve to confirm that while Blanco might have tried to convey an image of inclusiveness and nonprejudice, trying to render invisible the role of African cultures in Puerto Rican society amounts to a racist gesture in and of itself.

In a similar vein, Emilio Belaval in *Los problemas de la cultura puertorriqueña* (1933) echoes Blanco's Hispanophile perspective when he asserts, "We are Spanish through and through, and in our national makeup there is a respectable amount of Spanish-ness."[10] Through his exaltation of the so-called inherent *españolismo* of Puerto Rican culture, Belaval mirrors the ideology of *blanqueamiento* that was dominant at the time. Problematic claims such as "the Puerto Rican black is, nevertheless, the whitest black in the Americas" reflect his desire to whiten and Europeanize the Puerto Rican population.[11] Even more disconcerting is Belaval's readiness to negate the existence of a Puerto Rican black population: "I expect tourists to experience utmost disappointment. We don't have blacks, or gauchos, or 'bandoleros,' or Indians."[12] Blanco's and Belaval's postures echo those of a long line of Puerto Rican intellectuals who have given shape to the "Puerto Rican paradox," that is, the fact that the "mixture is embraced, provided that the essence of Puerto Rican society and culture is still rooted in Spain and later in the Americas" (A. Torres 287).

Today, while many Puerto Ricans would like to assume that racial democracy has been achieved on the island (Santiago-Díaz 27), even the seemingly trivial racialization of particular localities (coastal towns, urban spaces, the street, *caseríos* [projects]) attests to the prevailing racism that continues to mar this society. The (imaginary) circumscription of the Afro–Puerto Rican element to specific areas—which has historical roots that date to the eighteenth and nineteenth centuries—has also promoted the conflation of race and class, leading to the widespread racialization of certain indicators of social status (A. Torres 297). For instance, Puerto Rican ethnography has traditionally conceived of the island's sociocultural makeup in terms of oppositional binaries such as mountain/coast, white/black, European/African (Quintero Rivera 1986; Duany 1984; Torres 1998; Santiago-Díaz 2007; Rivero 2005). As Arlene Torres argues, "These symbolically charged categories perpetuate the construction of a black identity that is tied to a coastal plantation economy that relied on a black and enslaved labor force and a romanticized *jíbaro* identity of 'white' peasants in the mountainous interior of the island" (293). The danger of such binaries, as Torres herself points out, is that in ignoring evidence that blacks and *mulatos* lived, worked, and moved across various sociogeographic settings, "the historical contributions of free black people prior to the abolition of slavery and thereafter is left unwritten" (293). One of the most ignominious repercussions of this division has been the virtual erasure of the *jíbaro negro* (the black highland peasant) from Puerto Rican social memory, a topic to which I return in more detail in chapter 3.

I view the oppositional categories mountain/coast, white/black—a creation of the intellectual elites that were in large part officialized by the disciplines of historiography and ethnography—as another manifestation of a *frontera intranacional*. These types of binaries have perpetuated a division between the African (mostly from the French- and English-speaking Caribbean) and the European (mostly Catalans, Corsicans, Mallorcans, and French) elements of the island's population, with ramifications that we can witness to this day.[13] For instance, a contemporary analogue is the polarity between *urbanizaciones* (neighborhoods) and *caseríos*, as Arlene Torres reminds us, where the former is not typically seen as a place where black people live, despite the "phenotypical variation" that can be found in that setting (296). The common perception that "poor, dispossessed, and dark-skinned Puerto Ricans reside in *arrabales*, sectors of towns or villages with substandard housing, and in *caseríos*, public housing complexes," in turn has fueled the notion that they are to blame for the island's social ills (296).

In the past few decades, the influx of Caribbean migrants of African descent to Puerto Rico has heightened tensions surrounding racial issues. Among these groups, the case of Dominicans stands out due to the sheer magnitude of their migration to the island beginning in the mid-1960s. Dominican migrants, whether legal or undocumented, are mostly regarded as *black* and have thus endured a great deal of racism in Puerto Rico. Duany views "the popular conflation of the term *negro* (black) with *dominicano* (Dominican)" as evidence of the "growing ethnicization of racial stigmas on the Island, as well as the continuing perception that being black is foreign to national identity" (*Puerto Rican* 27). In other words, the exclusion of black Puerto Ricans from the national imaginary has been intensified as a result of the presence of an "other" (Dominican migrant) against whom the "Puerto Rican identity" is constructed as nonblack.

This brief discussion about the perception of Dominican migrants serves a twofold purpose: it challenges *la gran familia* by drawing attention to the *frontera intranacional* that has been erected between the local Puerto Rican population and various immigrant groups; and it mirrors the perception of Puerto Rican (return) migrants on the island, who have also become scapegoats for the island's social ills. In some cases, their exclusion from the contemporary national imaginary parallels that of blacks, *mulatos*, Dominicans, and other minorities. The backlash against Puerto Rican return migrants that began to be felt in the 1970s and 1980s (Duany 2002; Pérez 2004; Flores 2009) is thus indicative of the marginal position of this community vis-à-vis *la gran familia puertorriqueña*.

In fact, I would argue that the myth has been reactivated by neonationalist sectors during the past few decades in an effort to attenuate what Juan Flores calls the *migratory counterstreams* that the island has experienced since the advent of full-fledged return migration (*Diaspora* 33).[14] *Hispanismo* has therefore resurfaced as a key instrument in the demarcation of a boundary (linguistic, racial, class-based) that divides a so-called authentic *puertorriqueñidad* from its seemingly myriad "copies." Because in the insular imaginary migrants have been chiefly perceived as lower-class, dark-skinned, and non–Spanish speaking, they have for the most part remained outside the limits of the local "imagined community," to borrow Benedict Anderson's term. Prevalent perceptions of this group have their roots in the socioeconomic history of Puerto Rican migration to the United States, in particular the conditions that propelled the Great Migration, when a great majority of those who relocated to the mainland were poor, black, and *mulato* unskilled workers. The demographic profile of that specific migratory wave—the most significant in Puerto Rican history—led to what could be called the racialization of the diaspora.

Over time, the *frontera intranacional* that has been erected between the island and the diaspora has been rendered even more complex by the gradual intensification of linguistic nationalism. In Negrón-Muntaner's view, proponents of language nationalism on the island have overstated the role of Spanish in "an attempt to uphold the frontier allegedly separating the island from the United States, and islander elites from U.S./lower-class Puerto Ricans" ("English" 280). In other words, Spanish has been used as a measure of *puertorriqueñidad* by conservative sectors, and in this way they have excluded a large percentage of the population from the island's imaginary in the name of the "nation."

The highly transmigratory character of the Puerto Rican population has had incalculable repercussions for communities inside and outside the island, not only as a result of the physical relocation and resettlement of a great percentage of migrants, but also because of the continuous flow of ideas and practices between both sides, or what Flores refers to as *cultural remittances*. According to Flores, this term describes how, "by means of return and circulatory migration and multiple conduits of mediated and direct communications, cultural customs and practices, ideological orientations, forms of artistic expression, and ideas of group identity acquired in diaspora settings are remitted to homeland societies" (*Diaspora* 44). Of central concern among the island's nationalist elites has been the infiltration of what they consider destabilizing racial discourses in the past decades, particularly the development of a black racial consciousness that has made its way from the diaspora back to the island.

For instance, an awareness of the historical ties that unite Puerto Ricans and African Americans on the mainland—particularly evident in their collaboration during the civil rights movements in the 1960s and 1970s—has developed among some U.S. Puerto Ricans, who have come to see themselves as part of a broader African diasporan movement as a result of their own racialization on U.S. soil.[15] In other words, the experiences of many black and *mulato* Puerto Ricans as a racialized minority on the mainland has fostered new attitudes toward race that are spilling over to their homeland communities. As Flores puts it, "In our time, the very foundations of Dominican, Puerto Rican, and even Cuban national ideologies are being shaken by the remittance of Afro-Dominican, Afro–Puerto Rican, and Afro-Cuban identities. These are borne in decidedly new ways by return migrants and their children as they resurface in home-country settings after a veritable apprenticeship in black consciousness acquired in working-class diaspora 'hoods' in the United States" (*Diaspora* 47). Basically, Flores is reminding us of the unanticipated yet profound cultural impact that the life experiences of migrants in the United States can have in home countries, including the historically racist societies of the Spanish-speaking Caribbean.

The possible destabilization of racial and other social paradigms through daily practices and cultural expressions brought by return migrants to Puerto Rico should not be understated given its potentially "explosive" impact (Flores 144). One illustration is the current standing of the neonationalist intellectual; according to Pabón, "the metaphor of the intellectual as 'legislator' is presently facing a crisis."[16] Pabón highlights the threat that return migration constitutes to this group's hegemony as it calls into question their capacity to define the limits/borders of the nation. The vulnerability of this intellectual sector is evident in the way they have deployed *hispanismo* as a strategy to devalue U.S. Puerto Rican cultural production.

Much like their predecessors in the 1930s and 1950s, some neonationalist intellectuals (i.e., *puertorriqueñistas*) have adopted a discourse that recuperates *hispanismo* as the ultimate measuring stick of Puerto Rican identity. Contemporary cultural and national debates continue to center on issues such as language, race, and place of residence in conceptualizing the "essence" of Puerto Rican identity. The presence of 4.6 people of Puerto Rican origin or descent living on the U.S. mainland—compared to 3.7 on the island—has rekindled a sense of urgency among those who conceive of the diaspora community as a menace to Puerto Rican culture. For those who subscribe to this posture, the migrant embodies that which is foreign, an *elemento perturbador* (disturbing element), to echo Blanco's words, that threatens to disrupt the so-called harmony of *la gran familia*.[17]

Ironically, diasporic Puerto Ricans tend to display a strong sense of cultural nationalism and often imagine themselves as part of the national family (Duany, *Puerto Rican* 31). Cultural practices and artistic expressions by U.S. Puerto Ricans—whether in English, Spanish, or Spanglish—speak to the common historical roots shared by communities on both sides. In many cases, particularly in U.S. Puerto Rican women's narratives, their discourse tends to challenge Hispanophilia through the assertion of their Puerto Rican origins. The following section examines the various ways in which two Puerto Rican authors engage in a challenge of Hispanophilia—from an insular and a diaspora perspective—that successfully debunks the cultural pillar of *la gran familia puertorriqueña*.

This myth represents a primary axis on which Ferré's *Maldito amor* and Ortíz Cofer's *Silent Dancing* develop their feminist constructions of the nation. Although the degree to which each text engages in a dialogue with the metanarrative of *la gran familia* varies, both works, consciously or unconsciously, question hegemonic constructions of the Puerto Rican nation that have been informed by this myth. The preoccupation of these texts with regard to the representation of the nation, each from an equally valid context and location, thus constitutes a crucial link between them.

House and Family as Metaphors of the Nation

More often than not, essentialist and exclusionary views of the nation have relied on notions of purity and contamination. Adamant defenders of a Puerto Rican "essence" often conceive of cultural purity as a function of bloodline purity. The correlation of these two aspects of identity traditionally has been crystallized in the image of the house that is prevalent in nationalist discourses. As Pabón reminds us, "The metaphor of the nation as house or home—the family metaphor, the stage of the primal scene of the nation—usually goes hand in hand with organic metaphors of identity."[18] This emblematic correspondence between house, family, and nation has been crucial to the development and dissemination of static notions of *puertorriqueñidad* since the late nineteenth century. Therefore, the recurrence of the image of *la casa* in Puerto Rican letters reflects its position as the privileged space of the great Puerto Rican family (Gelpí 107).

However, the implied correlation between house, family, and nation has come under scrutiny in the works of post-1970s writers, especially female writers, who have systematically contested the patriarchal order that this space symbolizes. Even a cursory look at the production of now-canonical female writers serves to confirm the central role that the metaphor of the house plays in contemporary literature: Magali García Ramis's *Felices días, Tío Sergio* (1986), Ana Lydia Vega's *El baúl de*

Miss Florence (1991), Olga Nolla's *La segunda hija* and *El manuscrito de Miramar* (1998), and Rosario Ferré's *Maldito amor, The House on the Lagoon* (1995), and *Eccentric Neighborhoods* (1998), to name a few.[19] Each one of these texts succeeds in destabilizing the image of *la casa patriarcal* to some degree, thus unveiling its failure to provide cohesion to the national myth and to preserve the "orden vertical antiguo" (traditional hierarchy) that it came to symbolize (Santiago-Díaz 218). The remainder of this chapter situates Ferré's *Maldito amor* as a counterpoint to Ortíz Cofer's *Silent Dancing* (1990) to demonstrate how these texts challenge hegemonic views of the nation, particularly through their interrogation of the patriarchal myth of *la gran familia puertorriqueña*. I believe that their challenge of *hispanismo*—one of the main principles of *la gran familia* that exalts whiteness, the Spanish language, Catholicism, and so on—constitutes a significant, yet overlooked, literary contact zone between the literature of Puerto Rican female authors from both sides. While the critique of *hispanismo* is a point of convergence between these corpuses, there are also divergences that result from the specific historical factors that have shaped their respective experiences. For instance, issues of race and class take precedence in insular production, whereas in the diaspora questions of language and race outweigh other concerns. In the end, this analysis seeks to unveil the connections between narrative texts from both sides, with a focus on the challenges they pose to *la gran familia* and their respective canons.

My focus on Ferré's *Maldito amor* and Ortíz Cofer's *Silent Dancing* stems from what I see as some relevant connections between these works. For instance, *Maldito amor* and *Silent Dancing* are the first short novels by these authors, published during the boom of Puerto Rican women's narrative in the 1980s and 1990s.[20] Interestingly, despite formal and linguistic differences, both texts are structured around the metaphors of the family and the house that destabilize hegemonic (i.e., patriarchal) views of the nation from a feminist perspective. The links between these two authors thus run deeper than meets the eye, given that as Suzanne Bost puts it, Rosario Ferré, Ana Lydia Vega, Judith Ortíz Cofer and Aurora Levins Morales "all belong to the first generation of self-proclaimed 'feminist' writers from Puerto Rico, emerging after the 1970s, and they cross an analysis of gender and sexuality with their analyses of nationality, race, and culture" (191). Ferré and Ortíz Cofer, as my analysis shows, are two of the pioneer female voices to openly challenge the patriarchal canons of the island and the diaspora respectively.

If Walls Could Talk: Dismantling Facades
in Rosario Ferré's *Maldito amor*

The icon of *la casa patriarcal*, which came to embody the patriarchal values associated with the myth of *la gran familia* in the 1930s, is both crystallized and undermined in Ferré's *Maldito amor* in a move that opened the literary floodgates to the dismantling of this national symbol. Locating the action of the narrative at the turn of the twentieth century allows Ferré to confront head-on the myth of the glorified hacienda and the alleged harmony that enveloped *la gran familia*. Contrary to what the members of the *generación del treinta* have claimed, the sociologist Quintero Rivera has argued that by the 1898 U.S. invasion, "the union of the Puerto Rican family had started to break".[21] An examination of the De la Valles' *casa patriarcal*, in terms of both its physical structure and the social hierarchy that it symbolizes, reveals the multiple ways in which the novel takes issue with the myth of *la gran familia*. As Ferré herself puts it in the foreword, "When I wrote *Sweet Diamond Dust* I wanted to do a parody of this paradise. The novel points out the fact that land on our island has always been limited. . . . Our haciendas were never vast like in Cuba; our landed bourgeoisie never rich" (viii).[22] Because Ferré's *Maldito amor* is one of the first post-1960s "extended narratives" (novellas) to destabilize the patriarchal canon from a feminist perspective, it is considered a milestone in Puerto Rican letters.

The De la Valle family estate in the fictitious town of Guamaní stands for the prototypical hacienda of the turn of the century, when the island was transferred from Spanish to American colonial hands. Its location at the heart of Central Justicia is also emblematic of the key role that the family plays in the town, and of their economic, political, and social capital. While the reader does not have access to a detailed description of the house, we learn that it was designed for the De la Valles by a French architect over a century before Don Julio and Doña Elvira's wedding. The inside of the *casona* was tastefully decorated with imported European pieces that served to reflect the privileged status of the family.

In addition to brief descriptions of the interior, the reader eventually learns certain details about its spatial dimensions—for instance, there is a *sótano* (basement) and a cottage in the backyard that serves as a servants' quarters. Although apparently trivial, these features prove significant, because as the novel suggests each space of the house is imbued with meaning, reflecting the hierarchy of power within *la gran familia*. In other words, while the family apparently coexists under the same roof, not everyone, especially those who do not share the De la Valle's bloodline, has equal access to all spaces. The configuration of the house thus reflects a conception of national identity that privileges the white/European upper-class ancestry of the De la Valles above all other markers of identity.

For instance, Titina, the old servant and last slave of Guamaní, lives in the cottage, and her access to the center of the house is contingent on her subordinate position as housemaid, despite the fact that she considers herself a member of the family (30). In a similar fashion, Gloria, who moves in to help care for an ailing Don Ubaldino, is also relegated to the *sótano,* and even her lover, Arístides de la Valle, objects to her presence at the dinner table. The marginalization of these characters to these peripheral spaces ultimately reflects the power differentials that keep them subordinated as nonmembers of the family but also as women of color—Titina is black, and Gloria is *mulata*—and thus serves to dismantle the myth of racial democracy embedded in *la gran familia.*

Maldito amor also examines a range of racial, class, political, and gender divisions that undermine the so-called unity of the great Puerto Rican family. Of paramount importance is the text's challenge and parody of the symbolic white/Hispanic patriarchal figure at the head of *la gran familia*, achieved by casting doubt on Don Ubaldino's and his family's claims to their *limpieza de sangre* (bloodline purity). Despite the fact that Don Hermenegildo emphasizes the De la Valles' European ancestry when writing Don Ubaldino's story, Doña Laura's testimony later in the novel unveils the fiction behind his efforts to "whiten" the family.

In contrast to Don Hermenegildo's claim that Don Ubaldino's father, Don Julio, was "un español prestigioso" (19), at her deathbed Doña Laura confesses what she had learned from Gloria, that is, that "Doña Elvira, educated in Paris amid silk cushions, had married a black man! That was the reason I could never find a single portrait, daguerrotype, or photograph of poor Don Julio Font in the house" (74).[23] Anyone familiar with the novel would agree that once Doña Laura discloses the secret of Don Julio's blackness, the source of the De la Valles' anxiety over their racial lineage becomes more clear to the reader. In fact, critics have overstated this point, but in doing so they have failed to look beyond the traditional understanding that most Puerto Ricans have of the label *negro,* potentially dismissing one of the criticisms put forth by the novel.

Rather than refer to the features and phenotype characteristic of most Africans who were brought to the Americas in the slave trade, the text's emphasis on Don Julio's blackness and Spanish origins could be pointing in a direction that has often been overlooked: the fact that "Moroccans were in Spain for eight hundred years, and those were the same people who came in boats to the Caribbean" (Hernández Cruz, unpublished interview). In other words, through the character of Don Julio *Maldito amor* playfully disrupts the equivalence between *white* and *Spanish* that underlies the concept of *hispanismo* by reminding us that a significant number of the Spaniards who settled in the Caribbean were of mixed sub-Saharan blood. In this sense, the ambiguity of Don Julio's race suggests the destabilization of the very foundation of Puerto Rican identity by rendering more complex its tripartite—Spanish (i.e. white), Taíno, and African (i.e., black)—roots.

Because his blackness is considered a threat to the De la Valles' legitimacy and power, particularly that of the town's *white* hero Don Ubaldino, it needs to remain concealed. Don Ubaldino's and his aunts' anxiety over protecting the image of their family's white/Spanish roots is immediately noticed by Doña Laura, who at first cannot understand their obsession (71). As she puts it, "When I first came to this house as a newlywed, I realized the family I had married into was a strange one indeed. . . . [The aunts] would spend days on end poring over a set of heavy parchment tomes bound in soddy, grimy goatskin, tracing the De la Valles' complicated family tree. With breathless amazement they would then proclaim to the world that such and such's grandmother was the daughter of Countess Tosspot, or that such and such's grandfather was the Marquis of Merdeland, grandson of the Duke of Feculence, and for that reason the De la Valles were direct descendants of the daughters of El Cid" (69–70).[24] Doña Laura's comment not only parodies the family's desire for *blanqueamiento* but also allows us to see the logic behind a series of symbolic "erasures" of Don Julio from the family genealogy. On the one hand, the conspicuous absence of images of Don Julio around the house is emblematic of the family's effort to conceal their shame regarding the interracial relationship between Doña Elvira and Don Julio, as well as the subsequent embarrassment behind Don Ubaldino's mixed racial heritage.

On the other hand, and perhaps more significant, is the total removal of Don Julio's name from the family pedigree, achieved by Don Ubaldino's substitution of his paternal last name, "Font," by his mother's maiden name. According to Doña Laura, what led her husband to reject his father's name had been "his desperate need to conceal this, not only before the beveled mirrors of Guamaní's casino but before the shaving mirror of his own *nécessaire*, [and which] had led him to pretend a purity of blood he didn't possess" (77).[25] Ironically, the act of privileging the maternal over the paternal name as a way to safeguard the family's social status ultimately undermines it. The artificial deletion of any traces of Don Ubaldino's paternal genealogy in the end has the effect of "bastardizing" the family. In traditional Puerto Rican society, where social legitimacy is maintained through patriarchal bloodlines, the paradoxical nature of this act bluntly exposes the racism at the core of Puerto Rican society's quest for whitening, or *blanqueamiento*.[26]

Race, as we will see, is not the only identity marker that threatens the family's cohesion. Class also plays a key role as a mechanism of exclusion, evident in the attitude that Don Ubaldino's aunts assume vis-à-vis his relationship with Doña Laura. As the latter explains, "This doesn't mean that we didn't have our little mishaps during our first years together, like for example when Doña Elvira and Doña Estefana found out about our impending marriage. From their standpoint, my last name wasn't patrician enough for a De la Valle" (66).[27] As the daughter of an immigrant merchant, Doña Laura's middle-class background is not well regarded by Don Ubaldino's aunts. Because she is perceived as a threat to the family's prestige, she is never fully accepted by her husband's aristocratic family.

Ironically, it is precisely Doña Laura's marginal position within the family that allows her to be critical and rebel against the hegemonic (precapitalist, Hispanophile, patriarchal, racist, and classist) order that the De la Valles symbolize. For instance, she decries their hypocrisy when she complains to Don Hermenegildo on her deathbed, "In spite of their living on a tight income (the mill, which Ubaldino had just bought from the northerners, was still just breaking even and the aunts had to earn their living giving piano lessons and embroidering lace shawls), the family's delirium of greatness made them unable to live without servants" (70).[28] In other words, the aunts seem to be stuck in the past, holding on to the prestige and social capital that was once associated with their family name, when in reality they now live by modest means.

Doña Laura's condemnation of the family's pomposity reveals common attitudes among the insular elite, not only regarding class, but also regarding race. She is the first to denounce the family's racism and to call attention to the reality of *mestizaje* that other members try to deny (Bustos Fernández 27). One day, on hearing the aunts discuss which families in Guamaní were truly white, Doña Laura confronted them. As she puts it, "One day I couldn't stand their ugly habit any longer, and asked them sarcastically if they didn't think they were really pushing the point, since in recent years there had been such a great number of intermarriages in Guamaní's haut monde that by now everybody was related and probably not a single family could be considered white" (70).[29] In addition to confronting her husband and his aunts about their "follón de abolengo" (fuss about their ancestry) (72), she does not hesitate to divulge the family's most well kept secret, which she learned after her husband's condition had worsened—that Don Julio Font was black. Her confession to Don Hermenegildo regarding Don Julio's blackness and her husband's mixed racial background thus constitutes a crucial way in which Doña Laura challenges the De la Valles' legitimacy and privileged social status.

While critics have analyzed the impact of race and class on this family's structure, especially in relation to the characters of Gloria and Doña Laura, the crucial intersection of race, gender, class, and politics, embodied in Gloria, has received less attention. It is no coincidence that Gloria is mostly defined by her sexuality, given that traditional views of the *mulata* in Puerto Rican and Caribbean cultures tend to envision her as a sensual, hip-swaying, seductive figure that embodies male desire but also anxieties about interracial mixing. Giving a new twist to the traditional stereotype of the hypersexual *mulata,* Ferré emphasizes the political divisions that undermine the image of *la gran familia.*[30] It could be argued that Gloria's characterization as object of desire of all the De la Valle men functions as an allegory of how the Puerto Rican people— mostly the lower/middle-class mestizo majority—have been courted by the three main political parties in their quest for power. She becomes the "prize" for which the De la Valle men must compete in order to prove their masculinity, and in that sense, her role is defined as the catalyst that sets in motion the power struggle waged between Don Ubaldino, Nicolás, and Arístides.

Gloria is originally introduced in the novel as Arístides's lover, although readers later learn that she married Nicolás, the De la Valles' firstborn and future owner of Central Justicia. After Gloria becomes pregnant with Nicolasito, it is suggested that the child could be Don Ubaldino's. The conflict that emerges regarding Gloria's ambiguous position within the family—always as object of desire—underscores the hatred that develops between the three men. As the narrative implies, Arístides's hatred for his brother Nicolás—certainly fueled by the latter's marriage to Gloria—leads him to assassinate his own brother by staging the airplane accident that takes Nicolás's life.

However, the love triangle that develops admits another reading: it signals Gloria's symbolic role as a political pawn. In fact, the debacle surrounding Gloria's position within the family unveils the fact that political divisions have always caused a rift among the De la Valles (82). For example, the struggle for Gloria unveils the political strife between the pro-statehood and pro-independence camps that Arístides and Nicolás represent respectively. While Arístides learns English and embraces the capitalist way—underscored by his friendships with Americans and his plan to sell Central Justicia to U.S. investors—Nicolás's anti-American stance echoes that of his father, Don Ubaldino, a representative of the nationalist *criollo* landowning elite. The family's fragmentation along political lines mirrors the partisan divisions that emerged after the U.S. invasion in 1898 and that continue to divide families today. Don Ubaldino, like many members of the landowning class, sought to maintain his power despite the escalation of American domination through the acquisition of land. Don Ubaldino's heroic "rescue" of the De la Valles' Central Justicia, the last *criollo*-owned sugar mill in Guamaní, from American hands epitomizes the struggle of the landowning elite to retain their power amid the structural transformations that followed the American invasion, and which threatened, and eventually collapsed, the semifeudal agrarian system implemented under Spanish colonial rule.

However, Don Ubaldino's opposition to the U.S. takeover of Guamaní extends beyond the issue of land to encompass even the most mundane details of daily life, which he also regards as evidence of the Americanization his country is undergoing. His rejection of all things American is evident in the following comment by Titina: "Niño Ubaldino was always an honorable man; he'd have let his right hand be cut off before he'd sell a single acre of land to the northerners. 'Manifest Destiny,' 'Big Stick policy,' the 'American Army Mule,' even 'Scott Emulsion,' 'Palmolive Soap,' 'Baseball,' and that wonderfully quaint invention, the 'toothbrush,' . . . all became hateful words to him, part of the same vocabulary with which he damned the heavens every morning" (22).[31] As this fragment suggests, even products such as Palmolive soap and the toothbrush are reminders of the extent to which Puerto Rican society is being transformed as a result of the American invasion. Not only are Puerto Ricans losing their land to the hands of U.S. investors, but they are also experiencing a sort of transculturation as the United States tries to impose its culture and customs on its new subjects. For Don Ubaldino, everything, from American foreign policy to household products, reminds him of the impending "downfall" of Puerto Rican culture.

While Don Ubaldino can be said to represent one end of the political spectrum—the archetypal national father figure—the text also provides counterexamples of alternative political stances. The fact that the members of the De la Valle family adopt different and often conflictive positions regarding the issue of the island's status vis-à-vis the United States challenges the vision of a united family/nation expounded by nationalist intellectuals. Perhaps occupying the opposite side of the spectrum are Don Ubaldino's daughters, who marry the sons of American investors. To a man who has vowed never to lose his land to the hands of these foreigners, "losing" his daughters to the enemy is nothing short of an act of treason. In fact, his grief is powerful enough to produce physical symptoms, as Titina observes: "When the girls began to grow up and they all married into those families that held shares of Snow White Mills . . . Niño Ubaldino became ill and was bedridden for more than a week" (22).[32] Don Ubaldino's response to his daughters' treason is to disinherit them, which opens a rift in the family.

Undoubtedly, these events constitute an allegorical representation of the internal divisions that formed along political lines, permanently disuniting the Puerto Rican nation. But also, Ferré's depiction of the daughters as a sort of Puerto Rican *Malinche* who marry the enemy can be read as an allegorical rendering of the complex and inevitable bond that has been created between Puerto Rico and the United States.[33] As a radical nationalist, Don Ubaldino considers his daughters' marriages an act of treason against the nation. Marital union with the enemy not only implies physical surrender of the woman/colonized nation to the man/colonizing power, but ultimately forebodes the extinction of the Puerto Rican nation. Paradoxically, what Don Ubaldino sees as his daughters' poor "choices" of partners is not presented in the text as acts of free will. The reader learns that the daughters had been consistently rejected by their upper-class social circle due to racial prejudice (Don Ubaldino's father was a black man), which made it virtually impossible for them to be courted by *criollo* men. Their marriages can be interpreted as acts of rebellion against the strict racial/social codes that regulated Puerto Rican women's romantic relationships—and, ultimately, their sexuality. In the end, the novel's portrayal of the various political postures that the members of the De la Valle family assume constitutes yet another dimension of the heterogeneity that the *generación del treinta* sought to conceal under the myth of the nation-family.

As stated at the beginning of this chapter, one of the main precepts of the myth of *la gran familia* is the notion of familial unity under the authority of a "benevolent" father figure. After demonstrating how *Maldito amor* questions the ideal of familial unity, I would like to turn my

attention to how the novel challenges the iconic image of the compassionate and caring father. To begin with, the original patriarch, Don Julio, is
depicted as a violent and greedy man who controls his wife, Doña Elvira,
through physical abuse. In a telling scene, after Doña Elvira learns that
a former slave of her father had lost his arm working at the sugar mill,
she rebukes her husband's actions: "'If you can't give that man back his
arm, at least have a pension paid out to him for the rest of his days.'
And she added that the accident had been his fault, because he had put
Don Calixto, who was old and half-blind, in charge of the supervision
of the mill's presses" (13).[34] Don Julio's reaction to what he considered
an affront on her part reveals the verbal and physical violence to which
his wife was subjected. As the narrator recounts, he screamed, "'From
today onward, in this house women may speak when chickens start to
pee, and I forbid you to go on meddling in other people's business.' And
as he struck her left and right, he added that her saintly De la Valles, like
the rest of Guamaní's hacienda owners of yore, had also been slave driv-
ers" (14).[35] As a result, Doña Elvira "se hundió en un silencio de niebla"
(sank into a foggy silence) from which she never managed to escape (25).

Don Ubaldino, the so-called hero of Guamaní, also defies the ideal
of the benevolent father figure by calling into question his public image
as an upstanding and incorruptible man. The dismantling of the honorable portrait that Don Hermenegildo, the novelist-turned-historian,
fabricates in his apology of Don Ubaldino occurs both at the personal
and the public level. On the one hand, Doña Laura's confession to Don
Hermenegildo on her deathbed undermines Don Ubaldino's moral principles. As she puts it, "Ubaldino and I had already begun to complete all
the above arrangements for a peaceful retirement, as befits the conclusion of a well-balanced life, when I made a frightful discovery. . . . During his political sojourns at the capital Ubaldino had contracted syphilis,
and I was terrified of becoming infected; I had nightmares that my spinal
cord would disintegrate, or that my body would break out in pustules,
and I refused to have marital relations with him" (72).[36] In uncovering
Don Ubaldino's syphilis, clearly the product of his philandering, Doña
Laura's testimony forces the reader to question his commitment to his
wife and family.

While some may argue that his personal life does not necessarily
compromise his political wherewithal, the text provides ample evidence
of Don Ubaldino's failure to live up to the standard of the righteous
political leader that Don Hermenegildo presents in his account. Earlier
I reviewed some of the predominant conceptions that the members of

the *generación del treinta* shared and disseminated regarding the *hacendado* as father figure. Among these, some notable descriptions characterize him as a "padre generoso" (Blanco) and as "árbitro de vida y de hacienda" who is "worshiped" by his peons (Belaval). Generally, the figure of the *hacendado* as *patriarca* rested on the assumption that he protected his peons and always valued their well-being above his own, just like a father is expected to do in relation to his own children. Contrary to Don Hermenegildo's portrayal of Don Ubaldino as Guamaní's patriarch, Gloria recalls a radically opposite vision of him: "He became just another politician, who could recite poems by heart about the tragic condition of a country that could now effectively rivet its heart to the whirling wheels of progress. . . . [He] fought fiercely against the northerners' efforts to democratize the town, against the right to strike, the minimum wage, and the eight-hour work day, striving to keep Guamaní's inhabitants in the same state of abject poverty they had known for centuries" (83).[37] Gloria's testimony thus parodies the figure of the hacendado as head of *la gran familia* of Guamaní by exposing the contradiction between his nationalistic/patriotic rhetoric and his egotistic conduct. While he sang the praises of the motherland, he objected to the passing of any laws or measures that would grant more rights to peons and that would therefore improve their conditions. Examined against his own actions—which reveal his greedy and self-serving motives—his words amount to no more than empty rhetoric that exposes his failure to live up to his popularity as the town's putative father figure.

The portrayal of Don Ubaldino that Gloria brings to light is not gratuitous but rather reflects widespread views about *hacendados* at that historical juncture, when they began to lose their hegemony. As José Luis González observes, the *hacendado*'s patriotic rhetoric amounted to no more than a desperate attempt to regain his control: "And when, besides that, it became evident that the new economic regime—that is the replacement of an hacienda-based to a plantation-based economy— meant the ruin of the hacendado class and the beginning of the political participation of the working class, the 'patriotic' rhetoric of the hacendados reached such a level of demagogy that even the liberal professional sector did not hesitate to ridicule it and condemn it."[38] As he points out, the escalation of the *hacendados'* patriotic rhetoric—which coincided with the increase of U.S. control of the land—sought to promote popular support in order to secure their hegemonic position. It was also at this critical moment that *hacendados* redeployed the myth of *la gran familia puertorriqueña* (Quintero Rivera, *Conflictos* 68). Yet their self-construction as "fathers" of the nation—which presupposed their interest in the well-being of their children/people—was challenged as their struggle to remain in power became apparent.

In addition to challenging the image of the "benevolent" and "righteous" father figure, *Maldito amor* undermines his power by portraying female characters that question his authority. The defiance of patriarchal authority takes multiple shapes in Ferré's text, as women engage in both major and minor acts of rebellion. Among these, Doña Laura's testament and Gloria's actions at the end of the novel stand out as overt acts of rebellion against the authority of the father and against the hacienda system.

Doña Laura's testament constitutes a speech act that challenges the patriarchal and Eurocentric order that the De la Valle family has tried to uphold against all odds. In this document, she overrides the authority of her husband, Don Ubaldino—embodied in his testament—by disowning her own children and designating her friend and daughter-in-law, Gloria, and her son, Nicolasito, as the legal heirs of Central Justicia. In part, Doña Laura's decision stems from the desire to put an end to what she sees as an anachronistic system that is contingent on exploitation. However, it is also the result of her personal vendetta against her own children, Arístides and his sisters, for their racist and snide remarks about Gloria during Don Ubaldino's funeral. As she confesses to Don Hermenegildo before her death, it was when she witnessed their hatred of Gloria that everything changed: "And then I screamed at the top of my voice, so that all Guamaní might hear me[,] . . . swearing at the top of my lungs that, in return for their inane pride and because the De la Valles' name was a farce and no one in that house really had any right to use it, when I died I'd disinherit all of them and leave my shares of Diamond Dust to Gloria Camprubí and her son" (80).[39] Convinced of the need to destroy an oppressive system that was often misrepresented as "just"—epitomized in the name Central Justicia—Doña Laura's symbolic erasure of Don Ubaldino's will constitutes an affront to dominant society on several dimensions. First, Doña Laura undermines patriarchal authority and disrupts its hierarchy by revoking her son Arístides's right to inherit Central Justicia and, in turn, appointing a woman and a child as the new rightful owners. Second, designating Gloria as Justicia's proprietor symbolically destabilizes class boundaries by placing a woman of lower social status at the center. And finally, and perhaps more important, Gloria's *mulatez* serves to disrupt the socio-racial order that privileges white/Eurocentric roots while denying or erasing African influences.

Doña Laura is aware that the execution of her testament will have the effect of distorting the paradigm of *la gran familia* by subverting the racial, class, and gender hierarchy on which it stands. The bold statement Doña Laura makes by naming Gloria her successor is further emphasized by the ambivalent position that the latter occupies within the family. The novel depicts Gloria as an object of desire for the three De la Valle men; she is Arístides's and possibly Don Ubaldino's lover, as well as Nicolás's wife. She also plays a central role in the family as Don Ubaldino's caregiver, Doña Laura's friend and confidant, and the mother of Nicolasito, the youngest heir to the family's fortune. Despite the multiple roles that Gloria plays in this context, she remains marginalized and is never fully accepted as an integral member of the family.

Maldito amor's closing scene, in which Gloria tears up Doña Laura's testament and gets ready to set the De la Valle house on fire while Don Hermenegildo and Arístides are still inside, represents the final debunking of the foundational myth of *la gran familia puertorriqueña*. Not only will Don Hermenegildo's ineludible death prevent the publication and dissemination of Don Ubaldino's glorified biography—putting an end to the propagation of that myth—but the destruction of the house seeks to eradicate the oppressive order that the hacienda system symbolizes. Gloria's intentions are clear when she tells Titina, "Listen to the cane stalks bursting around us like kindling, empty and dry like the gibberish of Don Hermenegildo's novel; rejoice with me because Diamond Dust will finally go up in smoke" (82).[40] Gloria's use of imagery associated with the slave trade (*látigos, azúcar, espaldas*) emphasizes her need as a woman of color to eradicate the oppression of racial minorities on the island. By rejecting Doña Laura's last wish that she and Nicolasito inherit the family property, this act of agency allows Gloria to rebel against the hegemonic order and patriarchal structures that the De la Valle family, including Doña Laura, come to represent. Gloria's final act of incinerating the house thus symbolizes her rebellion and her need to destroy all traces of the white elite's hacienda system that cemented her exclusion from the nation-family.

Vaivenes: Swinging Migrations in Judith Ortíz Cofer's *Silent Dancing*

While much has been written about the presence of the metanarrative of *la gran familia* in insular literary production, its effects on diaspora literature have yet to be scrutinized by scholars in the field. The lack of studies about the transposition of this myth from the island to the U.S.

mainland can be partly explained by the tendency to separate these two branches of Puerto Rican literature. This has led some U.S.-based academics to reject insular-centered critical approaches to the study of U.S. Puerto Rican literature, while it has also led some island-based critics to deny the connections between these two literary bodies.

The myth of *la gran familia*, however, has played a central role in U.S. Puerto Rican women's literature because it has remained an anchoring device in the diaspora's collective imaginary. While the myth was mostly deployed on the island by the Generation of 1930, it remained a key instrument in the advancement of insular cultural nationalism for decades. This period coincided with Muñoz Marín's industrialization campaign, Operation Bootstrap, and its cultural counterpart, Operation Serenity. Arlene Dávila has noted that the latter "aimed to provide a sense of spiritual balance to a society threatened by the rapid social change caused by the new economic policies" and that it "marked an important moment in the development of Puerto Rico's cultural nationalism, involving a romanticization and purification of culture by reference to an idealized past" (34). It is this return to a glorified past that links this historical juncture with *la gran familia* in order to portray an image of national unity. Because the reactivation of this metanarrative seems to coincide with the Great Migration, it is safe to assume that the myth remained a cornerstone of Puerto Rican identity in the diaspora, as the narratives of U.S. Puerto Rican authors illustrate.

The translocation of *la gran familia* to the cultural and literary terrain of the diaspora is evident in Ortíz Cofer's *Silent Dancing*, where the portrayal of a divided family stands against the ideal paradigm of the national family. *Silent Dancing* dismantles the paternalism underlying the core tenets of unity and racial harmony under a benevolent father figure, thus offering a counternarrative to hegemonic views of the nation-family. In contrast to Ferré's *Maldito amor*, however, the geographic, linguistic, and cultural fissures the family endures as a result of migration further complicate any static and island-centered views of the nation. In the end, the presence of the island as a cultural point of reference and the pivotal role of the metaphorical nation-family in Ortíz Cofer's text force us to rethink how familial ties between the island and the diaspora are asserted in many of the narratives by U.S. Puerto Rican female authors.

The rejection that many Puerto Rican migrants and those born or raised on the U.S. mainland have experienced when they return to the island speaks to the perceived cultural distance between these two segments of the Puerto Rican population. As pointed out above, the exclusion of diaspora Puerto Ricans from the island's collective imaginary is explained in part by the linguistic nationalism that is prevalent on the island. Because the myth of *la gran familia* is deeply rooted in *hispanismo*, those segments of the population that do not fit in this model tend to be excluded from the nation-family and viewed as "inauthentic" Puerto Ricans.

Those in the diaspora, however, often feel and see themselves as Puerto Ricans. Ortíz Cofer asserts, for instance, "I am not confused about my cultural identity. I know what I am because my *puertorricanness* was not awarded to me: it is part of me; it cannot be legislated out" (*Woman* 113). Other Puerto Rican authors on the mainland, such as Esmeralda Santiago, Alba Ambert, and Tato Laviera, among others, have also defended their Puerto Rican cultural background through their works. In the case of Ortíz Cofer, her cultural roots are an endless source of inspiration in her writing because, as she puts it, "in my mind, I have never abandoned the island of my birth, or perhaps that obsession called 'the Island' has never left me. It is the subject of much of my writing" (*Woman* 105). It is precisely because so many authors in the diaspora have emphasized the issue of cultural identity in their literature—specifically the assertion of their Puerto Rican roots—that one must be careful not to artificially draw a line between insular and diasporic production but rather acknowledge how the two sides complement each other.

It is my contention that the prevalence of the trope of the family in the semiautobiographical narratives of U.S. Puerto Rican women authors, such as *Silent Dancing*, challenges the exclusion of the diasporic subject from the insular imaginary by envisioning the reinsertion of the migrant in the national family.[41] Of course, critics who maintain a separation between these two branches of Puerto Rican literature will probably object to this view by insisting that my posture reflects the tendency to "colonize" diaspora production by subsuming it to that of the island. While it is true that my posture could be mistaken as yet another manifestation of this island-based "colonizing" impulse, it is not rooted in the belief that diaspora literature is subordinate to its island counterpart. Acknowledging that U.S. Puerto Rican production sometimes examines the construction of Puerto Rican identities inside as well as outside the island does not imply the discrediting or the devaluation of Puerto Rican identities forged in the diaspora. Rather, a more open perspective such as this allows us to not lose track of the historical fact that for the thousands of first- and one-and-a-half-generation Puerto Ricans who have migrated to the United States, Puerto Rico occupies a central role as their homeland.

How can we, as critics, dismiss this reality in the name of a "non-island-centered" identity? Bost's assertion that "the number of writers who affirm their ties to the island challenge[s] any binary opposition between island and mainland" problematizes the tendency to maintain a division between the two sides (191). In fact, the degree to which many diaspora narratives have been written from what we can call an island-centered perspective, that is, the extent to which they focus on life on the island and its history, indicates an impulse to retrace both family and diaspora roots back to their homeland. This inclination is evident in *Silent Dancing*, when the adult narrator reflects on her yearly visits to her mother after she moved back to the island: "I planned to request stories about the town and its old people, something that we both enjoy for different reasons: [My mother] likes recalling the old days, and I have an insatiable curiosity about the history and the people of the Island which have become prominent features in my work" (153). The interest that this and other texts by U.S. Puerto Rican female authors display regarding the island's history, myths, and culture ironically has resulted in the recuperation of silenced chapters of Puerto Rican history (such as the history of migration), as well as in the recovery and preservation of popular folklore that in some cases has been virtually erased from the island's collective memory. As the analysis that follows intends to show, one of the myths that authors in the diaspora have also grappled with, contested, and rewritten is the metanarrative of *la gran familia puertorriqueña*. My examination of Ortíz Cofer's *Silent Dancing* seeks to demonstrate how diaspora narratives complement and complicate the perspective of *la gran familia* found in works such as *Maldito amor*, produced by island-based authors.

As stated earlier, the trope of the house has been consistently used in Puerto Rican literature to represent the family, and thus the nation, given the metonymic relationship between these concepts. While *Maldito amor* and *Silent Dancing* both make use of this metaphor, there are significant differences in the way that each text depicts this space that are reflective of the particular experiences, socioeconomic status, and family histories of the authors. In Ferré's novel, the hacienda or family estate situated in the midst of a sugarcane plantation reflects the social and economic capital of the De la Valle family. The luxuriously furnished interior of the house, decorated with French and Spanish antiques, is to be a reminder of the family's *limpieza de sangre* and of the legacy of power that they brought with them to the New World. This large house often conveys a lack of warmth, energy, and friendliness.

In contrast, the depiction in Ortíz Cofer's text reflects the lower-middle-class rural background of the family. This is the case with the two spaces that are home to the narrator-protagonist as her family moves back and forth between the mountains of Puerto Rico and urban New Jersey as a result of her father's career with the U.S. Navy. On the island, where she spends half of her childhood, her grandmother Mamá's robin's egg blue house sitting on top of a hill "was a large parlor built by [her] grandfather to his wife's exact specifications so that it was always cool, facing away from the sun" (14). Similar to the De la Valles' house, Mamá's house stands out in its landscape; the former above the *cañaveral* (sugarcane field), the latter on top of a hill, each representing Puerto Rico's two main economies prior to the modernization campaign in the 1940s, the sugarcane plantation economy of the coastal towns and the mountainous region's agricultural economy. The prominent position that both houses occupy is also symbolic of the families' advantageous economic status: the former as owners of Central Justicia, the latter as a result of the income they received from the military, which transformed them into the envy of the town (40).

According to the narrator-protagonist, Mamá's house is "like a chambered nautilus; it has many rooms, yet it is not a mansion. Its proportions are small and its design simple" (23). It is also "a place built for children," already "made child-proof" by Mamá's eight children (53). Despite seeming large with respect to their community's standards, Mamá's house is a highly functional space, built by her own husband to raise a large family—in contrast to the De la Valles' hacienda, which was constructed by a French architect and built to impress. Descriptions of the interior of both houses also speak to the differences between the two socioeconomic sectors that these families represent. While the De la Valles' house was furnished with French and Spanish antiques that reflected their social status, and which created a sober and snobbish atmosphere, Mamá's house was unpretentiously and practically decorated. For instance, the living room was "furnished with several mahogany rocking chairs, acquired at the births of her children, and one intricately carved rocker that had passed down to Mamá at the death of her own mother" (14). Although at first this description of the living room might appear too austere, the text constantly highlights the warm, friendly, and child-centered atmosphere of Mamá's home, offering a stark contrast to the family house in Ferré's novel.

Also, whereas in *Maldito amor* certain objects (such as the "the twelve leather shields that were once supposed to belong to Charlemagne's Knights" or "the Episcopal canopy [of Doña Laura's bed]") become superficial symbols of power for the family by evoking their so-called *limpieza de sangre*, the objects found in Mamá's house conjure up a different kind of power (65).[42] Mamá's bedroom, which the protagonist-narrator remembers as a "throne-room with a massive four-poster bed in its center," was the epicenter of her dominion (24). The bedroom "contained all of Mama's symbols of power. On her dresser instead of cosmetics there were jars filled with herbs. . . . And there was also the monstrous chifforobe she kept locked with a little golden key she did not hide. . . . On the wall above the bed hung a heavy silver crucifix" (24–25). The walls of the bedroom were covered with objects sent by her children from the United States. "Each year more items were added as the family moved and dispersed, and every object in the room had a story attached to it, a *cuento* which Mamá would bestow on anyone who received the privilege of a day alone with her" (25). In other words, the objects in Mamá's bedroom evoke an unconventional kind of power, one that stems from her interior and that does not rely on appearances or violence: her wisdom. Her grandmother's knowledge of herbal cures, her faith in God, and the wisdom she has cultivated through the years have cemented her image as "a wise empress" (24).

The objects and pictures that Mamá displays on the wall constitute a visual representation of each member's life trajectory. In telling the family's history, these walls trace each person's origin back to Mamá's house on the island. This presents an interesting contrast to what we see in *Maldito amor*, where Ubaldino and his aunts like to map out the family's history through the use of old bloodline books that trace their origins back to Spain. The juxtaposition of the living/talking wall at Mamá's house and the ancient books used by the De la Valles to outline their histories accentuates a crucial distinction between Puerto Rican literature produced on the island and that produced on the mainland: the former has displayed an anxiety regarding its European origins; the latter has focused on asserting ties to the island.

The fact that each year more objects are added to Mamá's wall to mark changes in the family's trajectory underscores a more organic and fluid conception of the family as an ever-changing and ever-expanding unit. This view is also reflected in the history of the house itself, "a house that has grown organically, according to the needs of its inhabitants" (23). In the chapter titled "More Room," which I have analyzed elsewhere, the protagonist-narrator chronicles the history behind the house reaffirming its central importance as "the place of our origin" (23).[43] This chapter tells the story of the grandmother who, according to what the narrator-protagonist had been told, had a very peculiar way of letting her husband know when she was pregnant: "He had built her a house too confining for her taste. So, when she discovered her first pregnancy, she supposedly drew plans for another room. . . . Every time a child was due, she would demand, *more space, more space*" (27). As the family expanded, the grandmother found it necessary to offset the reduction of her physical—and emotional—space by having more rooms added to the house. The more children she had, the more space she demanded, until she finally realized that "if she had any more children, her dreams and her plans would have to be permanently forgotten, because she would be a chronically ill woman" (27). Throughout her life she had complied with cultural norms and expectations by assuming her roles as mother and wife, but upon giving birth to her eighth child, she found herself having to challenge those roles in order to protect her health. One day, according to the narrator, she asked her husband to build a large room in the back of the house, and, of course, "he did so in joyful anticipation" (27). However, the grandmother's "belly did not grow" (27), and when the anxious husband told his wife that the new room was ready, she simply replied, "Good, it's for *you*" (28).

"More Room" calls attention to the house, and particularly the bedroom, as the location to which women have been confined by tradition. The gradual expansion of the house parallels the growth of the grandmother's body, and her multiple pregnancies point to a sort of organic relationship between woman and house. In addition, the grandmother's claiming of the intimate space of the bedroom suggests a practical as well as a symbolic act of defiance. On the one hand, taking control of the bedroom allows her to carry out her decision to avoid becoming pregnant again by foregoing intimate relations with her husband. On the other hand, it represents the sense of autonomy and personal freedom that she comes to experience as a result of her decision. Thus the text reconfigures the space of the bedroom into a metaphor of female independence and freedom, which contrasts with its traditional value as a symbol of women's subordination within the institution of marriage. Her husband's banishment from this space ultimately allows the grandmother to have "a room of her own" and to regain control of her body.

This *cuento*, told and retold by Mamá to her daughters and granddaughters, is a powerful testimony to her struggle to discover her sense of self and space. She defies tradition by claiming the right to control her body and her sexuality. Similar to Doña Laura, Mamá challenges the ideal of submission, specifically sexual compliance that defines wifehood in Puerto Rican patriarchal society. The main difference, however, lies in the fact that Mamá continues to love her husband and sees her decision as a form of self-sacrifice for the sake of her family. While Doña Laura and Mamá both claim the right to control their bodies in order to preserve their health, these women's experiences lead them to assume contrasting stances regarding their marriages.

In addition to challenging the myth of female submission, "More Room" questions the myth of the dominant father, which is central to Puerto Rican national discourse. Instead of the traditional authoritarian father figure, the text presents an easygoing husband who seems to obey his wife, as the episode of his expulsion from the bedroom illustrates. His marginalization from the family, in both physical and metaphorical terms, belies representations of the father as a pivotal figure. The grandmother's appropriation of the bedroom—"the heart of the house"— rearticulates the house as a female domain since the father figure is symbolically and physically displaced from its center. Banished to the room he had built adjacent to the main house, the grandfather is seemingly divested of his patriarchal authority.[44]

The central role that Mamá's house plays in the life of the protagonist is evident in the first chapter's title, "Casa." In addition to describing some of its structural features, this chapter describes what usually goes on inside as a way to highlight it as a feminine space. References to the kitchen and rockers, symbolic of women's prescribed roles as homemakers and mothers, serve to emphasize the expectation that women remain "inside" their private world, similar to its function in *Maldito amor*. These ideas in themselves are not new. We are all familiar with the correlation that exists between home and a series of concepts that range from privacy and protection to confinement and submission. What is new, at least in terms of Puerto Rican letters, is how *Silent Dancing* resignifies *la casa* by underscoring its potential as a source of female empowerment. The chapter's depiction of female relatives gathered for midafternoon coffee and storytelling speaks to the positive value ascribed to the home in this text: "We loved best the quiet hours in the afternoon when the men were still at work and the boys had gone to play serious basketball at the park. Then Mamá's house belonged only to us women. The aroma of coffee perking in the kitchen, the mesmerizing creaks and groans of the rockers, and the women telling their lives in *cuentos* are forever woven into the fabric of my imagination, braided like my hair that day I felt my grandmother's hands teaching me about strength, her voice convincing me of the power of story-telling" (19). The absence of men during the workday renders it an exclusively feminine space characterized by warmth and friendship but above all freedom.

As paradoxical as this may sound, Mamá's house transforms itself into a site of female liberation. This image of *la casa* contrasts sharply with the sense of encroachment and isolation that characterizes the De la Valles household; there it creates a sort of *insularismo* that regulates and delimits female agency. In Ferré's novel, female characters rarely cultivate friendships, nor are they depicted as supporting each other. In addition, most conversations between the aunts are limited to the reiteration of the family's European lineage. So while in *Maldito amor* women listen to each other defend their *limpieza de sangre*, at Mamá's house women listen to each other tell *cuentos*, "the morality and cautionary tales told by the women in [the narrator's] family for generations" (15). In contrast to *Maldito amor*'s recycled patriarchal discourse of *la gran familia*—deployed to disempower women—in *Silent Dancing* the backdrop of the house serves women to teach each other how to be strong and how to survive in a patriarchal world, subverting the stereotype of the submissive woman and rebelling against patriarchy through storytelling.

Kevane and Heredia have stressed storytelling as "one common technique that is shaping the form of contemporary Latina literature" (8). Because, as they put it, this oral tradition is "specifically tied to cultural heritage," it represents yet another strategy used by Latina authors, including U.S. Puerto Ricans, to assert their ties to their cultures of origin and thus claim their space within their respective "national families" (8). An example is the tale of María Sabida, which, the narrator says, taught her "how to use the power of words to conquer her fears" (*Woman* 75). The act of narrating this story about female empowerment, however, has a much broader implication in that it signals a desire to reconnect with the culture of origin. In telling the tale of Maria Sabida, which can be traced back to Puerto Rico's oral folklore at the turn of the century, Ortíz Cofer virtually rescues a piece of popular wisdom from oblivion.[45] This tale exemplifies the tendency among U.S. Puerto Rican female authors to delve into insular history, myths, and folklore as they examine their personal histories.

The correlation between storytelling and homeland is underscored not just through the image of the grandmother as storyteller—Mamá representing tradition and ancestral ties—but specifically through the vision of her telling her stories under the mango tree. As the narrator puts it, "The most amazing thing about that tree was the throne it had made for Mamá. On the trunk there was a smooth seat-like projection. It was perfect for a storyteller. She would take her place on the throne and lean back" (74). The evocation of regal imagery not only exalts the importance of the grandmother as storyteller, but it is also framed as a projection of her previous depictions as "empress" of the family. Above all, however, the image of the grandmother sitting on her "trunk throne" metaphorizes the interconnection of oral traditions (stories) and cultural roots (mango tree) through the symbolic visual fusion of the grandmother into the tree. Mamá, like the trunk of the tree, is the backbone of the family and the direct link to the homeland and ancestral roots.

Years later, the narrator would recall how "it was under that mango tree that [she] first began to feel the power of words" (76). The mango tree is also tied to memories of her first return to the island as a young child. Amid the cultural shock she and her brother experienced in Mamá's house, sitting under the mango tree to hear her grandmother tell stories provided her a refuge from the overwhelming reality inside. As she puts it, "Our solitary life in New Jersey, where we spent our days inside a small dark apartment watching television and waiting for our father to come home on leave from the navy, had not prepared us for life in Mamá's house or for the multitude of cousins, aunts and uncles pulling us into their loud conversations and rough games" (75). However, "Mamá would lead us to the mango tree, there to spin the web of her *cuentos* over us, making us forget the heat, the mosquitos, our past in a foreign country, and even the threat of the first day of school looming just ahead" (76). It would not be long before she felt comfortable enough to join "Mamá's tribe" or before she began to associate her grandmother's house and *cuentos* with freedom while equating life in New Jersey with confinement. In sharp contrast to the secluded life they led in the United States, Puerto Rico set them free: "Mamá freed the three of us like pigeons from a cage. I saw her as my liberator and my model. Her stories were parables from which to glean the *Truth*" (18). What is clear in this comment is that Mamá's house allows the protagonist-narrator to experience various dimensions of freedom, among which imagination and physical liberty leave an indelible mark on her.

Later in the text, the narrator's memories of her return to the island as a teenager clash with those of her earlier childhood. She recalls, "At fifteen, resentful of having once again been yanked from my environment of Paterson, New Jersey[,] . . . I felt smothered by the familial press of Mamá's house. It was a place where a demand for privacy was considered rude, where people asked where you were going if you tried to walk out of a room, where an adolescent girl was watched every minute by the women who acted as if you carried some kind of time-bomb in your body that might go off at any minute" (139). Observing how the narrator's perception of Mamá's house transforms over time ultimately renders it ambiguous. Static associations between Puerto Rico/freedom and New Jersey/captivity are destabilized through the subversion of these binaries as a result of the narrator's coming-of-age. In other words, her entrance into womanhood triggers her awareness of the strict parameters and gender roles that she must subscribe to as a Puerto Rican woman. It is this awareness, in part accelerated by her diaspora experience, what ultimately leads to her questioning and challenging of the patriarchal myth of *la gran familia puertorriqueña.*

One of the central claims of this study is that the works produced by insular and U.S. Puerto Rican female authors during the narrative boom of the 1980s and 1990s exhibit a literary contact zone that has been overlooked by most critics in the field: the interrogation of *la gran familia puertorriqueña.* Although the particular focus, concerns, or methodology may vary, *la gran familia* always emerges as a pivotal center of their narratives. This is possible, I argue, because the diaspora writers analyzed here—mostly first- and one-and-a-half-generation—were also exposed, directly or indirectly, to the government's national rhetoric that revitalized the myth during the *muñocista* era. *Silent Dancing* is no exception, as we will see; it offers ample evidence of engaging in a critical dialogue with that metanarrative, particularly its claims of harmony and racial democracy under a "benevolent" father figure.

Although race also surfaces in *Silent Dancing* as a way to call into question the ideal of *la gran familia*, it does not play the prominent role that it does in Ferré's novel. The first significant allusion to race emerges in regard to the distinct backgrounds of the narrator's parents. She remarks about their wedding picture, "His light brown curls frame his cherubic, well-scrubbed face; his pale, scholarly appearance contrasts with his bride's sultry beauty, dark skin and sensuous features" (38). Although their families represent two opposite sides of the racial spectrum, the narrator admits that her mother was eventually "accepted by a good family of strict Spaniards whose name was old and respected, though their fortune had been lost long before [the narrator's] birth" (18). Although her father's European background is mentioned in passing, it is worth noting that it represents a key point of contact with *Maldito amor*, given that both texts evoke the anxiety of an already declining European landowning elite who sought to protect itself by excluding the racial Other from the family.

The fact that her young mother has to be "accepted" by her father's family—she does not naturally belong due to her racial difference—speaks to the taboo surrounding interracial relations in early-twentieth-century Puerto Rico, also a central issue in Ferré's novel. Referring to the inverse situation, in which a white woman establishes a relationship with a black man, Aparicio points out that "any sort of sexual intercourse between a 'proper' young lady and a man outside her class sector and racially darker is still taboo, for it supposedly disrupts the social order and the *limpieza de sangre* boundaries necessary to secure class stability" (*Listening* 57). Although this observation reflects the specific power differentials that emerge between white/female and black/male, such as Doña Elvira and Don Julio's relationship in Ferré's novel, it nevertheless underscores the phobia that interracial mixing has traditionally provoked among the white upper-class sectors of Puerto Rican society.[46]

In contrast to the positive welcome the narrator's mother received, the story of her father's sister, Aunt Felícita, represents a more palpable example of the profound racial divisions that prevailed at the time. According to rumors the narrator-protagonist heard as a child, Aunt Felícita fell madly in love with a young black man when she was sixteen years old. When he approached her father to ask for his blessing, "the old man pulled out his machete and threatened to cut Felícita's suitor in half with it if he ever came near the house again. He then beat both his daughter and wife (for raising a slut), and put them under house-arrest" (43). The man's violent reaction to the young couple and to his wife, underscores the threat that interracial mixing posed to Puerto Rico's patriarchal and Hispanophile social hierarchy at the time. The anxiety or "fear of cultural and racial pollution," as Ania Loomba explains, "prompts the most hysterical dogmas about racial difference and sexual behaviours because it suggests the instability of 'race' as a category. Sexuality is thus a means for the maintenance or erosion of racial difference. Women on both sides of the colonial divide demarcate both the innermost sanctums of race, culture and nation, as well as the porous frontiers through which these are penetrated" (159). In other words, women's sexuality and maternity potentially blur racial divisions, upsetting the racial order. In this sense, Felícita's defiance of racial and cultural norms thus marks her as a "porous border," the vehicle through which her family's *limpieza de sangre* is eroded. Because her attraction for a black man is construed as sexual deviance (reflected in her father's use of the epithet "puta"), it also reinforces the stereotype of sexual excess typically ascribed to blacks. The anxiety that this violent scene unveils not only questions the ideal of racial harmony embedded in *la gran familia* but also serves to dismantle the figure of the benevolent father that lies at the center of this foundational myth.

While Felícita's story exposes the violence hidden under the guise of paternalism, her story also reveals how blacks and women rebel against patriarchal authority. As the narrator recounts, "The result of his actions was an elopment [*sic*] in which half the town collaborated, raising money for the star-crossed lovers and helping them secure transportation and airline tickets to New York. Felícita left one night and did not return for many years after her father's death" (43). The lovers' elopement, and the town's complicity, constitutes an act of defiance against a rigidly structured system that has relied on violence to preserve white patriarchal authority. The lovers' move to New York is significant because, although it seems to gloss over the racial divisions and prejudice that also existed on the U.S. mainland, it suggests that distance from her father and her close-knit Puerto Rican rural community makes it possible for this interracial couple to survive.

The social taboo that their interracial relationship represents is evident in the aura of secrecy that surrounds Felícita's story, much like the silence that envelops Don Julio's racial identity in *Maldito amor*. Similar to Doña Laura, who remained unaware of the interracial relationship between her in-laws, Doña Elvira and Don Julio, the narrator-protagonist admits that she had to piece "[Felícita's] story together over the years" (42). While the silence regarding Felícita's past is a reflection of the racial politics of the times, it can also be explained as a result of the shame that its possibly incestuous nature provoked. The text suggests that perhaps the young black man was also the son of Felícita's father, a Spaniard who, like Don Julio in *Maldito amor*, had black mistresses with whom he fathered numerous illegitimate children. In this way, his daughter's relationship not only threatened the family's *limpieza de sangre*; it also jeopardized its lineage. Regardless of the reasons for his violent behavior, the fact remains that the father's actions unveil the racial fissures and the double standards of the times, thus undermining the myth of *la gran familia*.

While race, class, and gender divisions are also integral to the portrayal of the Puerto Rican family in *Silent Dancing*, one of the most significant contributions of this text is its unveiling of yet another fracture within the family, that caused by the diaspora. Because the treatment of migration and its repercussions on *la gran familia* has remained relatively limited in the production of island authors, diaspora literature offers an indispensable vehicle for enhancing our understanding of this phenomenon. Ortíz Cofer's semiautobiographical perspective in *Silent Dancing* offers a unique opportunity to explore not only migration as it has been traditionally understood but also the experience of return migration that distinguishes Puerto Ricans from other diasporan communities and that has been recently foregrounded in Flores's *The Diaspora Strikes Back* (2009).

Most U.S. Puerto Rican narratives by both male and female authors tend to expose the toll that migration takes on individuals, families, and society while focusing on their experience outside the island. More often than not, these works emphasize the everyday challenges faced by migrants in their effort to survive in their adopted society, a process that is often depicted as negative and corruptive. While adapting to their new reality is typically portrayed as a confusing and painful process, in most cases migration itself—the physical displacement from Puerto Rico to the U.S. mainland and vice versa—is not depicted as a recurring experience. In this sense, *Silent Dancing* offers a unique perspective in its focus on Puerto Rican return migration, a phenomenon that until recently has not received enough critical attention from scholars of Puerto Rican studies.

Delving deeper into this topic is of critical importance because, as Flores asserts, "the drama of migratory 'counter-streams' and the life experience of migrants settling back into or paying visits to their countries of origin and ancestral homelands is endemic to the contemporary period, and promises to grow in frequency and intensity in the foreseeable future" (33). Because the narrator-protagonist has to constantly renegotiate her identity as she moves back and forth between the island and the U.S. mainland, her observations reveal the complex dynamics that have emerged between people on the island and those in the diaspora in the decades following the Great Migration. Paradoxically, as her own experience shows, while the insular community has tended to emphasize the distance between them and their counterparts on the U.S. mainland, the latter has sought to reassert the bonds that tie them to their homeland.

The role of language in *Silent Dancing* reflects its significance as a marker of cultural identity as conceived from an island-centered perspective. The Hispanophilia that is at the center of nationalist discourses of identity has precluded the open acceptance of non-Spanish-speaking individuals within the symbolic Puerto Rican family. The obstacle that linguistic nationalism poses as an "othering" device is evident in the anxiety that the narrator-protagonist experiences as she is constantly forced to master either Spanish or English every time she relocates between Puerto Rico and New Jersey. The identity crisis that ensues crystallizes the dilemma typically faced by return migrants on encountering linguistic prejudice. As she explains, "As a Navy brat, shuttling between New Jersey and the pueblo, I was constantly made to feel like an oddball by my peers, who made fun of my two-way accent: a Spanish accent when I spoke English; and, when I spoke Spanish, I was told that I sounded like a 'Gringa.' Being the outsiders had already turned my brother and me into cultural chameleons" (17). Language therefore represents a key cultural marker that triggers her exclusion from dominant society in each context. By signaling her "difference," the text underscores the linguistic, territorial, and cultural fissures that have divided Puerto Ricans as a result of the diaspora. In showing how the narrator insists on asserting her Puerto Rican identity despite her accent, *Silent Dancing* unveils and questions the Hispanophilia behind *la gran familia*.

The narrator's own sense of displacement is a driving force throughout the text that propels her interest in exploring the idea of otherness, mainly through her interest in "all the eccentrics and 'crazies' of [the] pueblo" (17). As she explains, "Their weirdness was a measuring stick I used in my serious quest for a definition of 'normal'" (17). The presence of characters in the text that seem to exist on the fringes of society— María la Loca, María Sabida, Marina, Salvatore, and Providencia— attest to the protagonist's fascination with exploring otherness. While language is one of the main factors that make her feel like a tourist in her homeland, her difference is also a product of her family's socioeconomic standing. Her unique situation is evident in the way she is treated by the teacher when she is back in Puerto Rico: "I soon found myself crowned 'teacher's pet' without much effort on my part. I was a privileged child in her eyes simply because I lived in 'Nueva York,' and because my father was in the Navy. His name was an old one in our pueblo, associated with once-upon-a-time landed people and long-gone money. Status is judged by unique standards in a culture where, by definition, everyone is a second-class citizen. Remembrance of past glory is as good as titles and money. Old families living in decrepit old houses rank over factory workers living in modern comfort in cement houses—all the same" (56). While the aura of "privilege" that envelops her and her father's family is partly explained by their upper-class origins—another link with the De la Valles in *Maldito amor*—it is also a product of her experience as a migrant. The fact that migration is simultaneously perceived as an advantage and a disadvantage speaks to the ambiguity surrounding the image of the returnee, who simultaneously faces admiration and resentment in the home country (Flores, *Diaspora* 164). The experiences of the narrator-protagonist in *Silent Dancing* illustrate the bidirectional cultural flows between home and host societies, both of which are integral elements of the Puerto Rican national imaginary. In the end, one of *Silent Dancing*'s major contributions is the narrator's unyielding sense of *puertorriqueñidad,* which provides insight into "a new or different way of being of that nationality" that commonly emerges as a result of the return diaspora cycle (Flores 144).

In a gesture reminiscent of what transpires in Ferré's novel, *Silent Dancing* challenges the icon of the father that is at the center of *la gran familia* through the symbolic erasure of this figure, or at least his marginalization, from the domestic domain. This is certainly the case of the grandfather, who was exiled from his bedroom by Mamá. Described by the narrator as an *"alma de Dios*, a saintly, soft-spoken presence," Papá's personality and demeanor distances him from the archetypical authoritarian father figure associated with Puerto Rican patriarchy (26). To an extent, it can be said that his docility allows for a subversion of roles, granting all decision-making powers to his wife. According to the narrator, "He had, at a time determined by his wife, been banished to the back of the house to pursue his interests, and as for family politics, his position was one of quiet assent with his wife's wise decisions. He could have rebelled against this situation: in Puerto Rican society, the man is considered a small-letter god in his home. But, Papá, a gentle, scholarly man, preferred a laissez-faire approach" (31). The role swapping that takes place between Mamá and Papá calls into question the authority associated with the father, and, more important, it destabilizes the sacrosanct hierarchy of the patriarchal myth of *la gran familia*.

The figure of the narrator's father is more ambiguous in that it seems to simultaneously assert and challenge the model of the patriarchal figure. On the one hand, like the quintessential *hacendado*, he is a white/Spanish member of the former landowning elite who constantly seeks to assert his control over the family. On the other hand, he is almost always absent due to his career in the U.S. Navy, a fact that sometimes tends to jeopardize his authority. The respect he is able to command from his wife, despite being away, speaks volumes about the extent of his control over his family. Respect would even sometimes border on fear, as expressed by the protagonist when she admits, "My mother's greatest fear was that my brother or I would hurt ourselves while at Mamá's, and that she would be held accountable by my excessively protective father when he returned from his tour of duty in Europe" (80). Her mother's apparent fear of disappointing her husband exemplifies the power differentials between women and men: the mother fears her husband, even if he is absent most of the year.

Another manifestation of his power over her is the fact that he had given "strict orders . . . to keep the doors locked, the noise down, [themselves to themselves]," a command that drove the family into a state of deep isolation during the periods they lived in New Jersey (88). The solitude the father imposed on his family, in addition to an effort to protect them, was driven by his upward-bound mentality and his desire for assimilation. As the narrator recounts, her father was obsessed with moving the family out of the barrio, and especially El Building. But his greatest wish was his wife's "greatest fear," since being surrounded by the sounds and smells of Puerto Rican voices and cuisine gave her great comfort. Contrary to her husband's wish for assimilation, the mother "kept herself a 'native' in that apartment she rarely left," mainly by refusing to learn English and by re-creating "an environment in [their] home that was a comfort to her[,] . . . that meant *casa* to her" (127). Holding on to her culture, despite her husband's desire to Americanize, would prove to be a strategy of resistance against her husband's control.

While mostly conforming to the ideal of the submissive wife, the mother of the protagonist in *Silent Dancing* occasionally rebels against her husband by engaging in small daily acts of defiance. Specifically, these are framed as her defense of Puerto Rican cultural practices when they are in New Jersey. One way in which the narrator's mother challenges her husband's authority is by refusing to cook Puerto Rican dishes using packaged foods whose contents she is unable to read. Although her husband prefers that she go grocery shopping at the (American) supermarket, she always opts to buy her ingredients at La Bodega, a small Puerto Rican grocery store. The family's excursions to the store during the week, when the father is away at the Navy Yard, constitute an act of defiance at multiple levels. As the narrator explains, "We would linger at La Bodega, for it was there that mother breathed best, taking in the familiar aromas of the foods she knew from Mamá's kitchen, and it was also there that she got to speak to the other women of El Building without violating outright Father's dictates against fraternizing with our neighbors" (91). Therefore, the act of cooking, typically associated with the realm of the feminine, is transformed into a weapon against both the husband's authority and the ideology of cultural assimilation that he represents. It is through these daily acts of rebellion that the narrator's mother exemplifies how women in patriarchal societies are victims but constantly engage in strategies of defiance against the system of masculine domination.

The father's absences have multiple repercussions on the family. The narrator confesses that "each time he came home he was a quieter man. It was as if he were drowning in silence and no one could save him" (128). In other words, even when he is physically present, he remains emotionally absent. It is due to this almost complete absence of the father (literal and figurative) that *Silent Dancing* succeeds in subverting the paradigm by positing Mamá's matriarchal home—*la casa matriarcal*—as the center of the family's existence. It is precisely because it stands for female empowerment by overturning the gender power hierarchy (albeit to an extent) that Mamá's house does not share the same fate that many a *casa patriarcal* have endured in the narratives of Puerto Rican female authors on the island, as evinced in *Maldito amor*. Yet, despite being left standing in the end, Mamá's house does not embody the total liberation from or substitution of patriarchy. The symbolic erasure of the father in Ortíz Cofer's text does not translate into the eradication of the system of patriarchal domination given that the code of values followed by the women in the family continues to be patriarchal in its very essence.

Thus far my analysis of Ferré's *Maldito amor* and Ortíz Cofer's *Silent Dancing* shows some of the connections that can be found between the narratives of insular and mainland women authors, connections that allow us to speak of a Puerto Rican *transinsular* corpus. As I demonstrate, the foundational myth of *la gran familia puertorriqueña* provides an axis for these authors' critiques of patriarchal views of the nation-family. *Maldito amor* directly engages with this national metanarrative and subverts the ideal of a unified family by showing how *la gran familia* is profoundly divided across racial, class, gender, and political lines. In addition, it questions the benevolent father figure at the center of the myth by unveiling the role that violence plays in cementing his power.

Silent Dancing also engages in a dialogue with the myth of *la gran familia* and challenges some of its main precepts. Similar to *Maldito amor*, this semiautobiographical text illustrates how issues of race, class, and gender affect the Puerto Rican nation-family. More important, perhaps, this text addresses how migration represents another dimension of the multilayered ruptures that subvert the ideal of *la gran familia*. The narrative's focus on displacement and the emergence of a hybrid Puerto Rican self ultimately serves to destabilize static concepts of national identity, thus broadening the definition of what it means to be Puerto Rican. The narrator's focus on the family, the island, and its collective myths and histories, underscores her desire to reclaim a space within the nation-family. But in addition, *Maldito amor*'s and *Silent Dancing*'s emphasis on the past points to the role that history—especially glorified versions of it—also play in the narratives of female authors in and outside the island, the focus of my analysis in chapter 3.

3 Retrieving the Past

The "Silenced" Narrate

Literature in a sense is the nation's diary, telling the story of its past, present, and future.

—Gregory Jusdanis

"TODA MEMORIA ES SIEMPRE una memoria rota, es decir, fracturada, fragmentada" (Every memory is always a broken memory, that is to say, fractured, fragmented), declares Carlos Pabón, echoing the title of one of Arcadio Díaz Quiñones's most influential essays, "La memoria rota" (The broken memory) (239). Throughout the twentieth century Puerto Rico's *memoria* seems to have suffered multiple fractures, many of which remained neglected until the advent of *la nueva historia*, a revisionist current that gave birth to the concept of "history from below."[1] This impulse of rediscovery led a new generation of historians to challenge dominant versions of the past—many of which had been cemented by the *generación del treinta*—and to delve into the history of those sectors of society that had been previously written out of official records.

Yet, despite the revisionist revolution of *la nueva historia*, one fracture in the nation's memory that continued to be overlooked was the history of the Puerto Rican diaspora. Díaz Quiñones, one of the first to denounce this glaring omission, states in "La memoria rota," "Migration has been another great absentee. In Puerto Rican historiography—both in 'old' history as well as in the 'new' history—the study of migration has been conspicuous by its absence."[2] In a country where migration had been officially promoted by the government, and some would even say "imposed on," thousands of lower- and working-class people displaced by the explosive combination of colonialism and modernization (i.e., Operation Bootstrap), the rupture of the memory of migration seems paradoxical at best.

The history of the Puerto Rican diaspora began to be formally written in the 1970s from outside the island, when the Centro de Estudios Puertorriqueños (Center for Puerto Rican Studies) at Hunter College in

New York made it one of its primary missions. To this day, the history of the diaspora remains mostly marginalized as a bona fide academic subject of inquiry on the island, where it is rarely or minimally taught at the high school or college level. Despite gestures by some contemporary academics, the dearth of historical studies, as well as the tendency to treat the diaspora as tangential to the island's history, is indicative of the progress that has yet to be made. A recent groundbreaking step toward a more holistic conception of Puerto Rican history is César Ayala and Rafael Bernabé's *Puerto Rico in the American Century: A History since 1898.* The authors state in the introduction, "We have tried to tell the history of the diaspora as it unfolded in constant interaction with events on the island" (11). This transinsular approach to Puerto Rican history helps to decompartmentalize these narratives and avoids presenting the diaspora as a mere "appendix" to island history (Ayala and Bernabé 11). In so doing, it provides a sound model for future, more balanced efforts in Puerto Rican studies.

Writing against *la vieja historia*: Island Voices

La nueva historia brought with it a new impulse to revisit the island's canonical histories and to challenge the versions of the past that had been cemented by the *generación del treinta*. In addition to revolutionizing Puerto Rican historiography, the advent of *la nueva historia* had other, equally significant repercussions, including a literary revolution that produced what is commonly known as *la nueva narrativa*. Rosario Ferré, Magali García Ramis, Carmen Lugo Filippi, Olga Nolla, Ana Lydia Vega, Juan Antonio Ramos, Carmelo Rodríguez Torres, Edgardo Rodríguez Juliá, Manuel Ramos Otero, and Edgardo Sanabria Santaliz became some of the most recognized figures of this group, also known as *los narradores del 70.*

In general most of these authors have systematically sought to uncover and present alternative versions of the past in their works ("history from below"), but in the case of female authors, *la gran familia* has emerged as a focal point in the demythification of the past. The floodgates were opened in 1986, when two of the island's key literary figures, Rosario Ferré and Magali García Ramis, published their first novels, *Maldito amor* and *Felices días, Tío Sergio,* respectively.[3] Written from a feminist perspective, both works defy what Gelpí has called the "paternalist discourse" of the canon and dismantle idealized versions of the past through their incursions into two pivotal historical periods, the dawn of the twentieth century and the *muñocista* era of the mid-twentieth century.[4]

An interest in revisiting the original *gran familia* that was revered in the works of the *treintistas* (members of the Generation of 1930) led not only Ferré but also other authors such as Ana Lydia Vega to explore the hacienda era. Vega's short novel, *El baúl de Miss Florence: Fragmentos para un novelón romántico*, from her collection, *Falsas crónicas del sur* (1991) provides an interesting point of contrast to Ferré's *Maldito amor*. These texts not only engage in a dialogue with this foundational myth that informed *la vieja historia* but also debunk the glorified hacienda that served as its primary metaphor. Set in the mid-nineteenth and early twentieth century, respectively, these narratives defy representations of an idealized preindustrial and pre-American past by unveiling the violence concealed within the democratic model of *la gran familia*. *La casa* surfaces as a polyvalent metaphor that stands for the family as well as the nation and its history. In both Vega's and Ferré's short novels, the hacienda—a symbol of economic, social, and political capital—ultimately collapses, signifying the debunking of this foundational myth.

Concealed versions, unexplored histories, silenced voices, a critique of historiography, and, perhaps above all, parody are some of the central concerns present in post-1970s narratives by Puerto Rican women authors. Both Vega's *El baúl de Miss Florence* and Ferré's *Maldito amor* privilege parody precisely because *there is* a Puerto Rican insular canon and a historiographic tradition that makes possible, and facilitates, the use of this literary device. Yazmín Pérez Torres has proposed reading Vega's entire collection, *Falsas crónicas del sur*, as a partial example of historiographic metafiction given its self-reflectivity, its parodic intertextuality, and its self-awareness of its historical dimension (571).[5] Understanding parody as a way to "enshrine the past and to question it" (6), as well as "one of the major ways in which women both use and abuse, set up and then challenge male traditions in art" (19), it can be said that women's literature is engaged in a dialogue with historical and literary canonical texts written by men. It is through this intertextual dialogue that they convey their critique, as Hutcheon explains: "Intertextual parody of canonical classics is one mode of reappropriating and reformulating—with significant changes—the dominant white, male, middle-class, European culture. It does not reject it, for it cannot. It signals its dependence by its *use* of the canon, but asserts its rebellion through ironic *abuse* of it" (12). The use of intertextual parody is evident in *Falsas crónicas del sur*, where historical discourse is parodied in several ways, including the juxtaposition of the terms "false"/fiction and "chronicles"/history in its title. Furthermore, *El baúl de Miss Florence* blurs the borders between fiction, chronicle, and diary and inscribes the text within the frame of the romance, a genre considered the antithesis of history and associated with the realm of the feminine. Pérez Torres has observed that "as its metafictional and satirical title suggests, the text tries to parody the genre of the romantic novel. . . . The ontological status of the tale is complicated by being a romantic novel written in the form of a diary, framed by another narration that is a story (or a short novel?)." [6]

As Vega has noted, the inspiration she found in history, legends, and oral traditions is the basis of *Falsas crónicas del sur*: "I delved deeply into the dense universe of public libraries and private archives to confirm the proteic multiplicity of 'the facts' and the disconcerting ambiguity of perspectives. On top of the ever-changing versions of lived or heard events, I constructed these that I now submit to your imagination."[7] Vega's text destabilizes History by incorporating nonconventional techniques such as multiple voices, diaries, gossip, and letters in her narrative.

Some of these same techniques can be found in *Maldito amor*, another text that exemplifies historiographic metafiction. While some may argue that *Maldito amor* does not fit squarely within Hutcheon's definition of historiographic metafiction (a type of fiction that is at once historical and metafictional) given that the story and its characters are not modeled after real-life events or people, it shares enough points of contact with this concept. Besides being a highly parodical text loosely set in a particular historical period (the turn of the twentieth century), its intertextuality, or what Hutcheon prefers to call *interdiscursivity* (to signal a much broader range of discourses), is evident in the novel's parodical treatment of a number of Puerto Rican metanarratives such as *la gran familia* and the myth of racial democracy.

In this parody, *la gran familia* and the hacienda function as the main intertexts. Similar to Vega's *El baúl*, one way in which the novel destabilizes History is by blurring generic borders through the incorporation of melodrama, gossip, and fiction in Don Hermenegildo's narrative. The capacity of this novelist-turned-historian, a parodic representation of the traditional historian, to narrate the life of Don Ubaldino is called into question not only by his own verbosity and melodramatic tone but also by the multiple voices (mostly feminine) that challenge his sanitized version of Don Ubaldino's life.

As critics have pointed out, the representation of the leader/hero in Vega's and Ferré's narratives constitutes another challenge to traditional histories, insofar as it demythifies the quintessential—mostly white male—figures that seem to crowd the annals of History. At the same time, because in these texts those same men are the owners and patriarchs of their haciendas, both narratives defy the stereotype of the benevolent father that is central to *la gran familia*. In *El baúl* this is achieved by exposing incriminating details about two specific men: Samuel Morse and his son-in law, Edward Lind. The story centers on the experiences of Miss Florence, an English governess who works for the Lind family in Hacienda La Enriqueta. This is also where the daughter of the renowned inventor of the telegraph, Samuel Morse, lived with her husband, Edward, and their children. Thus, indirectly, the narrative traces Morse's connection to the actual town of Arroyo, where La Enriqueta was located.

According to the narrator, Morse visited his daughter in December 1858, during which time he installed the first telegraph line on the island, immediately turning Arroyo into a showcase of modernity. Until the publication of the story, Morse had remained a local legend: he was "el incontestable super-héroe arroyano" (Arroyo's indisputable superhero) ("Nosotros" 108). While he had been celebrated by the people of Arroyo for having put their town on the map, Morse's reputation and his family's were called into question as a result of the publication of Vega's story. She explains the impact that her version of the events, which sought to reveal what had been previously concealed, had on her readers:

> "El baúl de Miss Florence," the tale I have just alluded to, brings into focus the pro-slavery and decidedly anti-abolitionist ideology of this illustrious inventor and his family. The tale, in addition, rubbed salt on the wound, underscoring the misdeeds of his son-in-law, Edward Lind, in the famous and opulent Hacienda Enriqueta, in the old days located on the road from Arroyo to Patillas. Some readers from Arroyo, a town with a high concentration of blacks, having found out that their adored hero was no more than an absolute racist slave driver, screamed bloody murder. Immediately there were protests to dethrone Don Sami and replace him with some other local hero from Arroyo.[8]

The intense debate (or "guerra civil," according to Vega) following the publication of *El baúl* illustrates, on the one hand, the links between fiction and history and, on the other, the power of literature to destabilize History.

Maldito amor shares with *El baúl* the impulse to challenge the patriarchal discourse of History through its demythification of Don Ubaldino.

Although Don Hermenegildo is aware of details that cast doubts on his portrayal of Don Ubaldino, he chooses to keep them out of his account: "But it's better to forget these unhappy events, erasing them with the edifying accounts of his heroic exploits" (24).[9] In order for Don Hermenegildo to construct a heroic image of Don Ubaldino, he must produce a sanitized version of his past. Interestingly, Don Ubaldino's demythification occurs simultaneously with his glorification: the text presents other characters who provide alternative versions of Don Hermenegildo's discourse. It is through these other voices that we learn about Don Ubaldino's infidelities to his wife (82), his contraction of syphilis during his political campaigns (74), the double standards of his political agenda (83), and finally, the corruption that led to his demise (82). By excluding these facts from his account, the novelist/historian protects the reputation of Don Ubaldino while the novel itself debunks the figure of the benevolent father that is central to the myth of *la gran familia*.

The ultimate metaphor for the collapse of this foundational myth, in both *El baúl* and *Maldito amor*, is the destruction of the hacienda, the symbolic bastion of *la gran familia*. Two key historical events, each represented respectively by Vega and Ferré, jeopardized the hacienda economy: the agriculture crisis of 1865–1875 and the American invasion of 1898.[10] In *El baúl*, Miss Florence's description of Hacienda La Enriqueta upon her return to the island in 1886 speaks to the repercussions of the former, which was directly related to the abolition of slavery (1873):

> When I reached the turn in the drive and stood for a moment in the thick undergrowth that obscured what had once been the perfect design of the gardens, I suddenly caught sight of the spectral outline of the house. The mid-afternoon sun lit the scene, revealing to me the desolating vision that my incredulous eyes in vain attempted to discredit: Its roof sunken, its woodwork fallen and rotting, its regal staircase mutilated, its doors and windows hidden by enormous boards, the princely mansion of La Enriqueta stood, its death-throes long past, like a soulless body amid the green of the trees.[11] (241)

Images of abandonment, decay, mutilation, and deterioration become even more poignant when Miss Florence likens the ruins of La Enriqueta to a *cuerpo sin alma* (lifeless body). The personification of La Enriqueta serves to underscore the hacienda as metaphor of *la gran familia*, and its destruction parallels that of the deceased Lind family (all suicide victims).

Although in *Maldito amor* the reader does not witness the destruction of the De la Valles' *casa patriarcal*, as is the case in *El baúl*, the narrative hints at the imminent destruction of the house at the hands of Gloria, who at the end of the story is setting the house on fire, or so it is implied through her various references to fire. For instance, in the last section of the novel, Gloria says to Titina, "Listen to the cane stalks bursting around us like kindling. . . . [R]ejoice with me because Diamond Dust will finally go up in smoke"—a clear indication that she has already set fire to the house (83).[12] In addition, she expresses her satisfaction in the fate that awaits Don Hermenegildo, who according to her has come to the house "a cebarse impunemente de nuestras entrañas" (to take advantage of us) (81). The ambiguity of the term *cebarse,* which is also associated with fire, and her reference to "the river of blue benzine that we poured a minute ago" (82) are evidence of her role in the final destruction of the house.[13] So, unlike La Enriqueta's demise following the agriculture crisis and the abolition of slavery, the final downfall of the De la Valles' hacienda is mainly portrayed as a result of individual agency. Gloria, a *mulata* who occupies a marginal and ambiguous position throughout the novel, wants to burn down the house out of revenge. On the one hand, she does not want the family estate and its Central Justicia to be sold to U.S. investors by Arístides, the De la Valles' surviving son. On the other hand, the burning of the house, with both Arístides and the novelist/historian Don Hermenegildo still inside, is an act of retaliation against two men who have victimized her on various levels.

Keenly aware of the sanitized version of the family's past that Don Hermenegildo is writing, she seeks to put an end to his deception. When Gloria says to Titina, "We'll still have the satisfaction of knowing that nobody will believe his tale about the man he maintained was a leader and a statesman, and who had been corrupt for so long," it is Gloria who has the last word (82).[14] Unlike other characters, whose voices are absorbed and manipulated by Don Hermenegildo's account, Gloria's voice is not mediated by him. In being the last person to speak within the frame of the narrative and in the act of burning the house, Gloria transforms her image from victim to agent. But perhaps more important, the destruction of the house unequivocally signals the debunking of the authority conferred to dominant history and the totalizing metaphor of *la gran familia.*

As this brief digression into *El baúl* and *Maldito amor* seeks to demonstrate, a number of narratives by island female authors establish a dialogue with the historical and literary canons. Rejecting the Eurocentric, androcentric, and traditional approach of *la vieja historia,* their works challenge official versions of the past through the use of literary devices that include but are not limited to fragmentation, parody, and intertextuality. In the end, many of these narratives deconstruct the trope of *la gran familia* by showing that *la casa patriarcal* is no longer standing.

Life Writing against the Void: Diaspora Perspectives

While island women's literature parodies and engages in an intertextual dialogue with official versions of the past, U.S. Puerto Rican women's literature displays a less critical approach to dominant histories. This is mostly explained by the fact that authors in the diaspora, unlike those on the island, do not tend to construct their narratives against a standing canon but rather write in the absence of a U.S. Puerto Rican historiographic tradition. The sense of "writing against the void" has been echoed by several U.S. Puerto Rican authors, among them the pioneer Latina writer Nicholasa Mohr. She admits, "It was that sense of being invisible in society that I felt while growing up that has compelled me to produce a body of work that would confront the reader with the truth of my existence and my community's impact on the larger society" ("Journey" 83). Esmeralda Santiago reiterates this point: "When I came to New York and made it my business to learn English, I read everything I could get my hands on. At that time I wanted to find stories about teenagers, about young people who were going through the same kinds of things that I was going through. . . . In the process of reading these books about young people, I discovered that I didn't exist in the literature of the United States. . . . I think that I was driven to be a writer because I didn't exist in the literature, and therefore didn't exist in the culture" (Kevane and Heredia 129). As Mohr's and Santiago's testimonies demonstrate, it is the historical "void" in which U.S. Puerto Ricans found themselves that partly fueled their desire to write and thus participate in a process of historical recovery. While some may argue that authors on the island are also engaged in the recuperation of the histories of marginal social sectors, it is important to keep in mind that those on the mainland have been doing so without the validation that an existing historiographic tradition may confer. Therefore, in writing their own stories they are often writing the history of their community. This interconnection between the personal and the collective is emphasized by Acosta-Belén and Santiago when they point out that cultural expressions such as literature "create a link with the past and the countries of ancestry" (187) that, as Stuart Hall suggests, is important for migrant groups in the process of constructing "a historical memory of their experiences in the host society as a way of validating who they are, and where they came from" (in Acosta-Belén and Santiago 187).

In addition to the relative invisibility that has characterized the condition of Puerto Ricans in the diaspora—which has kept them outside U.S. official history—they have remained marginal to the island historical record.[15] While recently some strides have been made to educate the public on the island about migration, not all material published is bound to change existing stereotypes. For example, in *Puerto Rico: Su transformación en el tiempo* (2008), a history textbook by Mario R. Cancel and Héctor Feliciano Ramos, Puerto Rican migration to the mainland is addressed in chapters 4 and 17. But the positive step that the inclusion of these sections might represent in creating more awareness about the roots and causes of the Puerto Rican diaspora is called into question by the following observation: "Others have remained marginalized, actively forming unemployment benefit lines and clinging to governmental aid. Many have become school dropouts, addicts, and criminals. Unfortunately, a negative image of Puerto Ricans living in the United States has long been projected both in the mainland and in Puerto Rico."[16] Paradoxically, the authors' lamentation about the negative perception of diaspora Puerto Ricans on the island is reflected in their own narrative. The lack of significant coverage of the advances that this community has made in the past few decades thus speaks to the lack of awareness that exists regarding the history of Puerto Rican migrants on the mainland.

Given that the migrant experience "is still occluded from the national history," as Flores points out, or tends to be misrepresented, as in the above example, literature has the potential to mend the broken memory of migration (*Bomba* 50). Vicki L. Ruíz echoes this idea: "Through poetry, short stories, and novels, Latina writers engender region in ways that are instructive for historians" (3). For this reason we can say that, in addition to the benefits that we typically associate with literature, U.S. Puerto Rican literary production can help remedy the historical void that has erased the diaspora experience from Puerto Rican official histories, can fill a gap in U.S. dominant narratives, and can provide a source of validation for that community.

"Self-life-writing," an umbrella term that includes a wide range of literary models (autobiography, memoir, letters, journals, testimonies, and personal essays) has emerged as a key mode of expression in the diaspora. The prevalence of self-life-writings among U.S. Puerto Ricans is telling of the "extremely close and dynamic relation between narrative and identity," given that, as Paul John Eakin explains, in talking about ourselves, "we perform a work of self-construction" (*Living* 2). To this, I would add the power of validation that comes from the act of writing. Reflecting on the trajectory of her literary production, Nicholasa Mohr shares the insight she gained:

> Finally, as I was writing *Felita* I realized that *Nilda, El Bronx Remembered*, and *In Nueva York* follow a chronological order. They go from World War II to the time I was hanging around in the streets of El Bronx as a kid in the late forties and fifties, up to the Vietnam War. Suddenly I realized that I had unconsciously done three books on my personal history because there was nothing about Latinos here and certainly nothing about Puerto Ricans. It wasn't until my fourth book that I could write about contemporary times. It is as if I had to validate my existence as a Latina in the United States, my personal history. (Kevane and Heredia 90)

Mohr's awareness of the connection between personal and collective history reveals the tight connection that exists between self and community, and how these are intertwined in ethnic self-life-writings, potentially enhancing both the group's social memory and its sense of historical continuity. In contrast to the literature produced by island-based authors, which does not possess a solid tradition of personal and/or growing-up narratives, the preference among U.S. Puerto Rican authors for this particular model has served as a link to other ethnic and minority literatures in the United States.[17] Teasing out the possible reasons that account for this substantial divergence between both branches of Puerto Rican literature can shed new light on the roles that they each play within their respective local communities.

Eakin's assertion that "an account of an individual's life can provide access to history" captures the potential interconnection that can emerge between self-life-writing and history (*Touching* 141). Simon Dentith and Philip Dodd also echo this claim when they affirm that autobiography has been "a form used through history by marginalized groups . . . and thus [has become] a source of knowledge and experience about those groups unavailable in standard histories" (6). In fact, the prevalence of this genre among minorities, who are typically excluded from standard histories, is indicative of the central role that autobiographical writings can play in the process of historicizing their experiences. After all, as Sánchez Korrol puts it, "in the final analysis, isn't the big story made up of the personal accounts of each and every one of us?" ("The Star" 211).

However, the connection between autobiography and history is not widely embraced, particularly among historians, who "have largely resisted this view, granting autobiography a peripheral place at best in the study of history when not discrediting its claims to referential truth altogether" (Eakin, *Touching* 142). The implied correlation between autobiography and collective history is also likely to be disputed by scholars of traditional autobiography studies, who depart from the understanding that individualism, not community, is the focus of this literary genre.

Recently, scholarship focusing on ethnic and female self-life-writings has challenged established definitions of this genre as protagonist centered. Martin Japtok, for instance, has argued that in contrast to the traditional autobiography and the bildungsroman (which he finds similar enough to be considered the same), "their ethnic equivalents seem to give more room to others" (25). In a similar fashion, scholars of women's autobiography are also destabilizing conventional conceptions of the genre. Nellie McKay, for example, sees the connection between self and community as a distinctive feature of women's and minority autobiography:

> Scholars interested in minority group or women's autobiography have begun to challenge many of the epistemological assumptions of white Western male critics who are concerned only with the autobiographies of white Western male subjects. These scholars have denied the universality of the criteria put forth by several of the most prestigious "deans" of the genre as requirements for the successful production of autobiography, particularly the view that individualism is the most important factor in the Western autobiographical endeavor. Scholars opposed to this view have demonstrated that for those outside the dominant group, identification with community is pervasive for the unalienated self in life and writing. (175)

The recent reevaluation of autobiography as it has evolved among marginalized sectors is pushing the limits and expanding traditional and more constrictive definitions. As a result, the deeply intertwined relation between self and community, self-life-writing and social memory, has been garnering more attention.

Studies have proven that narration, as a vehicle for articulating that past, is a crucial step in the construction of social memory. This is because social memory in itself is "not a 'natural' result of historical experience" but rather "a product of a great deal of work by large numbers of people, all securing (mostly) public articulation of the past." (Irwin-Zarecka 67).[18] Because, as Fentress and Wickham note, it is the act of talking or writing about personal memories that actually transforms them into social memories, it can be argued that self-life-writings by U.S. Puerto Rican authors help to transform individual memories into social memories (ix). As individual pieces of a much larger puzzle, each self-life-writing aids in the reconstruction of their community's past.

As pointed out above, ethnic and female autobiographies are intricately connected to the bildungsroman, or coming-of-age narrative, a genre that "focuses on the relations of a protagonist with the wider environment" (Japtok 21). In addition to poetry, the bildungsroman has been one of the most cultivated genres among U.S. Puerto Rican writers. The post-1960s explosion of this genre was undoubtedly influenced by the civil rights movements and their focus on bringing visibility to those disenfranchised by the system. It is in this context that Piri Thomas's *Down These Mean Streets* (1967) was published, becoming an instant best-seller at the time. Thomas's success led to the emergence of a number of U.S. Puerto Rican authors who published personal narratives that offered firsthand testimonies of urban life in the barrios. Most narratives written by men are characterized by violence and dismal depictions of street life in the ghetto. Coming-of-age narratives by female U.S. Puerto Rican authors, on the other hand, tend to focus on the home and to "explore the unequal power relations between men and women and relationships among women family members, especially of different generations" (Acosta-Belén and Santiago 197). The distinct ways that male and female authors choose to narrate their life stories reflect how gender and sex intersect with the construction of national and cultural identities. In emphasizing home versus street, inside versus outside, and intimate versus public, female authors are also challenging the patriarchal U.S. Puerto Rican canon that for decades validated the male immigrant experience while rendering invisible that of females in the diaspora.

Another crucial difference between male- and female-authored personal narratives—which has been neglected by critical scholarship on U.S. Puerto Rican literature—is the fact that memories and scenes of life on the island are of paramount importance in most women's coming-of-age narratives. Ortíz Cofer's *Silent Dancing*, Santiago's *When I Was Puerto Rican*, and Ambert's *A Perfect Silence* are just a few examples of personal narratives in which depictions of life on the island are central to the plot and are often contrasted with life on the U.S. mainland. The prevalence of self-life-writings and the recurrence of the island motif in U.S. Puerto Rican women's narratives are two aspects that deserve more critical attention. In other words, it is important to consider the role that the island plays in the recovery of memory. Without a doubt, the assertion of familial ties and the tracing of genealogical/cultural roots back to

Puerto Rico could be seen as a reaffirmation of the island as a privileged (i.e., "authentic") site of Puerto Rican identity. Given that the exclusion of diaspora literature from the island corpus is predicated precisely on this notion, it is possible to view the widespread presence of the island motif as a strategy of cultural affirmation against claims of "inauthenticity" based on distance from that "center." By highlighting the links between childhood, memory, and the island, I am not asserting an equivalence between nation and location; rather, I want to point out a common thread connecting the life-writings of U.S. Puerto Rican women authors examined here. After all, it is clear that their narratives propose the articulation of a Puerto Rican identity beyond the island's borders.

The fact that autobiographies and bildungsroman are common among stateside Puerto Rican authors while scarce among island-based authors makes *Felices días* stand out from the rest of the insular corpus. In *Literatura y paternalismo*, Gelpí poses a key question, that is, why is *Felices días* written as a bildungsroman in a tradition that does not tend to cultivate this genre? Moreover, why is it that one of the only coming-of-age novels of insular letters emerges following the island's modernization crisis (80)? And furthermore, why is there a lack of self-life-writings among island authors?

According to Gelpí, the lack of personal narratives results from the fact that insular literature is one "that strives to construct the nation as a family, where it is 'illegal' to use the personal 'I,' both within texts as well as in their presentation. This prohibition has an impact, of course, on the genres authorized and promoted by that literature: thus the marginalization of lyric poetry or the minimal development of autobiographical texts."[19] In addition, Japtok's observation regarding the typical emergence of autobiography and the bildungsroman in the context of crisis or instability, and indeed as a "response to those conditions," sheds light on the popularity of these forms among ethnic, migrant, and other marginalized communities. Its focus on the search for the definition of identity also fits within this framework given that minorities often face long-term instability in the dominant society and routinely search for ways to assert their identity in a culture that has opted to make them invisible.

However, the fact that self-life-writing did not become a popular literary model on the island does not mean that people on the island have not confronted their share of crises or that questions of identity are not central to the insular corpus. As most people familiar with insular Puerto Rican literature are aware of, national and cultural identity are two of this literature's principal topics. Yet for many island-born/based authors, perhaps because of being raised in the context of island culture where Puerto Ricans are the majority—and where their *puertorriqueñidad* is unquestioned—the issues of transculturation and hybridity do not take the center stage ascribed to them in the diaspora.

And this is, in fact, what distinguishes the experience of Magali García Ramis and the potential reason for her decision to write *Felices días* as a personal narrative that draws on the bildungsroman. As she explains in her interview with Negrón-Muntaner, "I would say that in my case, not feeling Puerto Rican was due to the cultural influence of my [Spanish] family and to my American Catholic school, which made me feel embarrassed to be Puerto Rican. I didn't want anything to do with Puerto Rico, I only wanted to be American. When I graduated, I only spoke English."[20] Growing up under the strong influence of Spanish (home) and American (school) cultures during the culturally turbulent 1950s and later on developing a consciousness about the fact that, as García Ramis puts it, "I, my siblings and cousins were part of a first Puerto Rican generation, in my family, because our parents were the children of Spaniards, Dominicans, or Cubans," seems to have led the author to explore the issue of her Puerto Rican identity.[21] Because the degree of American cultural influence was substantial during her formative years and because her contact with outside society had been severely curtailed by her family, her individual experience actually displays significant parallels to that of many authors in the diaspora. In these cases, the "cultural bubble" created at the home often triggers the subject's identity crisis—told and retold in (semi)autobiographical narratives that follow the model of the bildungsroman, where physical and psychological coming-of-age mirrors the protagonist's increasing sense of cultural/political awareness.

An analysis of García Ramis's *Felices días* and Esmeralda Santiago's *When I Was Puerto Rican* can be beneficial in helping us reflect on how Puerto Rican female authors from both sides engage with questions about the past, history, and cultural identity. As (semi)autobiographical narratives written in the first person, these texts privilege the feminine voice of their narrator-protagonists, thus underscoring their agency as historical subjects. The customary exclusion of women and other minorities from Puerto Rico's official histories—not to mention from the literary canon—is challenged through Lidia's and Negi's acts of telling their stories. In addition to the repercussions that this process may have at the individual level, personal accounts of the past provide a lens through which to examine the historical junctures that mark and shape the life experiences of these characters. The fact that in both works the characters' coming-of-age occurs in San Juan during the 1940s and 1950s, a key period of Puerto Rican history marked by industrialization and massive migration, represents another point of contact between these novels. In a sense, they could be seen as representing two sides of the same coin—*Felices días* providing a glimpse into the life of a middle-class urban adolescent girl living on the island, and *When I Was Puerto Rican* presenting an alternate view of that time from the perspective of a rural migrant young girl. In addition, their experiences growing up in upscale Miramar, Santurce (Lidia), and in El Mangle shantytown and poor areas of Santurce (Negi) also provide a glimpse of the sociospatial dialectics that Quiles Rodríguez argues existed in Santurce (*San Juan* 2).[22] Certainly looking back to this formative period in Lidia's and Negi's lives challenges claims of a monolithic Puerto Rican identity by emphasizing the multiple locations from which such an identity can be constructed. Both novels narrate equally valuable Puerto Rican experiences, thus giving voice to the history of an entire generation growing up in the 1950s.[23]

The concern that García Ramis's and Santiago's texts display regarding the construction of the past, and its glorification, is only one of the dimensions of *la gran familia* with which these novels actively engage.[24] Despite the similarities that link these texts—first-person female narrators, coming-of-age narratives set in the 1950s and 1960s, and an interest in documenting the past—they display significant differences in the way that each one relates to the myth of *la gran familia*. Reflecting on the potential reasons for those differences can shed light on the way that we have traditionally conceived of the relation between insular and diaspora literatures. In other words, it is crucial to ask what accounts for the various levels of intertextuality that these corpuses display in relation to *la gran familia*.

Unearthing the Past in Magali García Ramis's *Felices días, Tío Sergio*

Chronologically positioned after *El baúl* and *Maldito amor*, *Felices días* takes place in the mid-twentieth century, long after the Spanish-based hacienda economy portrayed in Ferré's and Vega's texts was supplanted by U.S.-propelled industrialization. Locating the action of the novel at this particular juncture allows for an examination of a more recent chapter of Puerto Rican history and of the extent to which the myth of *la gran familia* was a key component in the collective imaginary of the period.

Felices días opens with Lidia's declaration, "Era en los tiempos de Muñoz Marín" (It was in the times of Muñoz Marín) (6), a comment that denotes a certain sense of urgency on the part of the narrator to frame the action within this specific historical period. The emphasis that the novel places on *el muñocismo* sets the stage for the text's dialogue with the metanarrative of *la gran familia*. Although this myth had been originally employed on the island by the Generation of 1930, it remained a key discourse of the populist ideology of Luis Muñoz Marín's government.

Muñoz Marín, whose Operation Bootstrap propelled the island's rapid industrialization and modernization, found it necessary to launch Operation Serenity as a cultural counterpoint to the radical changes that were taking place. So, while the former looked ahead to the technological advances associated with Americanization, the latter's gaze toward the past resulted from the need to remain connected to the roots of Puerto Rican culture. The return to a glorified past, a central principle of *la gran familia* that was promoted through Operation Serenity, represents a crucial yet understudied link between this myth and *el muñocismo*.

The tension between past and present/future that emerges from the contrast between these two distinct projects is mirrored in *Felices días*. In describing the Muñoz era, Lidia observes, "It was a time of hope that still smelled like new. It was a time of razing red clay mountains to build houses in suburbs, of dissecting every green mountain with asphalt roads, of blossoming cement and hotels, of inaugurating dams and electric power stations" (14).[25] The critical undertone of Lidia's retrospective observations reflects the disenchantment that followed the country's initial optimism, that is, before Puerto Ricans came to realize the impact that modernization (i.e. massive migration) would have.

The Walls around Us

Nowhere is the tension between the past and the present/future more palpable in García Ramis's novel than in the contrast established between life inside Villa Aurora, the Solís's *casona* in Santurce—the embodiment of tradition and history—and the world outside its walls. Similar to its function in Ferré's *Maldito amor* and Vega's *El baúl*, the house recurs as a totalizing metaphor in *Felices días*. It is the symbolic repository of history, genealogy, language, national identity, political affiliation, and female sexuality. While most studies have focused on the last two aspects, particularly the parallel between Lidia's emerging sexual and political consciousness, less attention has been devoted to the role that history—whether personal, familial, or national—plays in the novel.[26]

In the analysis that follows, I examine how *la gran familia* informs representations of the past that strengthen the family's own sense of historicity at the expense of members who remain excluded from their "imagined family," to echo Anderson's concept. In so doing, I unveil the contradictions inherent in *Felices días* as a text that assumes an apologetic stance vis-à-vis the figure of the Puerto Rican migrant (embodied in Tío Sergio) but fails to fully vindicate him by underscoring his otherness. Ironically, it is the marginalized Sergio who stands as the symbolic repository of Puerto Rican history and culture, and who ultimately succeeds in transmitting nationalist values to the younger generation, represented by Lidia and her siblings and cousins. The novel's emphasis on the role that the diaspora plays in "rescuing"/salvaging Puerto Rican cultural traditions and histories therefore challenges claims of inauthenticity used to undermine and exclude migrants from the insular national imaginary.

The house's location and structural features reflect the already defunct privileged status of the Solís family. In Lidia's words: "Almost all the houses in our street were two or three storey wooden structures with overhanging roofs, decorative towers and gables, and all the houses, from the Roja's, the smallest, to the Soto Morales', almost a mansion, had names inscribed at the bottom of the entrance gate or on small plaques embedded in the walls facing the street: Villa Mercedes, Villa Sol, Villa Margarita. Ours was Villa Aurora, the House of the Dawn" (47).[27] The family's debate over whether to install iron bars on the windows as a security measure is telling of the changes that were taking place during the 1940s and 1950s as new working- and lower-class barrios emerged in Santurce as a result of modernization.[28] For the Solís clan, representative of the old bourgeoisie, such transformations attest to their precarious position, now threatened by "undesirable" elements.

Interestingly, the fear of vulnerability parallels the family's anxiety regarding their European ancestry and social standing; iron bars protect them from the outside world, while "imaginary boundaries" (racism, classism, etc.) are erected to safeguard the family's illusion of *limpieza de sangre* and prestige. The relationship between the inside and the outside is also negotiated within the space of *el balcón* (the front porch), which faces the street.[29] In one of the opening scenes, the narrator reflects on the importance of this space in their lives: "we were always on the front porch watching the people who ventured out under the terrible sun, listening from afar to the kids on the street playing all the dangerous games in the world—street, kids, and world forbidden to us—and keeping an eye out for Margara" (15).[30] *El balcón* becomes a primordial site for the children's worldly education. The function of *el balcón* has been examined by Edwin R. Quiles Rodríguez, who states, "The front porch marked the limit with the surrounding environment and provided visibility to those who usually remained inside the house: women, children, and the elderly. For children, it consisted of an educational space, their first exposure to city life. The balcony, the border of the private, was a place to hang out where everyday activity was in constant flux."[31] As descendants of the old bourgeoisie, the Solís children are not allowed to either play on the street or engage in contact with street kids. While this separation is ensured by keeping them confined to the house, the balcony's location as a transitional space will allow the children restricted contact with the proscribed outside (i.e., contaminated) world.

The Eurocentrism and Hispanophilia associated with the myth of *la gran familia* are replicated in the family's efforts to reconstruct their own history. The house itself becomes a tabula rasa on which, through gestures such as the display of certain objects, the Solís write their own narrative. For instance, Lidia's comments about the number of portraits of her grandfather Papá, who was born and raised in Mallorca, speaks about their need to trace their genealogy back to Europe: "'My grandfather left 'for a few years' and never again saw his fatherland,' Sara F. would say in her most dramatic tone. 'Then he met Mamá.' 'Isn't it true she was French?' Andrés asked. 'No, no. Her mother was from the French islands, her father was Canarian, from the Canary Islands, Manuel Villegas y Castro, and her mother was Marie Dubois'" (48).[32] The emphasis that Mamá Sara—the matriarch of the family—and Lidia's aunts place on their Spanish roots is evident not only in the number of portraits of Papá displayed around the house but also in their obsessive performance of a Spanish identity. Lidia notes, "Seventy years after having left Spain, three generations later, my family intently discussed the legitimacy of the heirs to the Spanish throne" (95).[33] And while these conversations rekindled the adults' affective loyalties to Spain, the children were also obligated to perform their *Spanishness* in other ways. One instance takes place during a Halloween celebration at Casa de España.[34] Lidia's sarcasm when describing the scene pokes fun at her family's obsession with the performance of a Spanish identity. She describes the numerous pictures taken of them: "together, separate, making faces, showing off our costumes, placing two fingers behind each other's heads to give one another horns, standing very straight—looking like Spaniards, memorialized as Spaniards for future generations of Solises, white, respectable members of the Casa de España" (135).[35] Ironically, the aunts view the space of Casa de España as a validation of their Spanish identity, when in reality this location—a failed copy of an original (i.e., Spain)—underscores the performative nature of this desired identity.

Years later, after visiting Spain, Lidia admits, "Thus I was taken in pilgrimage to the land of our ancestors, because supposedly all our roots were in Europe. Some Spanish cousins seemed to me a bit too dark, but when I returned home and consulted with Andrés, he reminded me that the Moors were in Spain for 800 years, that I should not bother our family with such matters, and I, so civilized and ladylike, did not even mention it" (154).[36] The cynicism behind Lidia's words ("se suponía que") reveals her suspicion about the so-called racial purity of her family, similar to the role that Doña Laura plays in *Maldito amor* when she uncovers the *mestizaje* of the De la Valles. By underscoring the existence of her darker-skinned cousins—albeit just to Andrés—Lidia unveils the racial heterogeneity at the center of Spanish society, which has been traditionally rendered invisible in the Latin American imaginary because it views "whiteness" and "Europeanness" as synonymous. Disguised as an apparently trivial comment, Andrés's explanation complicates this paradigm of racial "purity" by drawing attention to Spain's own hybridity. In so doing, the novel opens up a literary space for a dialogue on the complexity of Puerto Rican historical roots that reaches beyond the Spanish-Taíno-African triad that underpins traditional discourses on identity.[37] How can the myth of racial purity (i.e., whiteness) be upheld when the "purity" of that source in itself is being called into question? Because *la gran familia* privileges the white/European roots of Puerto Rican identity—reflected in the Solís family's attitudes toward race—Lidia's observation and Andrés's response illustrate how *Felices días* undermines this myth.

The Fall of the House

When Tío Sergio reappears in the lives of the Solíses after his years-long absence, he is confronted with the reality of having to reinsert himself into a patriarchal yet female-run household. Being the only man living in the house serves to mark him as an other, as Lidia intimates: "He was a man, and for all we could remember from our lives, we had always lived among women. . . . [I]n our everyday world everything was organized, decided and carried out by women" (22).[38] The depiction of strong and independent female characters challenges the stereotypes of submission and financial dependence often associated with women in canonical (male-authored) Puerto Rican writings. As the narrator observes, "Above them all, and far above us, reigned Mamá Sara. Mamá Sara had a chair with a high back, like a queen, that she would place at the head of the dining room table, and she insisted on keeping the chair opposite her's empty, so that the Man, depending on who was visiting— Uncle Roberto, Monsignor Serrano, or even Cousin Germánico—could sit in it" (23).[39] In this highly symbolic description, the grandmother's thronelike chair embodies her matriarchal power, but her insistence on reserving the other end of the table for a Man, whoever that might be, undermines her own power and that of the other female members of the household by privileging the masculine (also conveyed through the capital *M*).

So, early on, García Ramis's novel suggests that female control does not imply the effacement of patriarchy. When Lidia states that Mamá Sara "dominated with her spirit our manless family," the underlying truth is that Mamá Sara becomes the embodiment of the patriarch within the family (24).[40] Unarguably, the lives of the Solís women are rigidly regulated by the patriarchal values at the core of *la gran familia*, which they reproduce and perpetuate through their upbringing practices. For instance, gender and sexuality are conceived according to traditional models of masculinity and femininity, where men are encouraged to perform their sexuality while women are expected to repress it. Tío Sergio's failed attempt to fit into the constrictive gender parameters prescribed by society, for instance, through his sexual encounter with Micaela, is one of the reasons for his ostracism. Lidia's behavior and defiance of "feminine values" also marks her otherness within the family and provides a strong connection between her and her uncle.

The correlation between Tío Sergio's return and Lidia's sexual and political awakening has been the center of a number of studies on García Ramis's novel. In most cases, the focus on Lidia has tended to overshadow the figure of Tío Sergio, who is portrayed in the novel as the scapegoat of the exclusionary discourses (homophobia, racism, classism, Catholicism, Hispanophilia) embedded in *la gran familia*. Besides the general lack of in-depth analysis in relation to this character, critics have tended to disregard and/or underplay Tío Sergio's history of migration to the U.S. mainland and thus have failed to question the implications of envisioning the other (nationalist, non-Catholic, homosexual, racially "impure") as a migrant subject. A closer look at the construction of this character in the text can offer an alternative reading of the novel as a reaffirmation of the ambiguous role that Puerto Rican migrants play in an insular collective imaginary that has been conditioned by the foundational myth of *la gran familia*.

When Lidia observes, "although he looked like us, he was a stranger," on seeing Tío Sergio step out of the taxi in front of Villa Aurora for the first time, her comment foreshadows the ambivalent position that will define him in relation to his family (20).[41] While he shares the Solís last name and looks (41), he doesn't seem to have much in common with the rest of the family, except with the children, who are attracted to and fascinated by his otherness. Lidia's remark about how their world had been perfectly organized and "incambiable" until the arrival of Tío Sergio, who brought with him an element of novelty (20), explains in part the children's attraction to this figure. Besides the fact that Tío Sergio is the only man in the house, his otherness is constituted as a function of three main elements: the objects he possesses and/or cherishes, the people he relates to, and his cultural practices. One of the first instances in which we see Tío Sergio is when Lidia imagines him walking on Riverside with a book by Miguel Hernández (1910–42), a Spanish Civil War poet who wrote against fascism. His broken compass—always pointing south—is another valuable object that his cousin Andrés gave him and that he later passes down to Quique (139). While the compass represents a direct link to his ancestors (and the family history), it can also be seen as a reminder of the spiritual and cultural connection he maintains to the island despite living on the U.S. mainland. However, the broken compass pointer admits another reading: it mirrors Tío Sergio's tendency to spend time in the *sótano* (basement), the foundation of the house, where he liked to be alone and where his failed sexual encounter with Micaela took place (134). It is also there that he helps Lidia search for the skeletal remains of the family's dog, Negri, buried before the narrator was born and which she never finds. Searching for Negri's remains under the house can be seen as a metaphor for the search for the black ancestors, the silenced history that has been buried under the *casa nacional* that houses *la gran familia*.

In addition, Tío Sergio's interest in finding and discovering family mementos awakens the children's interest in such objects, and thus in the family's past. Lidia recalls how "often, Uncle Sergio sat next to us to read or to search the shelves and bookstands that lined the room, and amongst Papá's old books and papers, for all the things without any value which families value most: faded photos from family trips, birthday cards, old eyeglasses, everything that had been left behind in the corners of the study for forty years" (49).[42] As the novel progresses, his need to unearth and to document the Solíses' history reaches a crescendo that corresponds with the family's upcoming move to the suburbs, the destruction of Villa Aurora, and, unbeknownst to anyone, his imminent return to New York. Lidia observes that one day, after having received several long-distance phone calls, Tío Sergio displayed a sense of urgency to see family pictures: "And then he asked to see the photos. He asked all of us to look for all the family pictures we could find, and he proceeded to look at them over and over again. . . . And Uncle Sergio started to organize them, to make copies of the very old ones, to have his favorite ones enlarged, and to write the names of people on them and the approximate dates when they were taken. . . . 'We have to take pictures of the house in case they knock it down,' he said. 'We have to prepare a family tree,' he told us" (140).[43] As this passage suggests, Tío Sergio understands the urgency of documenting the past, of recording the family's history before change erases any trace of what was. Key to our discussion is the parallel that the novel establishes between the house and the family. Similar to the Solíses' forthcoming move and the subsequent fall of the house that divides Lidia's existence into "la Casa de Antes" and "la Casa de Ahora" (132), so will the family be transformed by a move that symbolically distances them from their roots while bringing them even closer to an American identity. It is, in a sense, the impending decline of *la gran familia*, brought about by Operation Bootstrap.

Tío Sergio's relationships, or, more specifically, the people he chooses to relate to, are another channel through which his character is constructed as an other. Perhaps the most salient relationship is the one he sustains with neighbors Don Gabriel Tristani and his daughter Margara, shunned for decades by the rest of the Solís clan because of their political views. The solid wall that divides the two properties thus functions as a metaphor for the insurmountable ideological rift that divides the two families. Both Don Gabriel and Margara are marginalized for being nationalists, what the Solíses call "gente mala" (bad people). It is important to note that the family's rejection of their neighbors reflects the climate of fear that spread as a result of the 1948 enactment of Law 53, better known as *Ley de la Mordaza* (Gag Law), which prohibited expressions of dissent against the U.S. government. The widespread implementation of Law 53 to quell opposition fomented a sense of anxiety that in many cases translated into the ostracizing of entire segments of the population—basically anyone with pro-independence views—whether or not they advocated the use of violence. The fear of implication by association is part of what leads the Solís family to malign Don Gabriel and Margara.

For this reason, Tío Sergio's willingness to help these neighbors in times of need—during the storm and when Margara goes into labor—is viewed by the family (including their preconditioned children) not only as a risky undertaking but also, more important, as treason. For instance, when Tío Sergio helps Don Gabriel board up the windows before the storm, Tía Ele admonishes, "You didn't have to go there; don't look for trouble" (64).[44] Later on, when Lidia asks her mother the reason for their rejection, she explains, "It's not good to visit the Nationalists. . . . You shouldn't mingle with people like that because people will believe you are like them"—an implicit reference to *Ley de la Mordaza* (65).[45] While the Solíses make every effort to dissuade the children from interacting with the Tristanis, the mystery and secrecy that surrounds them enhances their interest, as Lidia hints when she confesses, "They were forbidden to us, but we wanted to see them" (85).[46] Margara's reputation as a "mujer callejera" (street woman) also compounds the perception of the Tristanis as the embodiment of "lo prohibido," which clearly augments the children's interest, as the first scene of defiance in the novel attests (7).

Tío Sergio's implied political affinity with the Tristanis is perceived by the rest of the family as one of the main reasons for his difference. The Solíses take pride in their Spanish ancestry, desire Americanization, and deride autochthonous (i.e., racially mixed, lower-class) manifestations of Puerto Rican culture. As Lidia puts it toward the end of the novel, "It was true that we barely knew a thing about our country, because none of them or anyone else had taught us anything about it. We had lived for so many years locked behind the sweet and sour fence of our family home where everything we inherited from the past was European and everything in our future was North American that we could not know who we were" (162).[47] In this sense, Tío Sergio's knowledge of Puerto Rican history and defense of its culture represents an immediate threat to the family, which has consistently sought to "protect" the children from any such influence by discouraging socialization with others, especially Tío Sergio. In addition to constantly reminding the children to give him space because he is a man, the family makes an effort to keep the children away from his influence.

One incident that seems to mark a drastic change in the family's attitude regarding the children's relationship with their uncle takes place when Andrés inquires about Segundo Ruiz Belvis (1829–1867), a Puerto Rican abolitionist and independence advocate, after walking past a school named after him. Nati, who at that moment tried to defame this national figure, becomes upset with Tío Sergio after he explains his importance to the children, which leads them to believe that something bad had just happened (64). Later on Lidia adds, "Years later, when we questioned them, my family denied ever having requested Uncle Sergio not to speak to us about Puerto Rican history, but we believe they did, because he never spoke to us again about any eminent Puerto Ricans and we never again asked him about them" (72).[48] Perceiving the potential "negative" effect that Tío Sergio could have, the family tries to distract the children by taking them to the movies or to Casa de España in order to minimize contact. Yet Tío Sergio's influence on the children was too strong to be easily uprooted. As Lidia reminds us, "Adults never suspect—or fail to imagine—the existence of close and powerful ties between children and forbidden people" (92).[49] In fact, the family's effort to divert the children's attraction from Tío Sergio backfires when they start to become interested in books about sex and Lidia becomes an avid reader of history books. The interdiction of Tío Sergio is thus linked to the awakening of a sexual and a historical conscience, especially in Lidia's character.

In addition to the objects he possesses/cherishes and the people he relates to, Tío Sergio's otherness is fashioned according to particular cultural practices, such as his musical preferences. Because music is reflective of cultural identity, Tío Sergio's preference for the music played on WKVM, "la estación de las sirvientas" (the maids' radio station), also serves to mark him as an other within the family. In contrast to his appreciation for popular genres such as *boleros*, *plenas*, and *danzas*, the Solíses' rejection of Puerto Rican popular music (lower class and racially mixed)—and their bias toward peninsular or American musical genres—reflects their need to assert their whiteness.

Lidia sees her preference for African-based musical forms such as the mambo and the merengue as a tie that will forever link her to her Tío Sergio, despite the fact that he is gone. It is the love that she feels toward this figure that inspires her to learn as many popular songs as possible, thinking that this would make him proud when he returns. Again, it is through Tío Sergio that she develops an awareness and appreciation for different types of Puerto Rican music, "all the music that my family rejected because they preferred to listen to Spanish *paso dobles* and songs from American movies" (159).[50] At one point, Lidia is forced out of the living room for playing popular music, which her family sees as an act of defiance against their supposed Spanish identity. For that reason, they buy her a "victrolita portátil" (portable record player), "so [she] would take [her] tunes someplace else" (159).[51] Lidia's eviction from the "sala"—a central space for interaction, the heart of the house—parallels Tío Sergio's ostracism from the family, who as the embodiment of Puerto Rican culture is perceived as a threatening element to the family.

Throughout the novel, Tío Sergio is portrayed as the embodiment of Puerto Rican culture: he knows the history and the music and displays a deep sense of patriotism. He is, however, a migrant, a figure typically shunned on the island for incarnating an "inauthentic" or "failed" Puerto Rican identity. Given the prejudices that have shaped insular views of the diaspora, it seems ironic, although not arbitrary, that García Ramis's novel presents the figure of the migrant as the champion of Puerto Rican culture. It goes without saying that Tío Sergio's patriotism calls into question prevailing stereotypes about Puerto Ricans in the diaspora, which are informed by static and territorially based notions of identity. As the text illustrates, national and cultural identity are not contingent on location; members of the Solís family, residing on the island, tend to identify themselves as European and to undermine their Puerto Rican identity, while Tío Sergio, a migrant, is portrayed as the personification of *puertorriqueñidad*.

As mentioned earlier, the correlation between Tío Sergio's arrival and the awakening of Lidia's sexual and political conscience has been the subject of most of the scholarship on *Felices días*. However, little attention has been paid to the intersection between eroticism, nationalism, and diasporic identity. Throughout the novel, Lidia displays an ever-increasing desire toward Tío Sergio that she is unable to act on or to satisfy for obvious reasons. An eroticized Tío Sergio represents "lo prohibido," the desire that must be repressed. At the same time, if we conceive of him as the embodiment of Puerto Ricanness, Lidia's erotic desire can be read as a manifestation of her longing for a sense of (Puerto Rican) cultural identity, which has been repressed and truncated by her family. Moreover, Lidia's desire for Tío Sergio mirrors the desire for the other that he represents as a migrant. In a sense, the novel portrays the contradictory attitudes underlying the exclusion of diaspora populations from the insular collective imaginary where the immigrant, as an other, becomes an object of desire.

Earlier in the novel, Lidia humorously summarizes the distinction between "el Bien" and "el Mal" that her family upholds as their moral compass:

On the good side were the Catholic, Apostolic and Roman Religion, the Pope, the United States, the Americans, Eisenhower, Europe, especially all the refined Europeans, Grace Kelly, white people, all the militaries, Franco, Evita Perón, opera, *zarzuelas*, everything Spanish. . . . On the evil side were the Communists, atheists, Protestants, Nazis, newly formed black African nations (because in the process they spilled European blood and killed nuns), Puerto Rican Nationalists and any Puerto Ricans in favor of independence, mambo, Trujillo, Batista, and the Mexican actress, María Felix, the wicked woman responsible for Jorge Negrete being in hell.[52] (41)

This tongue-in-cheek catalogue reflecting the Solís worldview, and which is meant to provide moral guidance to the children, not only pokes fun at the family's idiosyncrasies but also, and more important, serves to delegitimize the model of *la gran familia* by underscoring the contradictions, biases, and prejudices hidden underneath this paradigm of social harmony. In other words, this list underscores the principles of Hispanophilia, Catholicism, racism, classism, and sexism that have been associated with *la gran familia*. Even a cursory look makes it evident that Tío Sergio falls squarely under "el Mal": he's not a practicing Catholic, he's a Puerto Rican nationalist, and he may be a homosexual.[53] Although he is of white/European descent, his taste for Afro–Puerto Rican music and his sexual encounter with Micaela (the servant) constitute two very distinct ways that this character signals openness toward other races. Because the Solíses are prejudiced against blacks—although they deny it ("Nosotros no tenemos nada en contra de los negros")—their bigotry and opposition to interracial mixing leads them to perceive Tío Sergio's acceptance as a threat to their "white" identity (46, 116). It could be argued that he comes to represent a porous, and thus dangerous, link in the family chain, one through which "impure" outside elements (black, non-Catholic, lower class, nationalist, homosexual) can filter into the "pristine" fabric that makes up the Solís family. The fact that porousness is personified in the figure of a migrant speaks to the anxiety that the emergence of diasporic identities has generated on the island.

Toward the end of *Felices días, Tío Sergio*, Lidia makes reference to two events that leave an indelible impression on her for the rest of her life: the destruction of Villa Aurora and Tío Sergio's death in New York. I would like to argue that these two seemingly unrelated events are inextricably linked. The house, a remnant of a defunct colonial order, is demolished in the name of progress. While the family moves to the suburbs, where their new house has all the (American) amenities associated with progress (such as air conditioning), Villa Aurora is demolished in order to be replaced by an apartment building. These transformations—the relocation of upper-middle-class families to upscale suburbs and the urbanization of the greater San Juan vicinity—were among those that resulted from Muñoz Marín's Operation Bootstrap. The tearing down of the house, however, can also symbolize the collapse of that fantasy called *la gran familia*. If nothing else, the family's move to a modern cement house at the expense of the wooden *casona* that had belonged to the Solís family for generations can be seen as indicative of the family's shifting allegiances, evinced through their increasing acceptance of Anglo-American cultural influences. More broadly speaking, these changes mirror the rapid Americanization that transformed the socioeconomic and physical landscapes of Puerto Rican society during the 1940s and 1950s.

Along with these transformations, one of the ill effects of Operation Bootstrap was the rampant unemployment that led to the Great Migration (1946–1964). The fact that Tío Sergio's migration and return migration take place during this critical period is significant precisely because it offers a portrayal, albeit limited, of this specific migratory wave. More importantly, the novel depicts the marginalization faced by many migrants upon their return to the island by creating a compassionate representation of Tío Sergio while offering an unfavorable picture of the family. The fact that he is only capable of establishing a profound connection with the children speaks volumes about the difficulties that migrants tend to face while trying to reinsert themselves into the home society. Tío Sergio's failure to integrate, even at the familial level, highlights and makes more palpable his marginalization. Symbolically ejected from insular society—"he didn't seem to fit anywhere" (128)—he migrates again to New York, where he eventually dies like "a pariah, a rebel, and probably a homosexual" (165).[54] The fact that the house, a metaphor of *la gran familia*, is demolished shortly after his departure for the United States can be seen as a manifestation of the failure of this myth to abide amid the drastic changes taking place in Puerto Rican society. Although on the one hand García Ramis's novel paints a compelling picture of Tío Sergio—and thus of the figure of the migrant—by literally and symbolically trying to reincorporate him into the family, on the other hand, the text seems to reaffirm his exclusion. Tío Sergio's death signals the impossibility of return and the migrant's permanent exclusion from *la gran familia puertorriqueña*.

Mending a Broken Memory: Narrating the Diaspora in Esmeralda Santiago's *When I Was Puerto Rican*

The prevalence of (semi)autobiographical narratives among (mostly male) U.S. Puerto Rican and U.S. Latino authors in the 1960s and 1970s mirrors the emergence of a new awareness among minorities in the aftermath of the civil rights movements. That moment marked a period during which, as Aparicio observes, "Chicano and Latino authors were constituting themselves as historical subjects for the first time, articulating in public spaces the history that had not yet been told" ("Latino" 14). Their personal narratives offered a window into the past and present of the U.S. Latino subaltern subject, a way of recording what some have called history from below. Some years later, in the late 1980s and 1990; female-authored (semi)autobiographical narratives took central stage a ; U.S. Latina writers irrupted into the literary scene in a quest to challenge the patriarchal discourse of the U.S. Latino canon.[55] Doubly marginalized as women and ethnic minorities, U.S. Latinas began to narrate what I call "history from underneath below," a concept that seeks to highlight their twofold subordination within dominant society.

Among U.S. Puerto Rican female authors, Esmeralda Santiago struck a chord that garnered her relatively high visibility among critics of U.S. Latino/a literature with the publication of her autobiography, *When I Was Puerto Rican*. Celebrated by some and denounced by others, Santiago's text managed to incite a lively and sometimes heated debate regarding the construction of Puerto Rican identity in the diaspora. For instance, Sánchez González voices the position of one contingent when she condemns it for "simultaneously and aggressively embracing assimilationist tenets of the 'American dream'" (158). In fact, she reads it as a "failed allegory" that has resulted from "the publishing industry's commodification of ethnic market niche writers" (11). Meanwhile, Maritza Stanchich recognizes that despite its "obtuse, tacked-on *comemierda* [snobbish] ending[,] . . . the fact is that, while she may be social climbing, she is hardly trying to pass. Nor is her work devoid of important political and historical observations worth explicating through a post-Nuyorican lens" (120). While Sánchez González is right in pointing out the effect that market forces have had on the production and consumption of U.S. Latino/a texts, Santiago's underprivileged rural background "cannot be dismissed simply because [she has] published narratives of uplift" (Stanchich 119). Therefore, shrugging off her memoir as simply another "novel of assimilation," as Torres-Padilla puts it, fails to recognize the relevance of this text not only in the broader landscape of U.S. Puerto Rican literature but also in its capacity to fill historical voids in the insular and Anglo-American social memories (82).[56]

My proposal to read *When I Was Puerto Rican* as the "other side" of the story that complements García Ramis's depiction of urban life on the island during the 1950s is based on the fact that most of the plot takes place on the island, despite it being a personal narrative of migration and/or "assimilation." In fact, one of the greatest contributions of Santiago's text is that it offers a window into the life of a rural family precisely during a period in which rural communities were not only undergoing significant transformations as a result of Operation Bootstrap but were also being molded into the icon of *puertorriqueñidad* through Operation Serenity, and more specifically, through the programs established by DIVEDCO. Because Santiago's childhood in Puerto Rico (1948–1961) overlaps DIVEDCO's golden age (1952–1960), her coming-of-age narrative can provide a rare glimpse into the effects of *el muñocismo* in the peasantry's daily existence.

In her book *Negociaciones culturales: Los intelectuales y el proyecto pedagógico del estado muñocista* (2009), Catherine Marsh Kennerley examines the role DIVEDCO played as a key pedagogical instrument designed by the Muñoz Marín government to target mainly the rural populations. DIVEDCO's cultural products—films, books, and posters—were created mainly to teach highland communities about hygiene, eliminate superstition, and create a new democratic citizenry (Marsh Kennerley 100). Underpinning what came to be known as the PPD's *pedagogía jíbara*, however, was an impulse to rescue those campesino values deemed central to the definition of a Puerto Rican identity. An analysis of *When I Was Puerto Rican* that takes into consideration the climate engendered by Operation Serenity offers a new angle and expands on previous readings of this autobiography.

The focus of Santiago's text on her childhood years in Puerto Rico must not be taken for granted. Among other things, pondering the reasons for and repercussions of the text's pronounced emphasis on the island has the potential to overcome the *frontera intranacional* that divides insular from diasporic literary production. In fact, the presence and description of life on the island in a significant number of narratives by other U.S. Puerto Rican female authors—which marks a distinction from male autobiographical writings in the diaspora—speaks to the key function that memories of island life play in the construction of identities for first-generation migrants who came of age in the United States.[57]

While the presence of *la gran familia* is more discernible in the texts produced by island-based authors, I argue—at the risk of coming across as too "island centered"—that the myth also underlies the works of first-generation diaspora writers, particularly those who were part of the Great Migration. At that specific historical juncture, *la gran familia* had become part of the "cultural baggage" that migrants were bringing with them to the U.S. mainland.

When I Was Puerto Rican is one of the works that best exemplifies the place the island occupies in the diaspora imaginary. As a narrative in which life in the homeland takes precedence over depictions of experiences in the host society, this autobiography destabilizes the traditional model of the narrative of migration, whose focus tends to be the adaptation to the new environment. In this sense, claims of "assimilationist tendencies" in this text need to be reevaluated, or at least mitigated. Its asymmetrical structure (ten chapters are set in Puerto Rico, three in New York) can be seen as indicative of a desire to assert her ties to the island. The fact that most of the narration focuses on her experiences while growing up in the mountains of Puerto Rico renders her story emblematic of what Muñoz Marín's government was trying to accomplish in those decades, that is, positing the rural experience as the epitome of Puerto Rican identity. In this sense, it is paradoxical that Santiago's defense of her Puerto Rican identity has been disputed by conservative insular sectors, when the experience she recounts is mostly in consonance with *el muñocismo*'s quest to cement the *jíbaro* as the foundation of *puertorriqueñidad*.

Interestingly, most of the negative criticism about the book has resulted from the misreading of its title, which emphasizes a past identity through the use of the verbal past form. However, as the author explains in an interview with Carmen Dolores Hernández, many have failed to detect the irony behind the title: "It refers to my life as a Puerto Rican girl, when I had no idea that I would ever leave the island, that I would ever visit another culture, let alone live in it for ten or fifteen years. It really is a Puerto Rican life for most of the book" (*Puerto Rican Voices* 165). She adds, "When I came back to Puerto Rico, *los puertorriqueños mismos me negaron* because I was so Americanized, so it is an ironic comment and it is a way of starting a discussion about what is Puerto Ricanism. These degrees of Puerto Ricanism have to be addressed" (165). This idea is also expressed in her interview with Bridget Kevane and Juanita Heredia: "It was devastating to be denied an identity I had struggled so hard to uphold. . . . When I titled my book in the past tense, I was answering those who disputed my right to call myself Puerto Rican—You said I was not Puerto Rican enough for you. Read this book. Tell me this is not a Puerto Rican experience" (131). Indeed, it is the still ongoing debate regarding the construction of Puerto Rican identity at home and abroad that is one of the most productive outcomes of the publication of Santiago's autobiography.

One of the reasons for the title, the rejection Santiago felt on her return to the island, illustrates precisely the most significant way in which this text intersects with *la gran familia*: its questioning of the myth's exclusionary premises. If nothing else, Santiago's text highlights the fact that as a minor she was uprooted and forced to leave her homeland in order to remain with her mother. The psychological violence of this displacement is evident when the narrator admits, "The Puerto Rican *jíbara* who longed for the green quiet of a tropical afternoon was to become a hybrid who would never forgive the uprooting" (*When I Was* 209). With these words, she reminds the audience that growing up on the U.S. mainland was not a choice and therefore should not be an argument used to question her sense of Puerto Rican identity. Unfortunately, her tale echoes the experiences of thousands of young first-generation migrants, succinctly captured by Tato Laviera in his poem "nuyorican":

> yo soy tu hijo
> de una migración,
> pecado forzado,
> me mandaste a nacer nativo en otras tierras. (8–11)

By underscoring the intersecting economic, political, and social forces that propelled the massive displacement of Puerto Ricans after World War II, both Santiago and Laviera—to mention just a couple of examples—put the burden back on the home society that rejected the sons and daughters of the diaspora. As Acosta-Belén and Santiago remind us, migration was hardly a choice for many, since "the state actively promoted migration of 'surplus labor' as a method to increase the standard of living on the island, and emigration became the 'safety valve' that it was envisioned to be" (129).[58]

In this sense, *When I Was Puerto Rican* challenges the exclusion of the diasporic subject from the imagined national family by firmly asserting the author's island roots in an act that undermines the Hispanophile, androcentric, and racist discourses that underlie *la gran familia*, and which have served to marginalize the Other (i.e., women, blacks, homosexuals, migrants, foreigners). In recognizing and labeling her past as "Puerto Rican," she metaphorically reinserts herself in the narrative of the family. The most effective way in which Santiago accomplishes this is by accentuating her *campesina* or *jíbara* background, a common practice among migrants. According to Lillian Guerra, "By invoking the jíbaro as the symbolic habitus of the Puerto Rican soul, Puerto Rican migrants and their descendants actively and consciously locate the roots of their identity in the history of the island" (5). In her in-depth analysis of the *jíbaro* as a cultural symbol, Guerra describes this iconic figure as follows:

> Originally, the distinguishing features of a view of national identity—the jíbaro's white skin, Spanish culture, materially impoverished lifestyle, preference for political autonomy if not neutrality, and patriarchal masculinity—were defined, legitimized, and romanticized by discrete members of the elite for their own class purposes. Eventually, broad acceptance of the jíbaro by all classes came to represent not only a legitimation of a sense of Puerto Rican-ness, which all Puerto Ricans discursively shared, but also a form of contestation of the legitimacy of the North American colonial project and the corresponding colonial identity it assigned to Puerto Ricans. (14)

Because of the mythical proportions reached by the *jíbaro*—another foundational fiction that developed during the first few decades of the twentieth century—an emphasis on this origin constitutes an act of cultural assertion on the part of the migrant. Yet, as the above passage suggests, drawing on this figure invokes both continuity and rupture with the *jibarista* discourse that emerged on the island in the eighteenth century and continues to evolve to the present. On the one hand, Negi's original anti-Americanism, the family's abject poverty, and her trajectory from the mountains of Puerto Rico to San Juan and eventually to New York echoes the proverbial story of thousands of Puerto Rican *jíbaros* during the Great Migration—a story that had been previously depicted in canonical works such as René Marqués's *La carreta* (1951–1952) and that represents a point of contact with the long-standing *jibarista* narrative tradition.

On the other hand, Negi's Afro–Puerto Rican and female identity diverges from the traditional icon's portrayal as a white male, despite the fact that, as Dávila reminds us, he represents "the embodiment of all three ancestral heritages in a single Puerto Rican culture" (*Sponsored* 71). "Ironically," Dávila adds, "the dominant presentation of the *jíbaro* as a white peasant belies the historical reality of racial intermingling on the island—that is, the same foundational principle for the blending myth of nationality" (72). Because both women and blacks had been rendered invisible by the nationalist elite's appropriation of the *jíbaro* as a symbol of Puerto Rican-ness, Santiago's rendition of her peasant origins gives voice to an alternate *Afra-jíbara* experience, thereby challenging the Hispanophile and masculinist *jíbaro* discourse that developed on the island, by giving a voice to an alternate *Afra-jíbara* experience. In fact, I would like to suggest that the value of Santiago's memoir extends beyond the points already discussed to include the fact that this is the first *jíbara* memoir produced on or outside the island; as such it is the first literary work to defy, head-on, this iconic symbol of the Puerto Rican soul.

Besides engaging with the myth of the *jíbaro* and *la gran familia* in order to challenge her own exclusion as a diasporic subject, Santiago's autobiography intersects with the latter by dismantling the tenet of an idealized past, a common posture among nationalists, who "tended to idealize the preindustrial rural past under Spanish rule and to demonize U.S. industrial capitalism in the twentieth century" (Duany, *Puerto Rican* 19). Similar to the posture assumed by the island-based authors Ferré, Vega, and García Ramis vis-à-vis the glorification of the past in male canonical writings, it can be argued that Santiago challenges the tendency to romanticize Puerto Rican history. More precisely, it calls into question recent Hispanophile representations of the past that have been used to cast blame on return migrants for being conduits of American cultural infiltration on the island.

While the negative stereotype of the migrant as the embodiment of a "corrupted" (i.e., Americanized) Puerto Rican has precluded his or her inclusion in the insular national imaginary, Santiago's memoir unveils the artificiality of such claims by showing that Puerto Rico had been undergoing increasing Americanization since 1898, including "the propagation of North American values, business interests, and political proclivities [that] came to permeate everyday life in Puerto Rico" (Guerra 23). Guerra's observation is evident in Santiago's narrative, where the issue of colonialism and its cultural impact are the focus of the chapter, "The American Invasion of Macún," the most popular, anthologized, and critically examined section of the book. Because this chapter has often been used as a springboard for discussions about Puerto Rico's oppression under U.S. colonialism, and in order to avoid redundancy, I would like to propose a reading of this chapter that not only foregrounds the cultural violence effected by Americanization campaigns, but that seems to call into question the mechanisms, procedures, and effectiveness of DIVEDCO's educational program, one of the main off-shoots of Operation Serenity.

The chapter depicts the visit of an American and a Puerto Rican from San Juan who go to Macún's community center to give a talk about health and hygiene. The situation is reminiscent of the hundreds of community meetings held by DIVEDCO's administrators across the island to educate the rural populations on those topics during that same period. In fact, these types of meetings were such a central component of the program that the image of the *círculo democrático* (democratic circle) became one of the DIVEDCO's icons (Marsh Kennerley 179). While the image of people seated in a circle was meant to convey exactly that, democracy and equality among its participants, the depiction of meetings where participants were lectured to by an authority figure while they sat in rows (which does not allow them to see each other) usually represented a non-democratic process (Marsh Kennerley 180). Examined in this context, Santiago's representation of the community meeting challenges the ideal of democracy underpinning DIVEDCO's program in more than one way. That the meeting takes place indoors—as opposed to the traditional outdoor *círculo democrático*—also serves to highlight an atmosphere where democracy does not prevail, thus challenging the perception that *el muñocismo* successfully restored the campesino's agency.[59]

The perceived superiority of the American is evident not only in the physical arrangement of the meeting but also in the dynamics at play during the exchange that takes place between the two government officials and the audience. While the tone of this chapter can best be described as humorous, it addresses the important issue of colonial subordination and also the resistance of Puerto Ricans to the imposition of American practices. One of the chapter's most significant contributions is that it illustrates how, "steeped in the language of paternalism and scientific racism, the discourse of Americanization relied heavily on the notion that North Americans in their self-appointed role as parental guardians knew better than Puerto Ricans what was best for Puerto Rico" (Guerra 22). The condescending attitude of the American delegate reflects the dominant posture adopted by the U.S. government over Puerto Rican internal affairs. At the same time, the presence of Puerto Rican men from San Juan—representatives of Muñoz Marín's government—conveys the ideology of paternalism that *el muñocismo* proudly cultivated vis-à-vis the *jíbaro* population.

A poignant representation of the culture clash between the government officials and the community takes place when the American is talking about the nutritional value of nonindigenous products such as apples, pears, and broccoli. The lack of access to such products sends the audience into a state of confusion as they try to make sense of the American food pyramid and deliberate how to substitute Puerto Rican for American produce: "In heavily accented, hard to understand Castilian Spanish he described the necessity of eating portions of each of the foods on his chart every day. There were carrots and broccoli, iceberg lettuce, apples, pears, and peaches. . . . There was no rice on the chart, no beans, no salted codfish. . . . There were bananas but no plantains, potatoes but no *batatas*, cereal flakes but no oatmeal, bacon but no sausages" (66). After someone in the audience tells the American that those fruits and vegetables do not grow in Puerto Rico, he suggests that they substitute his recommendations with their native foods (66). The irrelevance of the American's suggestions to people's daily life is underscored when someone in the audience asks if "an apple is the same as a mango," to which he replies that "it is best not to make substitutions for the recommended foods" because that "would throw the whole thing off" (67).

While the American's intention may be honorable, that is, he is there to educate the people about their health, the way he conducts himself reflects the Anglocentrism that for more than a century has characterized U.S.-Puerto Rico colonial relations. It becomes clear that the Americans were not working *with* the Puerto Ricans to help them solve their problems but instead trying to impose their way of life on the islanders. As Negi's father summarizes it, the American way means that "they expect us to do things their way, even in our country" (73).

The presence of the American has an effect on the community; because of him, the boundary between *us* and *them* is clearly defined, providing a temporary sense of unity among the people of Macún.[60] Allegorically, the American stands for the United States as colonizer, and the people of Macún stand for Puerto Rico, the colonized. Since the Americanization campaign was put in effect across the island, all Puerto Ricans, regardless of class, race, or political affiliation, experienced the imposition of American culture. Puerto Ricans of all walks of life would have endured the implicit violence behind the United States efforts to rid them of their language, traditions, and culture. This segment of Santiago's narrative is pivotal because it speaks to the transculturation of Puerto Ricans on the island, prior to the Great Migration, and therefore dismantles the nationalist rhetoric that has turned migrants into the scapegoats of Puerto Rico's social ills (often considered an effect of American cultural infiltration).

Along the same lines, *When I Was Puerto Rican* challenges versions of the past—present in canonical insular and U.S. Puerto Rican works—that glorify life in the countryside as emblematic of a preindustrial Puerto Rico. Unarguably, this autobiography engages in, and has been criticized for, the romanticization of the countryside and of *jíbara* identity, which illustrates the extent to which "the land was so tied up with the jíbaro's culture and self-identity that one was virtually inseparable from the other" (Guerra 89). Yet, despite the tendency to paint a glorified picture of *el campo* (the countryside), Santiago's story reveals the hardships that the poor, rural, working classes faced as they tried to make a living under deplorable economic conditions. The poverty faced particularly by female single-headed households, as Santiago's text illustrates, not only serves to demythify life on the island (rural and urban) but also challenges the utopian myth of *la gran familia puertorriqueña*.

Partly as a result of the absence of Negi's father, and his disinterest in providing for his children, the family moves to Santurce seeking a better future. Their journey and experiences in this urban setting as members of the rural working class will mark a stark contrast to Lidia's middle-/upper-class experiences growing up in the same vicinity in *Felices días, Tío Sergio*. A significant distinction emerges through the metaphor of the house, which in the latter stands for rootedness, solidity, and tradition and in the former comes to signal itinerancy, precariousness, and economic disenfranchisement.[61] This is quite evident from the beginning of *When I Was Puerto Rican*, when the narrator describes her family's humble dwelling in the mountains, "a rectangle of rippled metal sheets on stilts hovering in the middle of a circle of red dirt" (7). The deplorable living conditions depicted in this passage attest to the level of disenfranchisement of rural populations that was still common during the mid-twentieth century.[62]

In Puerto Rican literature, the displacement of the *jíbaro* from the mountains to San Juan or New York is generally portrayed as a corrupting process that jeopardizes his spiritual "purity"—linked to the mountains, where the "rural soul of Spain [had been] transplanted onto Puerto Rican soil" (Guerra 84). For this reason, the *jíbaro's* displacement from the mountains, the source of his spirituality, would inevitably lead to the loss of innocence and values as he struggled to survive in the city's inhospitable environment. *When I Was Puerto Rican* revisits this pivotal trajectory through the eyes of Negi, whose shuttling between rural Macún and urban Santurce exemplifies the quintessential experience of the *jíbaro* in mid-twentieth-century Puerto Rico. Her family's displacement from the mountains to the city, where they reside in more than one place, reflects the massive displacement of the rural lower class to urban areas in search of work.

This precarious condition is evident in Santiago's description of their living environment and surroundings. In her text Macún acquires a sort of Eden-like character; it is a place where nature abounds and where children can play freely and happily because people look after one another. Santurce, in contrast, signals decadence, corruption, and excess, as the following quote illustrates: "The way to school took me over muddy sidewalks strewn with garbage, across narrow streets teeming with traffic, people, and stray dogs, and past bars with open doorways and loud jukeboxes that always played *boleros* about liquor and women" (38). Negi's new surroundings do not offer her the comfort and security that she grew used to in Macún: "'The city is different,' Mami told us on our first day. 'There are many mischievous people, so you have to be careful where you go and who you talk to'" (38). Surviving in the city implies a loss of innocence; Negi is no longer able to trust people since every person is a potential predator.

The decay that characterizes sections of Santurce is further accentuated in "El Mangle," a chapter reminiscent of José Luis González's foundational story "En el fondo del caño hay un negrito."[63] El Mangle, a reference to Caño Martín Peña (a shantytown in Santurce where wood and zinc houses were built on stilts over a lagoon), is where Negi truly experiences the decadence of the city. This decadence takes the form of putrefaction both in physical and in metaphorical terms. She describes her new home as follows: "The *barrio* floated on a black lagoon. Sewage drifted by in a surprising variety of shapes, sizes, and colors. It was easy to tell what people in El Mangle ate because pieces of food stuck to the turds that glided past" (133). She adds, "In El Mangle, we couldn't get away from the stench. The air smelled like the brewery, and the water like human waste. Food didn't taste good. The smell lived inside us, and even though Mami used a lot of garlic and oregano when she cooked, it didn't help. I could still taste shit when I ate" (137). As these quotes suggest, Negi's insistence on and reiteration of the image of human waste points to something more besides the physical reality of her living conditions in El Mangle. The ubiquitous image of excrement is symbolic of the abject misery and destitution in which they live. In addition, life in the city becomes demoralizing for Negi and her family, the same way it was perceived as devaluing for the *jíbaro*, an idea that is reinforced by the image of floating excrement that surrounds them and that Negi symbolically consumes.

This, I would argue, is one of the novel's most important contributions; its depiction of life in El Mangle offers a rare glimpse into one of the island's most neglected sectors. In contrast to the image that Muñoz Marín's government promoted of the island as *"vitrina de las Américas"* (showcase of the Americas)—clearly extolling the success of Operation Bootstrap—a less flattering reality emerged as the growth of slums in urban centers quickly revealed what some viewed as the "dark side" of Operation Bootstrap. In other words, the massive migration of rural workers to the city had led to the mushrooming of slums and shantytowns on the city's edges. As A. W. Maldonado explains, "The hope of industrialization had ignited a full-fledged 'revolution of rising expectations' throughout Puerto Rico, setting into motion a massive migration from the country to the cities and grotesquely inflating the horrid slums" (75). The extreme poverty that characterized the slums posed an unexpected challenge to Muñoz Marín's administration.

The magnitude of the problem posed by the *arrabal* (slum) is evident in the fact that this topic remained outside DIVEDCO's canon (Marsh Kennerley 111). As Marsh Kennerley explains, this was due to the clash between the agency's philosophy, the push of the government toward modernization, and the emergence of problems associated with city life. While some of the DIVEDCO intellectuals did attempt to publish materials about *el arrabal* and the city, the government opposed their plan, as this would have amounted to an act of self-condemnation and acceptance of Operation Bootstrap's failure. The fact that the topic of urban migration was all but excluded from the arsenal of DIVEDCO's cultural products is striking given the extent of migration from the mountains to the city and the fact that thousands of campesinos became victims of the industrialization process. Given DIVEDCO's official silence regarding the *arrabal*, and the fact that this agency had single-handedly transformed the *jíbaro* into the icon of *puertorriqueñidad*, Santiago's depiction of life in El Mangle acquires even more significance. If the *arrabal* had been forced to remain outside DIVEDCO's canon (against the opinion of some of the writers and film producers), despite being a central element of the *jíbaro*'s existence after migrating from the mountains, *When I Was Puerto Rican* reconstructs this experience, giving voice to those previously silenced. This is not to say that the *arrabal* and the city were absent from Puerto Rican literature up to this point. In fact, many of DIVEDCO's intellectuals published works on this subject (René Marqués, Pedro Juan Soto, Emilio Díaz Valcárcel), but unlike Santiago, their perspectives were those of outsiders given that they didn't live in the slums. For this reason, Santiago's narration of her firsthand experience living in a slum not only serves to recuperate a neglected side of *jíbaro* history but also calls into question the glorification of this icon. The novel points to the deceptiveness of governmental programs that paradoxically tried to safeguard the *jíbaro*'s lifestyle and values while promoting changes that threatened this very lifestyle.

While most of Santiago's autobiography focuses on her life in the island, the last few chapters offer a glimpse of her family's struggle for survival in New York. Following the common path taken by many displaced *jíbaros*, Negi's family eventually moves from the island to the U.S. Once again, the city is depicted in negative terms. Brooklyn, their neighborhood, is not a safe place; it is full of "gente mala," and "every day there were murders, rapes, muggings, knifings, and shootings. In Puerto Rico the crimes had always happened somewhere else, in cities far from Macún. But in Brooklyn bad things happened on [their] block" (252). Life in New York is thus characterized by fear, a fear that appears more extreme than the one Negi felt in Santurce. As she puts it, "Every man was a potential rapist, and every dark doorway was a potential hiding place for someone waiting to hurt me" (253). This fear forces the family into a state of isolation analogous to confinement: "There was nothing to do, nowhere to go, no one to talk to. The apartment was stifling" (222). In addition to these conditions, the depiction in Santiago's text of poverty, deprivation, substandard living conditions, discrimination, racism, visits to the welfare program offices, and the language barrier succeeds in personalizing experiences shared by the Puerto Rican community, as well as other minority groups, in the United States.

An interesting point of contrast between Santiago's and García Ramis's texts is the absence of the house—a solid structure that serves as a metaphor for tradition and an idealized past in many works by insular authors—which in Santiago's novel is supplanted by a multiplicity of dwellings. The hutlike dwellings that Negi's family inhabits in rural Macún and urban El Mangle, as well as their substandard project apartments in New York City, reflect the lower socioeconomic position of what was originally the Puerto Rican rural working class, and which became the social base of the Great Migration. In addition to serving as a metaphor for the precariousness that characterized the lives of many migrants, the constant movement between dwellings—or condition of itinerancy—marks a stark contrast between Santiago's and García Ramis's texts. While the Solíses' *casona* in Santurce was an emblem of their solid economic and social capital, the lack of an analogue in

Santiago's case emphasizes the itinerancy that often characterized their experiences on the island and beyond. Of course, these distinctions speak to the social class differences between authors from each side. But also, they signal their respective concerns according to their individual class, race, and gender positions.

In one of the most poignant moments in Santiago's narrative, Negi says, "Sometimes I lay in bed, in the unheated rooms full of beds and clothes and the rustle of sleeping bodies, terrified that what lay around the corner was no better than what we'd left behind, that being in Brooklyn was not a new life but a continuation of the old one" (247). In this crucial instance, Negi's perceptiveness leads to disillusion, an experience shared by thousands of other Puerto Rican migrants, who like her mother had been lured to the United States by the promise of a better life, only to find that conditions in the diaspora were often worse than those on the island. Santiago's demythification of migration is not a novel topic of the (U.S) Puerto Rican canon. In fact, both the literary production of the *generación del 1950*, a group of island authors who wrote extensively about Puerto Rico's transition from a rural to an industrial economy (Marqués, Soto, Valcárcel, etc.), and the literature produced in the diaspora in the 1960s and 1970s contributed to the demythification of migration. However, Santiago's text is the first personal account of this process to explicitly draw a parallel between the condition of the lower class on the island and its experience in the mainland. In questioning what has really changed for her family and at what cost, her narrative raises an important point from a unique perspective.

As I hope to have demonstrated, literature plays a central role in the diaspora community's process of historicization. Santiago's account of her life growing up in rural Puerto Rico and her subsequent migrations to San Juan and New York offers a firsthand vision of a process that affected thousands of Puerto Ricans. Because Santiago's personal experiences are representative of the collective experience of Puerto Ricans during this period, by writing her memories she transforms them into social memory, further strengthening the sense of collective identity of the diaspora community. Her story, in addition, has the potential to create awareness among island Puerto Ricans—particularly among younger generations who read it in history and literature courses—of the history behind the massive exodus that forever transformed that nation.

4 Patriarchal Foundations

Contesting Gender/Sexual Paradigms

It is not women who have a colonial status, but the colonies that have a woman's status.

—Maria Mies

IN ADDITION TO THE PRINCIPLES of harmony/racial democracy and a glorified past that have been the subjects of the two previous chapters, the claim of unity under an authoritarian, yet benevolent, father figure completes *la gran familia puertorriqueña*. The myth's reconceptualization of the hacienda economy as one sustained on the principles of justice and fairness has served to justify the perpetuation of patriarchy in Puerto Rican society. Today, the challenge to this system constitutes the most tangible literary contact zone between the literature of women authors on the island and that of the diaspora, and it demonstrates the benefits of applying a transnational comparative approach. However, as we will see through an analysis of selected works by Olga Nolla, Nicholasa Mohr, and Alba Ambert, there are significant divergences in the way that these writers have engaged in their critiques of patriarchy that reflect each group's unique concerns and experiences.

Of course, the androcentrism that is at the center of *la gran familia* does not exist in a vacuum; it is just another manifestation of what M. Jacqui Alexander and Chandra Talpade Mohanty call "universal patriarchy," which operates "in a transhistorical way to subordinate all women" (xix). While the origins and causes of women's subordination continue to be a source of debate, biological determinism has prevailed as a primary cause despite feminism's rejection of this concept, which some argue tends to obfuscate the historical, political, economic, and other social factors that have converged at specific junctures to shape inequality between the sexes. Because, as Maria Mies explains, women's "share in the creation and maintenance of life is usually defined as a function of their biology or 'nature,'" many have come to see "social inequalities or exploitative relations as 'natural', inborn, and hence, beyond the scope of social change" (68). For Pierre Bourdieu, this is all precisely at the root of the masculine order, its strength coming "from the fact that it combines and condenses two operations: *it legitimates a relationship of domination by embedding it in a biological nature that is itself a naturalized social construction*" (23). The challenge therefore lies in moving beyond the discursive trap of biological determinism in order to move toward conscientization (Freire, in Alexander xxxvii) and a more equal and just society.

The universal tendency to imagine and articulate the nation as female is grounded in the paradoxical exaltation of women, who are at once expected to reproduce the nation, both literally (birth) and figuratively (national values and traditions), but at the same time are considered its most significant threat (Loomba 1998; Alexander 2005; McClintock 1995).[1] More specifically, women's sexuality is considered dangerous (Craske 203). According to the logic presented by Alexander, women's sexual agency poses "a challenge to the ideological anchor of an originary nuclear family, a source of legitimation for the state, which perpetuates the fiction that the family is the cornerstone of society. . . . And because loyalty to the nation as citizen is perennially colonized within reproduction and heterosexuality, erotic autonomy brings with it the potential of undoing the nation entirely" (64). The control and discipline exerted over women's bodies by patriarchal figures in the domestic realm (fathers, brothers, uncles, cousins, husbands, etc.), and the "success" of this operation (of which the glorification of chastity and virginity are its main evidence), is therefore correlative to the nation's ability to survive.

This inextricable relationship between patriarchy and nation that is evident in the centrality of the heteropatriarchal family is further magnified in the context of (neo)colonialism.[2] In the case of Puerto Rico, where the construction of the *nation* has occurred in the context of colonial ties to the United States, this relationship manifests itself in the cult of *la gran familia*, a key heteropatriarchal unit that is meant to mirror the nation. Departing from the parallelism that has been established between woman and colony—drawn from their respective subordinate positions within the power structure—it follows that the strengthening of patriarchy within colonial society is seen as providing a countermeasure against the feminizing effects of U.S. colonization.[3] Thus, given the colonial condition of the island, the veneration of the authoritarian, yet benevolent, father figure that is central to the foundational myth of *la gran familia* acquires even greater importance.

However, the assertion and perpetuation of the father figure's authority is not a given but rather is contingent on the "social subordination of women and children within the domestic sphere" (McClintock 358). Within the model of *la gran familia*, women, children, and other marginalized groups are expected to abide by the law of the father. Ania Loomba describes the parallel dynamics between the heteropatriarchal family and the colonial situation as follows: "The colonial state cast itself as the *parens patriae*, controlling but also supposedly providing for its children. . . . The white man's burden was constructed as a parental one: that of 'looking after' those who were civilisationally underdeveloped (and hence figured as children), and of disciplining them into obedience" (216). Mirroring the dynamics inherent in any system of colonial domination, violence—in its myriad manifestations—constitutes a key mechanism to guarantee the success of the patriarchal power structure. In order to better grasp the magnitude of its reach, a broad conception of violence is central to understanding the obvious and the less palpable modes in which the patriarchal system exerts its power. Here, Bourdieu's take on the inner workings of the system of what he calls "masculine domination" proves indispensable to our discussion.

In his study *Masculine Domination*, Bourdieu examines the ways in which this heteropatriarchal system has been engrained in society's unconscious and the mechanisms and structures that keep men in a position of power over women. In addition to its most evident manifestation in the form of physical violence, which entails a wide range of practices and degrees of abuse (beatings, molestation, rape, female circumcision, widow immolation, and murder, among others), one of its most pervasive embodiments is what he refers to as *symbolic violence*, "a gentle violence, imperceptible and invisible even to its victims, exerted for the most part through the purely symbolic channels of communication and cognition (more precisely, misrecognition), recognition, or even feeling" (1). This sort of *soft violence*, as opposed to "hard"/"real"/physical violence, has been largely underestimated when in fact it can be more damaging given the surreptitious way in which it leads its victims to internalize their subordination, therefore facilitating and promoting its widespread reach (Alexander 1997; Bourdieu 2001).

Because symbolic domination works mostly at the subconscious level, it can sometimes defy logic. In his attempt to explain this apparent contradiction, Bourdieu states that "the paradoxical logic of masculine domination and feminine submissiveness, which can, without contradiction, be described as both *spontaneous and extorted*, cannot be understood until one takes account of the *durable effects* that the social order exerts on women (and men), that is to say, the dispositions spontaneously attuned to that order which it imposes on them" (37). And while these durable effects manifest in multiple forms and degrees across cultures, generally men and women are universally socialized to subscribe to their respective roles.

The commonplace view of these structures of power as "natural" has diverted attention from the fact that they are "*the product of an incessant (and therefore historical) labour of reproduction*" (Bourdieu 34). The role that institutions such as the family, the church, and schools have had in the active reproduction of gendered dispositions that sustain this system should not be overlooked. Among these, Bourdieu asserts that the "family undoubtedly played the most important part in the reproduction of masculine domination and the masculine vision; it is here that early experience of the sexual division of labour and the legitimate representation of that division, guaranteed by law and inscribed in language, imposes itself" (85).[4] Given the crucial role of the family in cementing the system of masculine domination, a closer look at the myth of *la gran familia puertorriqueña* seems conducive to elucidating the "inner workings" of this system.

I would like to propose an alternative reading of *la gran familia* as a manifestation of symbolic violence given this paradigm's successful reproduction (i.e., "durable effects") of the gendered dispositions that have and continue to perpetuate patriarchy. As previously stated, the model of *la gran familia* relies on the central figure of the *hacendado*/father—the pater familias—who governs his wife and children with an authoritarian yet benevolent hand. Under this model, the wife is expected to submit to the authority of her husband and to display certain attributes that connote subordination. Bourdieu's description of "*bodily emotions*—shame, humiliation, timidity, anxiety, guilt—or *passions* and *sentiments*—love, admiration, respect" as manifestations of the awareness of "the magical frontier between the dominant and the dominated" offers a striking parallel to the Latin(o) American concept of *marianismo* that inflects *la gran familia* (38).

Marianismo, the "other" side of machismo that is central to the construction of womanhood in Puerto Rican culture, is defined by María Pérez y González as follows:

Traditionally, a Puerto Rican woman's identity is rooted in the function she plays in the family—housekeeping, childbearing, and child rearing. She is socialized to adhere to the cultural concept known as *marianismo*, which emphasizes virtues attributed to La Virgen María (the Virgin Mary): obedience, submission, fidelity, meekness, and humility. The expectation is that women will remain virgins until they are married, after which they will bear children without any recourse to contraceptives and will show little interest in and enjoyment of sex—that is the function of a mistress or prostitute—*una mujer de la calle* (a "street" woman). (19)

To the extent that *marianismo* has been embedded in the fabric of the masculine-centered Puerto Rican culture and the myth of *la gran familia*, it has successfully operated as a self-regulatory or self-policing mechanism working in the interest of patriarchy. The moral and religious underpinnings of *marianismo* make it a desirable objective among many women, thus demonstrating the paradoxical "spontaneous and extorted" character of masculine domination.

While some may not fully agree with my reading of *marianismo* as an example of symbolic violence, it is paramount to remember how conditions of (neo)colonialism often lead to the magnification of patriarchal violence within the domestic sphere. As Loomba puts it, "Colonialism intensified patriarchal relations in colonised lands, often because native men, increasingly disenfranchised and excluded from the public sphere, became more tyrannical at home. They seized upon the home and the woman as emblems of their culture and nationality. The outside world could be Westernised but all was not lost if the domestic space retained its cultural purity" (168). In the U.S.-Puerto Rican colonial context, where the power of the male elite was usurped by their American colonizers, the defense of the nation came to rely substantially on the defense of values associated with *machismo*.[5]

While the Puerto Rican variant of *machismo* stresses "positive" values such as responsibility, courage, honor, and paternity, these standards of masculinity are often eclipsed by other less noble aspects (Rafael Ramírez 14, 21). *Don Juanismo*, sexual potency, exhibitionism, coprolalia (the use of dirty language), aggressiveness, the cult of virginity, and the sexual repression of women are some of the negative aspects of *machismo* that Puerto Rican women see as synonymous with masculinity (Ramírez 12). Perhaps because women's experience of subordination is mostly the product of the way in which masculine sexuality is conceptualized in Puerto Rican culture, women tend to "stress negative traits and to associate machismo with sexual issues," while men tend to emphasize *machismo*'s most positive aspects (Ramírez 21).[6]

Machismo is deeply rooted in Puerto Rican culture, dating back to the island's colonial ties to Spain. Aware that *machismo* and patriarchal ideology became dominant in all of Spanish America, Acosta-Belén convincingly argues that its level of entrenchment in Puerto Rican culture, as well as the lack of a feminist consciousness, was determined by the island's condition as one of Spain's most "backward" colonies.[7] And indeed, *machismo*'s centrality to the island's cultural composition is reflected in the fact that it became paramount to the definition of the nation, as evinced by René Marqués's desperate plea to defend it as the "last bulwark" of Puerto Rican culture (175).[8]

Because the exaltation of *machismo* as a national value is always contingent on *marianismo* (they are reciprocal), it follows that the defense of the former would have implicated the intensification of the latter through the heightening of internalized oppression. The same argument can also be made in relation to the escalation of patriarchal violence in the context of the diaspora, where the Puerto Rican male's disenfranchisement is compounded by his loss of status as a colonized subject in the land of the colonizer. And precisely because women from both sides have confronted the challenges and limitations of *machismo/marianismo*, their literature strongly reflects their denunciation of patriarchal violence in its "real" and symbolic manifestations.

Discursive Weapons against Masculine Domination

The analogy between woman and colony has become a key element in the discourse of Third World and postcolonial feminisms, where critics have advanced the concept of the *decolonization* of women as a top issue of their agenda (Alexander and Talpade Mohanty 1997; Mies and Bennholdt-Thomsen 1988). Recently this rhetoric has permeated the field of feminist literary studies and is contributing to reshaping the way we conceptualize the role of literature in (post)colonial societies. For example, in *Transnational Latina Narratives in the Twenty-First Century* (2009), Juanita Heredia suggests that Latina writers "are involved in a decolonizing process by writing and relocating subaltern cultures from their respective national heritages and the United States to the forefront in order to participate and combat modernizing (colonizing) efforts from hegemonic forms (i.e., governments, corporations, institutional power, and patriarchy)" (5). While Heredia's statement is certainly applicable to the U.S. Puerto Rican authors that are the subject of this study, I would like to extend it to encompass the literature produced by women on the island, where the equation between woman and colony is equally pertinent given Puerto Rico's colonial status.

Whether referring to women or colonies, it is crucial to keep in mind that "thinking 'out of' colonization happens only through action and reflection, through praxis," because in the end, "social transformation cannot remain at the level of ideas, it must engage in practice" (Alexander and Mohanty xxviii). Praxis, as I see it, is reflected in the act of writing because, as Rogers states, "writing anything is usually a form of social action" (90). Understanding writing as a form of action is thus paramount to understanding the potential role of literature in the decolonizing process. The link between writing and social action has long been recognized by critics of U.S. Puerto Rican literature who see "the 'anti-Establishment' character of this literature and its commitment to denouncing inequality and injustice in U.S. society . . . as a consciousness-raising tool for promoting social change among the writers' respective communities" (Acosta-Belén, "Beyond" 980). The denouncement of patriarchy and colonialism in the literature of women authors from the island and the mainland constitutes a strategy of resistance with a twofold effect: it is a vehicle for personal catharsis that can facilitate the creation of bonds between women; and it serves to create awareness about the multiple levels of oppression to which Puerto Rican women are exposed both as women and as colonial subjects.

The potentially cathartic and/or consciousness-raising effects of the literary texts that I analyze in this chapter, although difficult to measure quantitatively, are a form of social action that constitute a solid *contact zone* between Puerto Rican literature from both sides. The denouncement of violence, the challenge to the virgin/whore complex (also referred to as the *Ave/Eva* dichotomy), and the demythification of the home as a safe space are all present to varying degrees in this corpus.[9] Similarly, it is common to find challenges to *marianismo* and the prototype of the submissive woman that have traditionally characterized the portrayal of female characters in the literature of male Puerto Rican authors and also in other official narratives, such as those developed by policy makers in the continental United States.[10] And while some may argue that the portrayal of strong female characters is not the sole hallmark of women's narratives—after all there are very dominant females in the works of, for example, René Marqués, Pedro Juan Soto, and Luis Rafael Sánchez—the issue of female agency acquires central significance in the prose of women authors.

Alexander and Mohanty characterize agency as a situation in which "women do not imagine themselves as *victims* or *dependents* of governing structures but as agents of their own lives" (xxviii). They define agency as "the conscious and ongoing reproduction of the terms of one's existence while taking responsibility for this process" (xxviii). So agency, I want to argue, inflects Puerto Rican women's narratives in a way that is not consistently present in the narratives of their male counterparts. As my analysis of Olga Nolla's *La segunda hija*, Mohr's "Aunt Rosana's Rocker," and Alba Ambert's *A Perfect Silence* will demonstrate, female characters' transformation from victims to agents constitutes a strategy of resistance inscribed within the decolonization project.

However, it would be too simplistic to focus exclusively on the convergences that exist between both corpuses regarding the denunciation of patriarchy given the fact that these take place in distinct and divergent literary contexts. The differences that characterize the literature of each side attest to the "pluralistic nature of feminism, the differences among women, and the many forms feminism assumes within specific communities, social sectors, nations, races, and regions" (Bose and Acosta-Belén 1995). In other words, the formal and thematic differences that can be observed in the feminist writings of women on the island and on the mainland reflect a heterogeneity of experiences and remind us of the pitfalls that any homogenizing discourse—even feminism—can have by silencing and excluding Other voices.

On the island, the narratives of Ferré, Vega, Nolla, García Ramis, and Lugo Filippi can generally be characterized by the predominance of fiction as the preferred genre, the use of parody, an irreverent tone, explicit or suggestive sexual content, the placing of female characters outside the home in public spaces (streets, motels), and a focus on the denouncement of symbolic violence (as opposed to physical violence). In contrast, life-writing predominates among their counterparts on the mainland. Life writings often display a more serious tone, a more conservative (less explicit) posture toward female sexuality, an emphasis on storytelling, and a focus on "real"/physical violence as well as on symbolic violence. Although not all of these characteristics are present in all of their works, and in fact vary significantly within each group, these observations aim to highlight some noteworthy discontinuities that merit a deeper examination.

I consider some of these discontinuities reflective of the specific conditions that affect Puerto Rican women's lives in two distinct settings, where class, racial, and other variables are also played out differently. Taking into consideration not only the social status that on average describes each group (these particular writers from the island belong to the middle/upper class, whereas those from the mainland grew up in working-class families) is the first step we must take to better understand the conditions that have shaped the lives of these writers. The generic, stylistic, and thematic differences that their literatures display—despite the strong link that the criticism of patriarchy provides—support the notion of a plurality of feminisms by underscoring the need to take into account the concerns of each group. In the same way, given the heterogeneity of experiences and factors that shape individual experiences, one must refrain from reading these authors as representative of all Puerto Rican women in or outside the island.

Class positionality has proven to be a crucial determinant in shaping the literature of Puerto Rican women from both sides. The more privileged upbringing of figures such as Ferré and Nolla, who were born into the island elite, not only afforded them access to competitive educational opportunities, but ultimately shaped their feminist concerns more in alignment with those of so-called First World feminists. Their preference for fiction, their ongoing dialogue with canonical works, the irreverent tone and use of humor, and the focus on symbolic violence are all features of their works that show how the intersection of their class, race, gender, and sexual identities inform their literature. As women in a colonial society, they are challenging patriarchy and colonialism, but the challenges and issues they confront living on the island are not always the same as those faced by their counterparts on the mainland.

For diasporic writers in the United States, the intersection of class, race, gender, and sexuality is inflected by the context of the migratory/minority experience, which complicates some of the challenges they share with women on the island by the mere fact that they are subjected to both the patriarchal violence prevalent in their native culture and the oppression exerted on them as minorities within U.S. dominant society. While it is true that Puerto Ricans in the United States come from a wide range of social and economic backgrounds, a majority of the male and female writers who have actively published in the diaspora have working-class backgrounds. In fact, the lower/working-class positionality of most of these authors was central in defining the aesthetics and thematic concerns of what came to be known as Nuyorican literature in the 1960s and 1970s. So, in contrast to their counterparts on the island, who generally come from more privileged backgrounds, the experiences of female authors in the diaspora and the concerns their works raise tend to echo those of Third World feminism. As such, they display a preoccupation with issues of survival, "real"/physical violence, and education as a tool to overcome poverty, disenfranchisement, and patriarchal oppression. A desire to "teach each other" how to survive by example seems to inform their tendency to cultivate life-writings and storytelling as instruments in passing down knowledge from generation to generation. Although awareness of oppression is also central in the works of women authors on the island, in the diaspora, this awareness is inextricably linked to survival in the context of the migratory/minority experience.

Decolonizing Narratives: Writing from the Island and the Diaspora

Since the publication of Ferré's *Papeles de Pandora* and García Ramis's *La familia de todos nosotros* in 1976, the narrative of Puerto Rican female authors has systematically denounced and challenged the traditional representation of women in Puerto Rican canonical literature.[11] As Gelpí has pointed out, the production of authors such as Vega and Ferré marks a rupture with the canon, in particular with regard to the limiting and unidimensional portrayals of women characters. Much has been written about the negative and stereotypical depictions of women that circulate in the texts of canonical figures like René Marqués, Pedro Juan Soto, and José Luis González, to name just a few. As studies conducted by feminist critics have shown, female literary characters are often seen as submissive or castrating, materialist, and destroyers of traditional values (Acosta-Belén, "Ideology" 133).

The activation of the virgin/whore complex rooted in *marianismo* in male canonical writings severely constricted the representation of female subjectivity. This is especially evident in the works of the writers of the *generación del cincuenta* (Generation of 1950), who often reacted against the more active economic and social role that women began to play as a result of the changes brought about by modernization. The battle that was quickly played out in the terrain of women's bodies/lives mirrored the apparently contradictory impulse toward modernity on the one hand and the traditional values associated with the agrarian past on the other. This reflects what McClintock regards as the gendered nature of nationalisms. According to her, "Women are represented as the atavistic and authentic body of national tradition (inert, backward-looking and natural), embodying nationalism's conservative principle of continuity. Men, by contrast, represent the progressive agent of national modernity (forward-thrusting, potent and historic), embodying nationalism's progressive, or revolutionary principle of discontinuity" (359). In Puerto Rico's case, this translated into the solidification of gendered social norms that reflected this male/female division. This, coupled with the fact that the lens of colonialism posited modernity as synonymous with Americanization and tradition with *puertorriqueñidad*, rendered women's role as "symbolic bearers of the nation" perhaps even more crucial than ever before.

These dynamics were reflected in the cultural—both literary and visual—production of the time. This is the case with DIVEDCO's products, which on the one hand encouraged women to participate in the modernizing project but on the other stressed women's role in the home, especially the kitchen. Many of DIVEDCO's intellectuals, who were later recognized as the *generación del cincuenta*, conceived of the transformations brought about by *el muñocismo* as a threat to Puerto Rican "traditional" values; against the new "Anglo" matriarchal system stood Puerto Rican *machismo*, hailed by some as the ultimate national value. This is the reason Marqués praises Puerto Rican male writers; according to him, "Apparently, the writers are the only ones in Puerto Rican society who have aggressively rebelled against the disappearance of the last cultural bulwark from which one could still combat, in part, the collective docility: *machismo*, the creole version of the fusion and adaptation of two secular concepts, Spanish *honor* and the Roman paterfamilias" (48).[12] Informed by this conception of national culture, the depiction of women characters in canonical works either subscribed to the ideal of the *submissive* woman embedded in the myth of *la gran familia*—which posited her as an emblem of the nation—or was portrayed as breaking that ideal, thus becoming a traitor to the nation (i.e., Americanized).

The narratives of female authors that emerged after the 1970s offer evidence that "women writers are often especially aware of their task as producers of images that both participate in the dominant representations of their culture and simultaneously undermine and subvert those images by offering a re-vision of familiar scripts" (Lionnet 205). Faced with a wide range of either idyllic or negative depictions of women in the insular canon, women sought to provide alternate characterizations as a counterpoint to those produced by male authors. The creation of assertive and independent female characters who embraced their sexuality provided a more nuanced perspective of femininity that challenged the virgin/whore complex.

The dissonance between these more complex female characters and the traditional model of the submissive woman has magnified the irreconcilability of feminism and nationalism, presenting a true quandary for feminist authors on the island.[13] As Vega puts it in her essay "De bípeda desplumada a Escritora Puertorriqueña," "A Puerto Rican woman writer, what a huge mix-up. Slight contradictions emerge between these two evangelic missions."[14] In her typical sarcastic tone, Vega exposes the oxymoron of being a Puerto Rican woman author: she is expected to denounce *machismo* as a feminist writer but also expected to defend nationalist values (cemented on a patriarchal tradition). In denouncing the double subordination of Puerto Rican women, authors like Vega face the predicament of being attacked on two fronts.

Perhaps no other topic has received more critical attention than the portrayal of female sexuality in post-1970s women's narratives, a fact that highlights the centrality of this taboo subject in a highly masculine-dominated society. A plethora of scholarship on this subject has been produced in recent decades, most of it focusing on the works of Ferré and Vega, and those of García Ramis, Lugo Filippi, and Nolla to a lesser degree. Many of these studies tend to zero in on overt female sexuality as a metaphor for women's liberation, directly challenging the notion of female sexuality as problematic, sinful, and something that ought to be controlled (Craske 203). For example, referring to some of the stories from the collection *Vírgenes y mártires* by Vega and Lugo Filippi, the critic Margarite Fernández Olmos has pointed out the transformation of female characters in the past few decades: "There is a growth in these characters which is manifested in two ways: their economic power (limited as it is by their positions in the 'pink collar' professions) and their sexual liberation, both of which are surprising and disturbing to the male characters" ("Survival" 80).[15] In addition to exploring this topic, these studies have elucidated the role of race, gender, music, popular culture, and working-class positionality as strategies that challenge the canon. Some of these authors have broken some of its gender barriers by adopting a register that has been typically associated with lower-class males. Vega's and Ferré's works constitute the clearest examples of this trend. Their appropriation of the lower-class male register, including slang and sexual innuendo, is a mechanism that conveys a more forceful criticism of *machismo* and its multiple manifestations of violence, including the verbal abuse to which women are subjected. Given the scope of critical analyses devoted to Ferré and Vega, I have opted to focus on Olga Nolla's first novel, *La segunda hija* (1992), a text that in my view constitutes a foundational work in Puerto Rican women's literature but has not received the critical attention that it deserves.

Marianismo Unbounded: Defying Gender Paradigms in Olga Nolla's *La segunda hija*

In 1992 the Puerto Rican literary establishment was shaken up again, this time by Olga Nolla, who had gained recognition as a poet, editor of literary journals (*Zona de carga y descarga* and *Cupey*), and short fiction writer (*Porque nos queremos tanto*, 1989). The publication of her first novel, *La segunda hija*, would prove to have broad repercussions on the island's literary scene, as it ventured further than any of her predecessors's works in representing female sexuality. The novel's publication thus marked a groundbreaking moment in Puerto Rico's literary history. Its release caused such an uproar that it was censured "swiftly and viciously within a year of its publication" by the island's former secretary of education due to its "pornographic" content (Hintz 408).[16] Ironically, the banning of the book translated into more sales, although it did not result in a comparable degree of attention from academic circles, a fact that has left this innovative narrative practically unexamined.

While asserting that the novel is unconventional is an understatement—after all, it was banned on the island—the book seems to break various aspects of the mold of Puerto Rican women's literature, sometimes sharing some of the characteristics associated with diaspora female authors. Although *La segunda hija* clearly partakes in the development of female sexuality and explores symbolic violence, it departs from the narrative mold by eschewing parody and an irreverent tone. It shares, however, the paradigms of the bildungsroman and the coming-of-age novel that are also present in García Ramis's *Felices Días, Tío Sergio*, and which are a defining trait of female diaspora production. Unlike contemporaneous island narratives, and even those spanning the following two decades, Nolla's novel also distinguishes itself in its treatment of the migration experience, albeit in the context of an upper-class family that settles in Worcester, Massachusetts. These aspects of the novel, combined with the decidedly feminist impulse of the Puerto Rican women's narrative corpus, offer an opportunity to examine certain issues from a unique perspective. Like all works analyzed in the present study, *La segunda hija* challenges the foundational myth of *la gran familia* on various fronts; most important, the novel calls into question the paradigms of unity and patriarchal authority that are at the core of this myth. Given the focus of the present chapter, I will focus on the latter while paying attention to how the defiance of patriarchy in fact undermines the ideals of family harmony and cohesion.

La segunda hija is a text that engages in a forceful condemnation of Puerto Rican patriarchal society, particularly with regard to the dispensation of symbolic violence, palpable in the highly defined gender norms and expectations that affirm male dominance and its corollary, female submission. The restrictive conception of womanhood along the *Ave/Eva* axis that is central to the ideology of *marianismo* is scrutinized in the novel through the portrayal of female characters whose experiences stretch the boundaries of these polarities. The novel also seems to propose female transformation from victim to agent, although in the end it appears to undermine this very idea by privileging the more conventional vision of womanhood embodied by the protagonist.

Breaking the Mold: Three Generations of Women Defying Conventions

Although from the beginning the title *La segunda hija* points to the centrality of this particular character in the novel, the narrative's additional focus on the mother's and grandmother's histories provides some crucial points of continuity and discontinuity among three generations of women in the family. In one way or another, all these women are depicted as breaking the mold of Puerto Rican womanhood, illustrating how they rebel against the class, race, and gender standards that are imposed on them by their families and the wider society. Clara Ríos, the protagonist's grandmother, is the first one to transgress social expectations when as a young aristocratic woman she elopes with one of her father's peons. According to the homodiegetic narrator, "Old man Ríos never forgave her. He pulled all the tricks in the world in order to leave her without a cent. He died cursing his name and that of his wife for having given him such a daughter."[17] Her father's lack of forgiveness and contempt for his daughter (and later for his wife) reveal the rigid class and racial boundaries that were in place in that society and, more important, the threat that female sexuality and reproduction pose to the patriarchal hierarchical structure.

Clara's defiance of norms and customs leads others to see her as "loca" (crazy), or better yet, as "apasionada, voluntariosa" (passionate, determined), which according to the narrator is sometimes the same (31). The equation of crazy with passionate and strong-willed speaks volumes about the judgment that society passes on women who stray from predetermined patterns of behavior, and how the system in place works to marginalize them. Having rebelled against her father's authority, Clara becomes a victim of both symbolic and what we could call *economic* violence. Not only is her reputation tarnished and her links to her family severed, but she and her children are forced into a state of destitution when her father disinherits her.

Esmeralda, Clara's second daughter—note the parallel with the nameless protagonist—is the only one in the family who has a chance to escape the family's extreme poverty when upper-class Esteban Guarch marries her at sixteen. Years later, after having children and relocating to Worcester, Massachusetts, Esmeralda also transgresses the societal conventions when she abandons her family to live with another man. Esmeralda's infraction takes a toll on her relationship with everyone around her, but it decidedly severs the bond between her and her mother. While the protagonist-narrator often struggles with her feelings of love and hatred for her mother, Clara expresses only contempt, which leads the children to wonder, "¿por qué abuela no te quiere ya?" (why does Grandmother not love you anymore?) (25). The second daughter eventually comes to the conclusion that "men only want obedient women: that's why they insist so much, when we're little, that we be obedient. When women do as they please, men stop loving them; they punish them, that's it. Abuela thought like a man, that's what I think."[18] Women who dare to transgress their roles as mothers and wives are chastised—as Esmeralda's ostracism illustrates—not only by men but also by women who uphold the values of patriarchy, such as Abuela Clara.

Even years before Esmeralda makes the decision to leave her family, her behavior deviated from what was expected of her, compounding the tension between her and her mother, Clara. For instance, after the birth of Esmeralda's first daughter, Azucena, Clara moved in with her and Esteban and took over the responsibility of caring for the baby. Seeing Clara as their primary caretaker, the children refer to their grandmother as "mamá" and their own mother by her first name (35). As Esmeralda became relegated to a secondary place, the children developed deep bonds with Clara and their father, Esteban, a nurturing paternal figure who subverts the prototypical image of the authoritarian father figure. Even when physically present, Esmeralda displays attitudes that defy the stereotype of women's "natural" inclination toward motherhood. Not only does she always remain emotionally distant from her children, but she tends to disappear for stretches at a time, leaving her children constantly wondering where she is. Eventually, this behavior makes them immune to her absence, as illustrated by their reaction the day she abandoned the family: "When my mother left, we did not miss her during the first few days."[19]

As time goes by, however, the second daughter seems to be deeply affected by the emotional and physical absence of her mother Esmeralda. The overarching theme of the "search for the mother" emerges as the protagonist tries to come to terms with her failed mother-daughter relationship and seeks to overcome the hatred she has developed toward her (also shared by Clara and her older sister, Azucena). Toward the end of the novel, the narrator-protagonist's own experience taking care of her niece and nephew for the summer not only leads her to discover the joy of taking care of children but also gives her a new perspective on Esmeralda's attitudes and decisions:

> The residents of a house organize life around the children: one has to dress and bathe them, feed them, keep them amused, and love them. They are like gods: equally capricious, equally demanding. I knew these things because I always lived in a house full of children and relatives. But I hadn't realized it, because I was a god. Now, as a grown-up, my role is that of server. Many people don't like it to be this way, and that's why they don't like children. I understand that that is life, that that is how it should be: like Abuela, just like that. Esmeralda has never understood. Maybe that's why she's different, and maybe that's why I hate her.[20]

Esmeralda's failure as a mother, in the eyes of the second daughter, stems from her incapacity to mold to the demands of motherhood, in particular the selflessness and understanding that parenting requires. In the end, Esmeralda and the second daughter's relationship heals to a certain point, a dynamic also observed between Clara and Esmeralda. In both cases, the rapprochement that occurs between the protagonist and Esmeralda, and Clara and Esmeralda, stems from the latter's loss of her youngest daughter, who dies at an early age. This tragedy leads the second daughter and Clara to reconsider the respective roles they have played in Esmeralda's ostracism. The focus on Esmeralda's character, positioned at the center of the grandmother-mother-daughter triad (in a text where mother-daughter relationships take center stage), allows an additional reading of the title of the novel, given that it could also refer to Esmeralda, Clara's second daughter, and the epicenter of a great deal of conflict throughout the text.

To Be or Not to Be: *Ave/Eva* Duality

One of the novel's innovative takes on the issue of female subjectivity is the fact that the second daughter, who remains nameless throughout the novel, appears to simultaneously embody the *Ave/Eva* dichotomy.

Early on she is described as "distinta," "no dominante" (different, not domineering), and as someone who "se interesaba por los demás" (was interested in others), qualities that reflect the submission and selflessness typically associated with *marianismo* (2–4). She also displays traditional values regarding her sexuality, evident in scenes that depict her out on dates during her high school (20) and college years (39). In these cases, despite her dates' desperate attempts to engage in sexual acts with her, she upholds the value of chastity, which she breaks only when she falls in love with Juan Carlos. Toward the end of the novel, once her relationship with Juan Carlos has ended, she is depicted as striving for the traditional role of wife and mother that defines women in patriarchal societies. Her fantasies of transforming into the ideal wife and mother thus bring her back into alignment with the prescribed norms of *marianismo* after having distanced herself from this model during her affair with Juan Carlos.

While the characterization of the second daughter for the most part corresponds to the *Ave* model, she also comes to embody the *Eva* side of this polarity as a result of her romantic relationship with Juan Carlos. The graphic descriptions of their erotic encounters—which tend to emphasize female sexual pleasure and desire—call into question what is by and large her *Ave*-like depiction throughout the novel. I would like to argue that the intensity of her *Eva*-like portrayal stems from the fact that their relationship disrupts three central taboos: the suppression of female sexual pleasure and the interdictions associated with love affairs as well as with workplace romances. The reader first learns that the protagonist and Juan Carlos work in the same office, which automatically raises a red flag given the association of this type of liaison with the stereotype of the woman as temptress (*Eva*/whore). Shortly after, it becomes evident that the second daughter, to her detriment, is Juan Carlos's "other" woman and that their relationship amounts to no more than an affair—again tapping into the conventional image of the temptress as homewrecker.

Last, the text's vivid descriptions of female sexual desire and pleasure confront head-on the taboo of female sexuality in Puerto Rican and other Latin American patriarchal societies, which construct sexual enjoyment as "the preserve of men" (Craske 203). In fact, as Hintz has pointed out, the request to ban the novel in public schools came from two mothers who "wanted to protect their children as much as possible from the erotic thoughts that they themselves experienced" (414). While it is not my place to pass judgment on these women's mothering values and practices, their posture aligns with that of the Puerto Rican patriarchal society in its implementation of a double standard. If the same sexually explicit language had been used by a male character, or to describe a male protagonist's thoughts, most likely the novel would not have been labeled obscene (Hintz 414). Therefore, in a culture where the enjoyment of female sexuality is either suppressed (*Ave*) or constructed as a marker of indecency (*Eva*) by the ideology of *marianismo*, Nolla's defiant reappropriation of sexual discourse—traditionally a masculine privilege—is viewed as an affront to the very core of patriarchal Puerto Rican society. Taken together, the realistic and explicit portrayal of female pleasure and the relationship's rupture of the taboo surrounding the workplace affair combine to highlight the protagonist's *Eva*-like nature.

Nevertheless, a closer look at the second daughter's relationship with Juan Carlos undermines her apparent deviation from the model of *marianismo*. While it does not negate the discourse of female sexual pleasure associated with this character, it calls into question her motives for engaging in a relationship that by traditional standards is viewed as prohibited. The *Eva*-like behavior ascribed to the protagonist as a result of her affair with Juan Carlos is constantly subverted by the display of dispositions commonly linked to *marianismo*, such as innocence, subordination, and suffering. According to the narrator, Juan Carlos was "an expert player of workplace erotic games, a champion. She didn't know because she had recently arrived from Worcester and her early childhood had transpired in Jayuya. She fell head over heels in love with him."[21] Here, her naïveté regarding Juan Carlos's reputation is framed as a result of her recent arrival to the office, which marks her as an outsider. In addition, the mention of her childhood in the rural town of Jayuya seeks to magnify her innocence by tapping into the commonplace antithesis between the ideal of purity embodied by *el campo* and the corruption associated with *la ciudad*.

Her naïveté therefore transforms her into Juan Carlos's victim. In contrast to the image of the temptress who has the upper hand in a relationship, the second daughter is the one being seduced by the man and subordinates her needs and feelings to his. She suffers a great deal every time Juan Carlos makes excuses to not be seen with her in public—after all, he has an "official" girlfriend with whom he goes out—or when he refuses to meet her family. When she returns to Puerto Rico after attending her half sister's funeral in Worcester, he virtually ignores her and denies her any sort of emotional support, only to approach her and try to seduce her a few days later. The final betrayal occurs when Juan Carlos marries an old girlfriend when the second daughter is away in Worcester for the summer, putting an end to an "amor agujereado por la incertidumbre" (a love pierced by uncertainty) (85).

After the protagonist learns that Juan Carlos betrayed her, she falls into a state of depression that lasts weeks. The intensity of her pain not only reflects the strength of her feelings for Juan Carlos but also brings her closer to the model of the suffering woman embedded in *marianismo*. During this "mourning" period she relies on her friends and family to console and nurture her. She also leaves San Juan after resigning from her job and takes refuge in the mountains of Jayuya, where she had spent her early childhood years. The fact that it is her cathartic experience in the interior of the island that allows her to overcome her sorrow acquires a profound significance: it reiterates the correlation between the rural/urban and innocence/corruption dichotomies that are at the root of Puerto Rican conceptions of womanhood. In this sense, Nolla's portrayal of the second daughter echoes that of certain female characters in canonical works, where authors such as Marqués and Soto condemned the "corruptive" effects of modernization (i.e., Americanization) on traditional gender roles. In *La segunda hija*, the main character was temporarily "corrupted" by her love affair with Juan Carlos (i.e., she lost her virginity and openly enjoyed her sexuality) but was "cleansed" from her transgression by her return to the purity of *el campo*.

Her "purification" is further magnified by her visit to her sister's family home in Europe, where she spends a great deal of time with her niece and nephew. Her bond with them grows to such an extent that on her return to Puerto Rico she finds herself missing them above anything else. This experience, in addition to the time she spent with them the previous summer, leads her to desire wifehood and motherhood. As the homodiegetic narrator puts it: "She lived for years that single woman's life that so terrifies many women. Not the life of the divorced woman who raises two or three children, and works in an office, and has to go to court because the alimony does not arrive; the ex-husband remarried and does not want to pay it. It is instead the thirty-year-old single woman who feels pressure from her family to get married and if she doesn't she considers her life a failure" (89).[22] The narrator's words capture what is considered by many to be the essence of Puerto Rican womanhood: marriage and motherhood. Having reached her thirties without fulfilling these roles not only exposes the protagonist to disapproval, but more important, it chips away at her self-esteem by leading her to believe that her life is a failure. The protagonist's sense of incompleteness, which leads to her fairy tale–like fantasies, illustrates the "durable effects" and the internalization of the system of masculine domination by those who are its victims. The second daughter's belief in the impossibility of achieving self-realization outside traditional parameters of womanhood thus highlights what Bourdieu calls the "spontaneous and extorted" nature of patriarchy: she desires the typical life of a *gran señora* but it is unclear whether this is her genuine aspiration or the result of her socialization.

La segunda hija concludes with the narrator painting a picture of the protagonist's life. The use of the future tense is significant given the ambiguity it creates; it can be read as a testimony of her future, or it can be interpreted as plausibility. What is interesting, however, is how the end of the novel cements her characterization as the prototypical ideal woman: "She will marry a rich man ten years her senior; she will apply the knowledge she gained at the university and her professional experience to the administration of the household; she will give birth to a son. . . . She will feel fulfilled and will think again that life has meaning, and will be a positive factor in her husband's professional career."[23] According to the narrator, her husband will love her dearly because "she will become the woman he always dreamed of. She will be identical to his ideal."[24] With this, the second daughter transforms into the epitome of womanhood that the patriarchal system—here embodied by her husband—needs in order to perpetuate itself.

Suzanne Hintz has expressed her surprise regarding Nolla's construction of this character: "The protagonist's sought-after identity is the antithesis of the feminist search; it is an ironic conclusion to a novel written by an author who has always created literary works in which the woman/adult achieves some dominion over her own life and destiny (Ferré)" (411). She resolves this impasse by proposing a reading of the novel as "the other side of the feminine coin, the alternate perspective of women who do prefer to be mothers and homemakers" (411). While Hintz's reading is valuable, I would like to propose a different explanation. More than representing "the other side of the feminine coin," where the protagonist spontaneously subscribes to the mold of ideal womanhood, I see the narrator's final utterance as indicative of how the power of the system of masculine domination is both "spontaneous and extorted."

When the narrative voice concludes by saying, "Así, me imagino, tuvo que ser" (Like that, I imagine, it must have been), the employment of the verb *tener* problematizes the preceding narration of the protagonist's imagined future (94). The use of "tener" after "me imagino" not only serves to denote uncertainty, but it also insinuates the impossibility of diverging from the "only viable" script of Puerto Rican womanhood that has been ingrained in that culture through the centrality of *maria-nismo* and the ideal of *la gran familia puertorriqueña*. While the second daughter's compliance with this paradigm seems to undermine the feminist makeup of the novel, its "fairy tale" ending can also help strengthen its feminist objectives by arousing discomfort in the feminist reader. The ambiguity surrounding the ending allows the reader to interpret the novel as either condoning or denouncing the rigid ideals of womanhood that continue to exist in Puerto Rican culture.

Double Decolonization: Writings from the Diaspora

Although the explosion of U.S. Puerto Rican women's narratives did not take place until the 1980s, the story behind the publication of the first book-length narrative by a woman in the diaspora—Nicholasa Mohr's *Nilda* (1973)—encapsulates some of the challenges faced by female writers who had to break away from the shadow of their male counterparts. As Mohr recalls in an interview, the first time she submitted original work to be reviewed it became clear that the editor expected something along the lines of Piri Thomas's *Down These Mean Streets*: he said that she "should write something more exciting, about prostitutes, gang wars, and the seedier side of life" (Hernández, *Puerto Rican* 91). For female authors such as Mohr, breaking away from the narrative mold already sculpted by Puerto Rican male authors in the United States not only meant justifying and defending their choice to emphasize the home (as opposed to the streets) but also entailed altering the constrictive images of women that prevailed in male-authored narratives. In this sense, the literature of women authors on the U.S. mainland also represents a rupture vis-à-vis the male-centered diaspora canon.

Similar to the predicament of female authors on the island, those on the mainland faced the need to break down and challenge the virgin/whore complex rooted in *marianismo*. The high incidence of female characters who are either idealized as emblematic of traditional conceptions of womanhood or demonized for embodying female sexuality led many women authors to challenge this Manichaean vision of women by presenting complex characters and nuanced notions of femininity. The representation of a wide range of female subjectivities that defied the limits of traditional ones also raised an issue that was already present in insular literature: the apparent irreconcilability of feminist and nationalist agendas, in this case the defense of Puerto Rican culture in the United States.[25] According to Acosta-Belén, what distinguishes the literature of Puerto Rican women authors in the United States, and other women authors, is that "gender will be an essential factor in the search for expression and articulation of their own identity. This process also entails a confrontation with the caprices or vagaries of a patriarchal ideology within the culture of their own group, as well as in the culture of the broader society. As a result, their responses to and strategies against oppression are going to differ from those formulated by men" ("Beyond" 990).

During the civil rights movements, Latina feminists, including U.S. Puerto Ricans, found it difficult to advance their views on women's liberation as part of the broader agenda of the patriarchal Latino community, which sought more power and rights in dominant society. Caught between the choice to either remain "loyal" to their masculine-dominated culture or defend their rights as women, many of these authors had to face the consequence of being labeled "traitors" to their culture. As Ellen McCracken puts it, they have become part of the sub-subcultural movement of Latina fiction, which "contests both the 'dominant' culture of the U.S. mainstream as well as the 'parent' culture—the patriarchal blindspots of the Latino cultural 'renaissance' of the late 1960s and beyond" (152).

Interestingly, the choice by U.S. Puerto Rican women authors to privilege feminist concerns has not translated into the explicit treatment of eroticism and female sexuality, save a few exceptions, a trait that is more common in the works of authors on the island. Although sexuality is almost always present in diaspora literature, in general such experiences tend to be framed in the context of the adolescent girl's first erotic and/or sexual feelings (e.g., Negi's first kiss in *When I Was Puerto Rican* or the narrator's first love in *Silent Dancing*). This more innocent representation thus offers a sharp contrast to the more overt and defiant depiction of female sexuality present in island literature, where more often than not adult women challenge the conventions of *marianismo*, such as in Ferré's "Cuando las mujeres quieren a los hombres," Suzy Bermiúdez in Vega's "Pollito Chicken," and the main character in Nolla's *La segunda hija*, to name just a few.

Inextricably linked to female sexuality is the concept of motherhood. Generally, in the works of women authors in the diaspora, mother-daughter relationships, as well as family dynamics, have taken center stage. In most instances the works explore how these are shaped by migration and/or transculturation, often unveiling the conflict that emerges between the traditional values of the culture of origin (usually embodied by the mother) and the more unconventional ones associated with the host society (often embodied by the daughter). As Ortega and Saporta Sternbach have observed regarding Latina literature, "a cultural conflict is epitomized in relationship to sexuality, especially for second-generation Latinas who came to maturity during the so-called sexual revolution. The act of choosing and practicing her sexuality, and then writing about it, is often perceived as either an assimilation of the Anglo-gringo way of life or a loss of Latina values and culture" (12). This duality, and the need to reconcile the disparity of these two culturally different worlds, defines most of the works of U.S. Puerto Rican women authors, as *Silent Dancing, When I Was Puerto Rican,* and *Rituals of Survival* illustrate.

The experience of sexual abuse and violence against women and children is another context in which female sexuality is explored, and which marks another discontinuity with the narrative produced by women on the island. Although sexual violence is not evenly present in diaspora works, it figures with more frequency in U.S. Puerto Rican literature than it does on the island. It is important to attend to these discrepancies without falling into the trap of generalizing in either direction, for instance, by concluding that women on the island are not subjected to violence, or that all women in the diaspora are victims. Again, what accounts for the prevalence of violence in any society is determined by multiple factors. However, studies have shown the correlation between the incidence of domestic violence and the level of disenfranchisement that many minority communities experience in host societies.[26] By depicting the home as the background of domestic violence, these texts participate in the effort to demythify the home as a safe space for women. Both Santiago's *América's Dream* and Mohr's *Rituals of Survival* speak to the violence that permeates women's lives under *machismo* and portray their female characters as trying to break the cycle of violence that dominates their lives. This risk, certainly magnified for Puerto Rican women as victims of double colonization—"as colonial subjects and as women"—is one of the strongest validations of the role that literature can play as an instrument of survival (Matos Rodríguez, "Women's" 17).

Off Her Rocker? Reclaiming Female Agency in Nicholasa Mohr's "Aunt Rosana's Rocker"

One of the works in which the link between literature, social action, and survival is extremely palpable is Nicholasa Mohr's short story collection *Rituals of Survival: A Woman's Portfolio* (1985). As the title

suggests, this compilation of six short narratives focuses on the problematic of survival faced by Puerto Rican women of different generations and social backgrounds. The collection itself works as a portfolio
because it provides a range of scenarios where women are portrayed as
they embark on the process of transformation from victim to agent. The
portfolio-like quality of the text also highlights the role of storytelling
as a didactic instrument used among women in the diaspora (Puerto
Ricans and other U.S. Latinas) to teach and learn from each other's
experiences.

The story "Aunt Rosana's Rocker" stands out—both in the collection and in the context of diaspora literature—as one of the few narratives that openly addresses female sexuality, agency, and desire. As
indicated above, the literature produced outside the island has generally been less explicit than that produced on the island by some of the
authors examined here. This central difference between both corpuses
becomes more striking when one considers that the influence of mainstream American culture has produced a more liberal attitude toward
sexuality among second- and third-generation Puerto Rican women
on the mainland—as opposed to the more conservative attitude associated with the island. Precisely due to the relatively scarce attention that
the issue of female sexuality has received in the prose fiction of U.S.
Puerto Rican women authors, "Aunt Rosana's Rocker" provides us with
a unique optic through which to explore these issues in the context of
diaspora production. The analysis that follows looks at how this story
challenges the *Ave/Eva* complex, and the role that both symbolic and
"real"/physical violence plays in maintaining that duality. In addition, I
will explore how by deploying what Bourdieu calls the "weapons of the
weak," Zoraida is able to shift from victim to agent.

Because patriarchal Puerto Rican society is structured around the
machismo/marianismo dialectic, strict gender roles have played a key
part in securing the equilibrium of this system. The construction of
women's subjectivity based on the *Ave/Eva* dichotomy has thus been
central to holding this system in place, as evinced by the pervasiveness
of female characters who subscribe to either of these classifications in
the works of canonical (male) authors. The reduction of female subjectivity to these polar extremes has severely hindered the representation,
and therefore the understanding, of women as complex human beings.
The story also calls attention to the subordination of female sexuality
in Puerto Rican patriarchal culture, one of the ways in which masculine domination manifests itself.[27] "Aunt Rosana's Rocker" confronts

head-on this distorted and limiting view of women by presenting a character who, like the second daughter in Nolla's novel, embodies the two apparently irreconcilable sides of the *Ave/Eva* complex. Through Zoraida's performance of these two opposite roles, Mohr not only problematizes and satirizes the restrictive nature of the *Ave/Eva* model but also metaphorizes the ambivalence that characterizes the female subject under the masculine gaze.

Zoraida's *Ave/Eva* performance is principally delineated along the day/night temporal axis. During the day, Zoraida's demeanor brings her closer to the *Ave* model and in fact fashions her as the epitome of the Puerto Rican submissive woman; she is shy, meek, frail, sickly, and ladylike. Above all, she is a dedicated mother and homemaker who constantly endures her husband's verbal and physical abuse. In consonance with the *Ave* stereotype, she does not exhibit any interest in sex. Her husband Casto's complaints that she "always urged him to hurry" and "get it over with" serve to accentuate the stereotype of women as asexual beings advanced through *marianismo* (13).

At night, however, Zoraida transforms into the polar opposite of her daytime identity, as the beginning of the story illustrates. The text opens in medias res with Casto nervously pacing back and forth in the kitchen late at night after he has been awakened by the loud, seductive sounds coming from the bedroom, where his wife sleeps alone.[28] The reader soon learns that Zoraida has been experiencing frequent inexplicable "spells" during her sleep that make her behave as if she was having intercourse. Although at first Casto believes these episodes are the result of a fever, his concern eventually turns into anger and jealousy, as the following passage illustrates: "Why, her actions were lewd and vulgar, as if they were sexual, as it seemed, then this was not the kind of sex a decent husband and wife engage in. What was even harder for him to bear was her enjoyment. Yes, this was difficult, watching her total enjoyment of this whole disgusting business! And, to make matters more complicated, the next day, Zoraida seemed to remember nothing. In fact, during the day, she was normal again" (11). Zoraida's sexual gestures during her spells exceed the boundaries of what constitutes acceptable behavior in a male-dominated culture. In Casto's opinion, his wife becomes an animal: "she's just like an animal, no better than an alley cat in heat" (13). His tone of condemnation corroborates the fact that, as Edna Acosta-Belén reminds us, "in Puerto Rican culture (and in Latin American culture in general) there is a tendency to classify or judge women according to their sexual behavior" ("Puerto Rican" 16).

Interestingly, Casto's outrage at his wife's behavior takes on an air of ambiguity as he simultaneously becomes indignant when he realizes, "Never in all their years of marriage had she ever uttered such sounds . . . or shown any passion or much interest in doing it" (13). His ambivalence toward his wife's overt sexual behavior reflects the double standards inherent to the system of masculine domination, particularly regarding women's sexuality, which seeks to suppress it in so-called decent women while it tends to exalt it in the "easy" women who are casual sexual partners. Zoraida's implied autoeroticism is threatening to Casto for two reasons: her capacity to achieve sexual pleasure without him represents a challenge to his masculinity; and it attests to the possibility of attaining female sexual agency within a system of patriarchal domination.[29] The submissiveness that marks her as a victim during the day is put into question by the sexual behavior that she exhibits at night.

The threat that Zoraida's overt sexual behavior poses to Casto parodies the universal menace that female sexuality constitutes for any patriarchal order, because it is a reminder of the power that women's erotic autonomy has to "undo the nation," as Alexander reminds us (*Pedagogies* 64). Universal patriarchy has put into place myriad mechanisms to control this potential threat. From the implementation of psychological methods, such as directing women to internalize their subordination, to physical ones, such as the institution of marriage, domestic violence, and even witch-hunts, men have consistently tried to suppress women's sexuality because the legitimacy of the patriarchal system is contingent on men's control of women.[30]

Under such a system, uncontrolled and insatiable female sexuality becomes an unfathomable excess that can only be ascribed to metaphysical forces (i.e., madness, *espiritismo*), as exemplified by Casto's belief in his wife's possession by a spirit. Although madness itself has emerged as a central metaphor of women's subversion and resistance in the field of feminist studies—for instance in Sandra Gilbert and Susan Gubar's *The Madwoman in the Attic* (1979)—it fails to explain the complexity of the situation presented in Mohr's text. I concur with Marta Caminero-Santangelo's critique of madness as a failed metaphor of female empowerment. She states, "As an illusion of power that masks powerlessness, madness is thus the final removal of the madwoman from any field of agency" (12). Despite the flaws in the use of madness as a metaphor of resistance, Mohr's texts illustrates how it can succeed by instilling fear in others (as exemplified by Casto), thus guaranteeing a certain degree of autonomy. In addition, its success in this case relies on the fact that

Zoraida's episodes are constructed as performances; she is always in control, as I examine below. Another interesting aspect of Mohr's story is the conflation of madness and the supernatural (*espiritismo*), illustrative of what Bourdieu has referred to as the "weapons of the weak" (32). Magic, cunning, lies, and passivity are all forms of soft violence that "women use against the physical or symbolic violence of men" (Bourdieu 32).[31] Inscribing Zoraida's autoeroticism as a product of possession by a spirit (thus wild and uncontrollable) magnifies Casto's terror, to the point that he is forced to live in chastity, thus living up to a name that evidently pokes fun at the glorification of male sexuality in patriarchal cultures.

The story's depiction of this role reversal, where the woman is sexually active (independently) and the man is forced to be chaste out of fear, also works to uncover the double standards present in systems of masculine domination, where male sexuality is valued above female sexuality. This attitude is especially evident at those times when Casto summons his and her parents to a meeting demanding their support in recuperating his old (i.e., submissive) wife, an act that constitutes a form of symbolic violence given that it is meant to publicly humiliate her. Casto's attitude during such meetings is telling of the superiority of men over women under patriarchy, evident in the fact that he considers his wife's "spells" a violation of his sexual needs and rights: "Trying to control his anger, Casto had confessed that it had been a period of almost two months since he had normal and natural relations with his wife. He reminded them that he, as a man, had his needs, and this would surely make him ill, if it continued" (12). In yet another instance of role reversal, Casto succeeds in enlisting the help of his parents and in-laws by presenting himself as his wife's victim.

After confessing that he is "frightened of Zoraida," Casto agrees with his mother and in-laws to consult Doña Digna, the spiritualist (14). Although the visit appears to have immediate results—it seems to put an end to Zoraida's nightly spells—her pattern of inexplicable behavior continues under a different guise. She becomes even more silent and distant, but perhaps more important, she sits in her rocker—as if she were in a trance—when Casto wants intimacy. Most members of the family see Zoraida's avoidance of intimacy with Casto as a breach of her responsibility as a wife. Her "trances" are seen as manifestations of her madness, as is her silence, which constitutes a site of resistance against oppression. As the story shows, in alienating Zoraida from her husband and family, her madness allows her to rebel against societal demands and expectations. Both her silence and her madness allow Zoraida to redefine the limits of her personal space, limits that Casto respects only out of fear.

Unable to explain Zoraida's behavior toward her husband, her family interprets her attachment to the rocker as another confirmation of her madness. They believe that disposing of the rocker is the only way to bring Zoraida back to her senses and to force her to "act like a wife." Disregarding the attachment that Zoraida has for this heirloom, given to her by her great-aunt Rosana, Casto and his in-laws decide to throw the rocker away: "They were going to take away the rocker. She had always had it, ever since she could remember. When she was a little girl, her parents told her it was a part of their history. Part of Puerto Rico and her great Aunt Rosana who was very beautiful and had countless suitors. . . . Lately it had become the one place where she felt she could be herself, where she could really be free" (29). The removal of the rocker can be read as a metaphor for the symbolic violence that the masculine order wields against women. One way in which women have been disempowered has been through their virtual exclusion from canonical histories. The omission of women from historical narratives creates a void, a sense of disconnection from the past. Women, however, have tried to remedy this through other means such as the creation of myths, the practice of rituals, and storytelling, which create a sense of historical continuity and identity.

In the story, the rocker provides Zoraida with a sense of continuity and with an instrument through which she can fashion her identity, her subjectivity. It is an object that is symbolic of her past, her Puerto Rican roots, her female ancestors, female sexuality, and freedom. When Zoraida loses her rocker, she loses more than meets the eye: she loses her connection with her past, her sense of continuity, and her sense of self. For this reason, the removal of the rocker constitutes an act of violence, for she is forced to let go of a part of herself.

Her mother's complicity with Casto attests to the symbolic power of masculine domination, which, according to Bourdieu, "cannot be exercised without the contribution of those who undergo it and who only undergo it because they *construct* it as such" (40). In other words, her mother's contribution to Zoraida's oppression illustrates the key role that women play in the perpetuation of patriarchy through the practice of *horizontal violence*, that is, women's violence against women. Instead of supporting her daughter, helping her to stand up to her abusive husband, Zoraida's mother allies with Casto in order to coerce her to act "like a wife." By insisting that she needs to be sexually available to him because he supports her and their children, her mother reflects the inherent sexism of masculinist ideology, which tends to devalue women and/or represses their sexuality. Her posture exemplifies how women often perpetuate their subordination through the acceptance and reiteration of norms and values artificially formulated to promote masculine domination.

Zoraida's smirk after her mother's harangue suggests that, contrary to what she has made everyone believe, she is completely aware of her behavior. She tries to humor her mother by acknowledging her advice, but this facial gesture betrays her. What appeared to have been Zoraida's acts of madness or the result of being possessed by a spirit take on a new tenor when regarded as examples of the "weapons of the weak" and thus as products of her agency. In hindsight, the reader must question her behavior—the sexual spells at night and her trances while sitting in the rocker—and come to regard them as performances. Clearly, the intention behind such performances was to create distance between herself and Casto in order to achieve control of her own body. At first, through her spells, she was able to scare her husband away. Later, after seeing the spiritualist, she found yet another way to "escape her duties"—by sitting in her rocker and acting zombie-like when Casto made sexual advances. In the end, once the rocker is taken away, Zoraida simply pretends to be asleep when she wants to reclaim her space.

"Aunt Rosana's Rocker" depicts Zoraida's process of finding her own space, a safe space where she can reclaim control of her body and her sexuality. In the beginning, the bed represents that personal space that she seeks. In fact, she achieves control of her body only in the confines of the bed because Casto is too frightened by her spells to lie next to her. Unable to continue her performance after being cured by the spiritualist, Zoraida seeks refuge in the rocker that once belonged to her great-aunt. Again, it is within the restricted space of the rocker that Zoraida gains temporary control of her body. While sitting in the rocker she becomes silent, absent, and untouchable—sending Casto the message that he is powerless over her.

The limiting of Zoraida's personal space, signaled by the substitution of the rocker for the bed, could be interpreted as a reflection of the lack of personal space that Puerto Rican women enjoy due to constraints imposed by patriarchal culture. As the end of the story implies, once Zoraida does not control the space of the bed, or have access to the rocker, her sphere of control is limited to her own body. In other words, the amount of space available to her diminishes until her only refuge becomes her self.

"Aunt Rosana's Rocker" is a story that traces the process through which a female character comes to assert her sense of self. In this process, common objects such as the bed and the rocker—culturally associated with the realm of the feminine—are resignified as emblems of women's liberation. The bed, a typical symbol of marital union and thus a reminder of women's subordination, acquires a new significance in the story. Zoraida's reappropriation of the bed through her acts of madness resignifies this object by underscoring female sexual agency and undermining the conjugal sexual union when it becomes oppressive. In a similar fashion, the rocker's traditional association with the realm of the home—generally used by women to rock babies to sleep, to knit, to tell family stories—is challenged in the story. The rocker becomes her private space, a space where she sits erect, in control, active—as opposed to laying down, vulnerable, lax, and passive. Instead of signifying women's confinement to the private space of the house, the rocker is transformed into an emblem of freedom and an assertion of female sexuality; it is where Zoraida "enjoys sexual fantasies—her form of resistance to her husband's demands for sex" (McCracken 154). Mohr, according to McCracken, recodes "the rocking chair as the bearer of female familial tradition and the site of a temporary sexual liberation" (154). By resignifying everyday objects such as the bed and the rocker—objects culturally seen as symbols of women's subordination—Mohr's text underscores the many levels on which women can contest masculine domination in their struggle to assert their subjectivity.

As this analysis demonstrates, Mohr defies prevalent views of womanhood that serve to keep women in rigidly defined roles. More specifically, she targets the *Ave/Eva* dichotomy through her radical conflation of these polarities in a single female character that subscribes to the norms of *marianismo* during the day but challenges them at night. Her duality unveils women's sexual subordination within the institution of marriage in order to underscore the varied forms of symbolic and "real" violence that women face under systems of patriarchal domination. By restoring female sexual agency to her main character, Mohr challenges the ideal of the "submissive woman" that is prevalent in Puerto Rican culture. In this sense, the story articulates a new kind of sexual politics, restoring women's sexual agency and constructing female desire and pleasure independently of the male, thus illustrating a woman's erotic autonomy. As Zoraida struggles to assert herself vis-à-vis her domineering husband, she finds herself empowered by her performance as madwoman. Through madness she is able to find liberation, albeit momentary, as she takes control of certain objects and spaces typically associated with the realm of the feminine and refashions them as sites of resistance against masculine domination. Readers can only wonder if, finally faced with the reality that her body is her only refuge, Zoraida's final move will be a disappearing act.

Telling Her Story: Violence and Survival in Alba Ambert's *A Perfect Silence*

Alba Ambert's *A Perfect Silence* brings to the fore the intersection between violence and *marianismo*, the "other" side of *machismo*, in order to demonstrate how *marianismo* has contributed to the perpetuation of violence in patriarchal cultures. The emphasis on motherhood, central to *marianismo*, is based on the assumption that women are "naturally" loving, caring, and protective of children. Yet, as my analysis will prove, women often participate, either actively or passively, in multiple forms of child abuse. I argue that this work challenges traditional constructions of Puerto Rican womanhood cemented on *marianismo* by positing a female character as an abuser, a move that dismantles the stereotype of the maternal figure and shows how women are key agents in the perpetuation of machismo. Here, I draw on contemporary studies on the psychology of trauma in order to show that the novel, as written text, is symbolic of the transformation of traumatic memory into what Susan Brison calls "narrative memory," a process that evokes a shift from victim to agent.

A Perfect Silence, the second novel by the London-based Puerto Rican author Alba Ambert, is considered "the first Puerto Rican novel dealing with child abuse" (Hernández, "On Language" 59). Its focus on violence makes it a dark semiautobiographical narrative that traces the life of Blanca, an orphan who "falls through the cracks of the system" and is repeatedly abused at the hands of her paternal grandmother, Paquita, and other caregivers. The novel moves back and forth between the present, where we observe Blanca institutionalized due to severe mental illness, and the past, which traces Blanca's childhood story to provide a backdrop to her present condition. The alternation between past and present in the text mimics the therapeutic process that Blanca undergoes at the asylum, where conversations with her psychiatrist and other patients trigger memories of her traumatic past, an indispensable step in her healing process, as she admits: "I dig constantly within, to peel my layers of pain. My pain and my past are one" (225). In addition to temporal shifts in the narration, the action moves back and forth between Puerto Rico and the U.S. mainland, the two spaces where Blanca's life transpires. Although the end of the novel suggests that Blanca manages to transform herself from victim to agent, most of the narrative emphasizes how her sense of powerlessness and isolation in the face of violence—physical, sexual, and psychological—eventually leads to self-violence. Yet, while not a particularly uplifting story, Blanca's tale of abuse, healing, and survival can be a source of empowerment for those who have endured violence and the tyranny of silence that often accompanies it.

Contemporary narratives by U.S. Puerto Rican women tend to follow the model of the personal "success story." These texts paradoxically reinforce the myth of the American dream, despite the fact that the majority of Puerto Ricans in the United States struggle to overcome the obstacles associated with internal colonialism. According to Sánchez González, contemporary narratives differ from those of pioneer authors such as Luisa Capetillo, Pura Belpré, and Nicholasa Mohr, given that "these mainstreamed Latina feminist texts narrate personal experiences of the feminine condition to the near total exclusion of a collective predicament that entails growing problems with racism, poverty, reproductive rights, education, and colonial maldevelopment" (140).

Because *A Perfect Silence* is not framed around the formulaic "success story," nor is it unconcerned with the social ills affecting Puerto Rican communities on the island and the mainland, the novel is an exception to the trend proposed by Sánchez González. Although Blanca is relatively successful eventually—she studies at Harvard and becomes a teacher of bilingual education at a Boston high school—it is obvious that the memories of her past traumas continue to affect her in the present. Her release from the hospital at the end of the novel, which typically would be seen as a sign of health and progress, is mitigated by the fact that she partially fakes her recovery in order to be released. Freedom from the hospital does not translate into freedom from her past; she still carries with her the wounds that more than once have led her to attempt suicide. While the end of the novel offers a glimpse of hope when she opens that "outside door, the final door, the door that will open all doors," the guarded reader is left to wonder how Blanca, and her daughter, Taína, will fare in the end (234).

Blanca's depiction in the novel does not glorify the Puerto Rican woman's experience in the diaspora. In fact, the representation of Puerto

Rican women—especially those who have been victims of violence—is highly negative at times. Depicting the main character as the ultimate victim of patriarchy paradoxically serves to raise awareness about the taboo of child abuse and its long-term effects on those who endure it. The mere act of talking about such a silenced topic can have an empowering effect, such as Ambert recalls in an interview with Carmen Dolores Hernández:

> The reading unleashed something. Women started talking about child abuse, about how they had been abused as children and nobody wanted to talk about it. They were saying that finally there was a novel in Spanish, written by a Latina, that addressed this important issue because Puerto Ricans and other Latinos did not want to acknowledge that this problem existed. There was a Chicana lawyer there who talked about seeing instances of child abuse among Latinos all the time. We are all denying that child abuse happens among us. We want to believe that Puerto Ricans are perfect parents and never abuse their children. That's not true; child abuse happens in every society. ("On Language" 60)

As suggested above, the audience's reaction reveals the extent of the taboo surrounding the issue of child abuse in Puerto Rican and other U.S. Latino cultures, where traditional views of the family reflect the values of patriarchal ideology.

One of the novel's most salient accomplishments is the way in which it "breaks the silence" by shattering the traditional image of the Puerto Rican woman cemented on *marianismo* through the character of Paquita, Blanca's grandmother. The attributes associated with *marianismo* have also been transferred to, and are often more accentuated in, the figure of the grandmother, who plays a central role in U.S. Latina literature (Ortega 12). Due to the role of *marianismo* and "the cultural myths we project upon mothers and women in general—that mothers are child protectors and have unconditional love for the child and that women are often the victims of abuse but are not perpetrators of it," it is often difficult for U.S. Latino and Latin American cultures to accept that women are capable of abusing children (Duncan 21).

Ambert's *A Perfect Silence* dismantles this myth through the character of Paquita, who takes the role of Blanca's surrogate mother. Having lost her mother at the age of two, Blanca spends most of her childhood and teenage years in her grandmother's custody. Living with Paquita proves to be a lifelong traumatic experience for Blanca, given that she subjects her to years of relentless psychological, physical, and even sexual violence. For instance, Paquita humiliates Blanca by constantly reminding her that she is an orphan and by making her feel like a "piece of furniture" (222). In addition, despite not ever showing any affection toward Blanca, she forces her to call her "Mami" (45). Paquita also beats her regularly, and sometimes so severely that at least once Blanca ends up in the hospital (99). When Blanca reaches her teenage years, Paquita engages in acts of sexual abuse through the performance of frequent vaginal tests in order to "insure that she was not running around with any man" (152). This need to control and safeguard Blanca's virginity mirrors dominant ideas of female sexuality in patriarchal cultures.

Paquita's portrayal goes beyond the simple defiance of *marianismo* in order to posit her as the embodiment of patriarchal authority. Much of her behavior aligns her with the realm of the masculine, as both aggressiveness and violence are closely linked to *machismo* and the construction of Puerto Rican masculinity (Ramírez 71). In emphasizing the role that women can play as perpetrators of violence against children, *A Perfect Silence* thus undermines the stereotype of women as victims of patriarchal domination and exposes their complicity in its perpetuation. Women are not only victims within this system; they can also be victimizers. Children, however, are the real victims.

It can be argued that the relationship that develops between Paquita and Blanca parallels the dynamics between the typical abusive man and the victimized woman. For instance, as Nancy Kaser-Boyd points out, a characteristic of abusive men is their "strong need for control," which ultimately drives them to make all decisions for their family, including decisions about their partner's bodies (45). They also tend to be highly egocentric, they do not accept responsibility for their actions, they cannot control their emotions, and they do not usually show empathy toward others (45–47). The abuser's intense need for control is partly the result of his paranoia, which "is based on his history of abandonment by his parental objects during his childhood" (Celani 159). For this reason, Celani explains, he does "everything in his power to insure that he will not be abandoned again. He uses the independent style, which relies on action, activity, vigilance, to combat his vulnerability. His paranoia is designed to protect him from the humiliation and potential ego collapse that will occur if his partner leaves him" (159).

Paquita's frequent displays of egocentrism and her obsessive need to control those around her are traits she shares with the archetypal abusive man, as the following passage illustrates: "Paquita had an insatiable need to destroy. She was unable to accept the distinctive features of others, least of all in her own family. The blood they shared was an indissoluble bond that made them one, like a tribe or a web. She not only required their physical presence in her life, she demanded their minds and souls. Paquita pronounced herself the force ruling this unity and was willing to destroy whoever threatened her rule" (50). For the most part, Paquita uses violence and manipulation to exert control over those around her. She often fakes illness or assumes the role of a martyr when violence is not an option. Such is the case when she manipulates Blanca into moving back to Puerto Rico with her after the brutal beating that sends Blanca to the hospital and Paquita into self-imposed exile to Puerto Rico (121).

Blanca, on the other hand, displays qualities associated with the so-called battered woman syndrome, which is characterized by the formation of a bond between abuser and victim (Kaser-Boyd 47). As the narrator explains, the "years of beatings had achieved the irreversible mental bondage that would not allow [her] to break away" (122). Even when Paquita no longer has the physical strength to overpower Blanca, she still feels dominated by her grandmother: "The girl became the center of the old woman's center. So it was that Paquita controlled every second of her granddaughter's life and made the girl her reason to be and to exist. It was the girl who would sacrifice her youth to Paquita, who would love her, obey her, and never ever leave her" (123). Although as a child Blanca is completely dependent on her abusive grandmother, her inability to leave Paquita once she is older parallels the incapacity of abused women to leave their oppressors, often misunderstood as a "masochistic" impulse (Kaser-Boyd 47). This type of behavior is often the result of a psychological phenomenon called repetition compulsion, "the human pattern of unconsciously choosing marital partners, friends, or lovers who reject the individual in the very same manner that he [or she] was rejected in childhood" (Celani 143). For Blanca, this pattern becomes more pronounced when she establishes relationships with men as an adult.

The repetition of this pattern illustrates Paquita's success in socializing Blanca to be submissive through the use of violence. She often resorted to beatings in order to "train" the little girl, a "time-consuming enterprise," as she put it (71). Yet it pays off: "Slowly she fashioned her empire, locking in her subjects" (67). Blanca's absolute submissiveness at the hands of her grandmother thus evokes and denounces violence against women and children under systems of patriarchal domination, but perhaps more important, it challenges the positive value ascribed to submissiveness by *marianismo* by unveiling it as a key instrument of oppression.

In fact, *A Perfect Silence* demonstrates how patriarchal mechanisms of socialization engender and perpetuate violence and oppression. For instance, following her grandmother's escape to Puerto Rico after she beats Blanca, her father places her in the custody of Rafael, one of his coworkers. Rafael beats, starves, molests, and ultimately rapes Blanca while she lives with him and his family in the Bronx (119). The first time Rafael abuses her is indicative of the level to which Blanca has internalized her submission: "Blanca suspected that nothing nice could emerge from his request, but her years of unquestioned obedience to adults had indoctrinated her well" (109). Blanca's isolation is emphasized by the psychological violence to which she is subjected at the hands of Rafael, his wife, and their children. Cruelly mistreated by all of them, Blanca's dehumanization culminates in her rape as she is reduced to a sexual object.

Her internalized submission also emerges years later when she is raped by her driving instructor in Puerto Rico. After he sexually assaults Blanca, he becomes obsessed with her and forces her into an abusive relationship from which she cannot escape (168). Afraid of the "beatings he threatened to inflict," Blanca becomes paralyzed just like she used to in the past when her grandmother threatened to hurt her (168). The helplessness Blanca feels corresponds to a "learned pattern" among abused women that usually puts them at risk for subsequent victimization, according to Duncan (22). The narrator's assertion that "[Blanca] had grown accustomed to punishment" and that in fact "she expected it as her inescapable fate" (169) perhaps explains why Blanca stays in a relationship with a man who rapes her (167), forces her to have an abortion (175), and abuses her over the course of several years. Life with him proves to be a "repetition of patterns"; Blanca escapes her "grandmother's subjugation only to fall into the snare of an equally oppressive tyrant" (135).

The inhumane treatment and suffering that Blanca experiences both in Puerto Rico and in the United States challenges glorified images of the diaspora and the island—as land of opportunity and paradise respectively—that are prevalent in U.S. Puerto Rican literature. On the one hand, Blanca's abuse while living in the Bronx with Paquita and Rafael represents an aspect of the diaspora that has remained silenced in U.S. Puerto Rican literature despite the negative impact that it has on individuals, their families, and their communities. The prevalence and neglect of the reality of violence against children and women among immigrant communities speaks to the subordinate position that Puerto Ricans, despite being U.S. citizens, occupy in dominant society. Blanca's abuse, which spans several years, is not only a result of *machismo* but also of the level of disenfranchisement that Puerto Ricans experience on the mainland as a colonized people. On the other hand, the abuse Blanca faces while living in Puerto Rico also speaks to the lack of support for victims of violence in a culture that privileges masculine domination and that dismisses violence within the home as a "private matter."[32]

Although Blanca eventually manages to escape from both her grandmother and her abusive husband, memories of the violence she endured at their hands will have an impact on the rest of her life. In addition to suffering from physical, psychological, and sexual violence, Blanca becomes a victim of self-violence, which manifests itself in bouts of depression, self-hatred (153), self-mutilation (160), and repeated suicide attempts (160). These typical expressions of childhood abuse represent "reenactments of the trauma experience" or "expression[s] of emotional pain" (Duncan 10). By focusing on Blanca's last suicide attempt and her eventual institutionalization, the novel bridges the gap between Blanca's past and present while illustrating the cyclical nature of violence.

While Blanca's victimization is emphasized throughout most of the novel, the end hints at her newfound sense of agency. Earning a graduate degree from Harvard, securing a job as a bilingual education teacher in a Boston high school, and raising her daughter as a single mother are all modes of resistance against a system that stacked all the odds against her. Most important, however, is the sense of empowerment readers can derive from reading Blanca's story. The crucial role that giving voice to trauma plays in the healing process should not be underestimated. As Brison explains, "Narrative memory is not passively endured; rather, it is an act on the part of the narrator, a speech act that defuses traumatic memory, giving shape and a temporal order to the events recalled, establishing more control over their recalling, and helping the survivor remake a self" (40). *A Perfect Silence*, as written text, thus represents a form of therapeutic art that can be transformative not only to the author but to readers as well. Writing the novel, Ambert intimates, was "a way of getting many stories out," particularly her own story and those of women she has known (Hernández, "On Language" 59). Voicing those experiences thus serves to transform many traumatic memories into narrative memories by giving a voice to the truly voiceless, the real disenfranchised—abused children—through a speech act that resonates beyond ethnic, racial, and gender boundaries.

As this analysis illustrates, through literature, authors such as Nicholasa Mohr and Alba Ambert participate in the wider feminist project that seeks to create an awareness of the oppression to which women are subjected in patriarchal cultures. In this sense, much like their counterparts on the island, Puerto Rican women authors in the United States are using their literature as an instrument of social action. The denunciation of *machismo*'s double standards, strictly defined gender roles, conservative ideals of womanhood, and symbolic as well as physical violence against women are some of the elements that these two bodies of Puerto Rican women's literature have in common. It can be said that the struggle against masculine domination represents the strongest link that exists between women's literature on the island and the mainland. This is so because the ideology of *machismo* is central to the notion of Puerto Rican masculinity, both as it is conceived on the island and as it is conceived in the United States. Although it would be tempting to assume that Puerto Rican women in the United States have been liberated from *machismo* as a result of the influence of the less androcentric American Anglo culture (at least in relation to Latino/a and Latin American cultures), the prominent role that this topic plays in their literature indicates that this is not the case. While more sociological studies need to be conducted to explain what accounts for the incidence of Puerto Rican *machismo* in the United States, for the moment it is safe to say that more than ever, through their literature, U.S. Puerto Rican women authors are forcing us to acknowledge the many connections between U.S.-based and insular Puerto Ricans. The role that U.S. Puerto Rican women's literature—and Latina literature in general—plays as an agent of social change not only seeks to rearticulate the image of the U.S. Puerto Rican (both male and female) as an ethnic minority, but, perhaps more important, to redefine womanhood in the context of a U.S. Puerto Rican culture.

Epilogue

In 1957 DIVEDCO issued the booklet *La mujer y sus derechos* (Women and their rights), written and edited by René Marqués. Published immediately after *Los derechos del hombre* (The rights of man), *La mujer* sought to trace how far the struggle for women's rights had advanced and how much Puerto Rican women had gained in the process. The emphasis on women's role in society, including their rights and obligations as citizens, reflected the democratic ideals associated with *el muñocismo*. From early in his campaigns, Muñoz Marín had stressed the need for women to be "active" participants in the ELA's construction. However, the push toward the inclusion of women in civic and political processes posed a challenge to the patriarchal power structure on which his government had been built—namely, the myth of *la gran familia*—and also to the traditional values his government tried so hard to promote. In other words, women's participation was needed, but they were to remain subordinate to men's authority and fulfill the "natural" responsibilities conferred to them as women.

The condescending tone and content that characterize *La mujer y sus derechos* illustrates how *el muñocismo* achieved that precarious balance between women's rights and patriarchal values. In the booklet's introduction, the narrator (Marqués) states, "The woman, already triumphant in the struggle, has wisely learnt to benefit from legal rights. But, even more wisely, she has not allowed the enjoyment of the right to equality in front of the law to deprive her of the two primordial missions for which God put her on earth: love and maternity."[1] It is clear that the text overplays the more advantageous position of Puerto Rican women at that historical juncture, but this type of comment, which abounds throughout the narrative, amounts to no more than empty talk. Its duplicity lies in the fact that the text recycles traditional discourses

regarding women's "natural" and "God-given" character and disposi-
tion toward motherhood. This idea is reiterated in the chapter "La mujer
en el Puerto Rico de hoy" (The woman in today's Puerto Rico), where
the narrator states, "It is amazing how woman in today's Puerto Rico,
without neglecting her sacred duties as wife and mother, has been able
to become so useful and active in her duties as a citizen."[2] Women are
not exactly commended for being agents of progress but rather for "successfully" juggling wifehood, motherhood, and their responsibilities as
citizens without compromising the first two. The booklet, disguised as a
sort of apology to women, in reality serves to perpetuate the notion that
women's first and foremost responsibilities are to her family.

Ten years later, in 1967, the booklet *La familia* would restate the
same sexist principles that were patently manifested in *La mujer y sus
derechos*. For instance, the chapter titled "El matrimonio" (Matrimony)
clearly advocates the gendered division of labor. For example: "In order
for the mother to devote herself to the noble task of motherhood, the
man assumes the responsibility of relieving her of the economic burden.
That is to say, within marriage it is the man's responsibility to support
the family. He provides economic comfort to the woman."[3] Never mind
that women are expected to limit their aspirations to being homemakers,
they still should be grateful that they are no longer "un cero a la izqui-
erda" (less than nothing). According to the narrator, "The woman is a
human being with a right to vote in political elections, communal decisions, and the handling of household problems, and marriage relations."[4]
While these rights and privileges have certainly been crucial to women's
empowerment, the basic patriarchal structure of the home and the family would continue to be promoted as the basis of Puerto Rican society.

In 2006 the Instituto de Cultura Puertorriqueña published the booklet *Las mujeres en Puerto Rico,* written by Norma Valle Ferrer, in its
Cuadernos de Cultura series, which sought to "promote, circulate, and
salvage the cultural manifestations of Puerto Rico."[5] The publication
of *Las mujeres* is more significant than it may appear at first sight, as it
constitutes "an update of the *Libro del Pueblo* about women's rights."[6]
Almost half a century later, the ICP had allowed a woman to write
and update this essay on the history of Puerto Rican women from an
openly feminist perspective that would call into question the patriarchal
values and norms that had informed DIVEDCO's series. The booklet
would also provide more concrete details about the history of women's
rights and achievements in the Puerto Rican context in specific sections such as "Educación y sufragio" (Education and suffrage), "Los

años sesenta" (The sixties), "Logros a diferentes niveles" (Various levels of achievements), and "Pioneras en la cultura" (Cultural pioneers). The author takes issue with the patriarchal ideology that hindered women's advancement. Speaking about the past, she affirms, "At that time, it was a prevalent belief that women should not be educated, should not be taught how to read, because *machista* culture upheld that education would spoil women and they would stop being submissive and self-sacrificing mothers."[7] Although this quote refers specifically to the Spanish colonial period, it is interesting to note that it seems to mirror the same discriminatory attitudes present in *La mujer y sus derechos* and *La familia*, two texts that underscore the sexism embedded in Puerto Rican notions of identity.

What in my view constitutes one of the greatest contributions of *Las mujeres en Puerto Rico* is that it aims to set the record straight by not only celebrating the advances made by women in Puerto Rican society but also acknowledging the hurdles they continue to face in the present. The author reminds us, "Nevertheless, women still do not receive equal pay. . . . They continue being bare and crude sexual objects in advertising and the media in general."[8] The road to equality, according to her, is filled with obstacles, many of which are very difficult to overcome, such as extreme poverty and domestic violence (38–39). In conclusion, she declares that "There is still a deficit of democracy in women's lives, even when they have resisted and fought for their equality."[9] This negative assessment of Puerto Rican women's condition is certainly more in line with the daily lives of women than the falsely enthusiastic image put forth in the 1950s by the book's precursor, *La mujer y sus derechos*.

I have taken the time to reflect on these products of the ICP for a couple of reasons. First, comparing the two books produced by DIVEDCO in the 1950s and 1960s with the recently published *Las mujeres en Puerto Rico* can shed light on the transformations that women's lives have undergone in the past fifty years. In fact, the booklets' narratives accurately mirror the sexual and gender discourses that characterized Puerto Rican literature at those historical junctures. The changes that took place between the publication of Marqués's *La mujer* and *La familia* and Valle Ferrer's *Las mujeres* allowed Puerto Rican women to carve out their own literary space and to make the move from poetry to narrative, from celebrating love and nature to denouncing *machismo* and reclaiming their agency.

Second, these booklets allow us to reflect on the power of the word and the image as instruments in the construction of a national consensus.

Originally designed to instruct the rural and working-class public and to promote the cementing of a collective imaginary, DIVEDCO's booklets often relied on the metaphor of *la gran familia*, and along with it, underscored the subordinate position that women were expected to assume in the name of the nation. In conjunction with the films and posters that accompanied them, the booklets became key instruments in the dissemination of the patriarchal ideology underlying *el muñocismo*. The widespread reach of these "educational" cultural products ensured that most of the rural and working-class population—which constituted the majority of those who participated in the Great Migration—were likely to be exposed to Muñoz Marín's discourse of the "nation as family," which would later resurface in the literature produced in the diaspora. *La gran familia*, therefore, constitutes a link between the island and mainland communities, a sort of *contact zone* that has played a role in the cultural production of both sides and which forces us to call into question the tendency to accentuate the differences between them.

It is difficult to believe that after decades of steady publication by Puerto Rican women authors, virtually no book-length studies have delved into the relation that exists between these two branches of Puerto Rican literature. The reluctance to examine these literatures in light of each other responds not only to the palpable differences between them, especially in terms of language, but also to less perceptible ideological factors such as identity politics. The *frontera intranacional* that has been erected between those who have left and those who have stayed has precluded the emergence of a sense of solidarity or union between the two sides, which in turn has been reflected in their respective cultural productions and their reception, or lack thereof, by the opposite camp. *Family Matters* calls into question this naturalized division by demonstrating that more connections exist between these two branches of Puerto Rican literature than we have cared to acknowledge.

My analysis of insular and U.S. Puerto Rican women's narratives shows that both the continuities and discontinuities found in these two corpuses can reveal much about how each side has internalized their history and the perceptions they have of women's struggles. While it is true that there are significant differences between the narratives produced on each side, there are also links that have remained mostly unexplored until now. The presence of the myth of *la gran familia puertorriqueña*, as I see it, constitutes the most compelling tie between insular and U.S. Puerto Rican women's narratives produced in the last decades of the twentieth century. It is important to emphasize the temporal coordinates that delimit the present study because the social and historical factors that were in place in order for these two literatures to converge will not always be present.

The women authors who have been the subject of my analysis were all influenced, in one way or another, by the transformations brought on by *el muñocismo*. Muñoz Marín's paradoxical push toward modernization and simultaneous grip on the past as a catalyst for national unity had consequences that we are trying to unravel to this day. Cultural production, especially literature, was undoubtedly shaped or affected by the ideology behind cultural nationalism promoted by the PPD. This is evident in the cultural production of DIVEDCO, and even the works produced by the male intellectuals associated with this program. The emergence of *la gran familia puertorriqueña* and the figure of the *jíbaro* as emblematic of a Puerto Rican identity seeped into and was reflected in all modes of artistic production. Because many Puerto Ricans at that time were likely to have internalized to some degree the cultural nationalism promoted by Muñoz Marín's government, even those who migrated would have partaken in this shared sense of collective identity. Because Ferré, Vega, García Ramis, Nolla, Ortíz Cofer, Santiago, and Ambert all came of age during *el muñocismo*—whether on the island or on the U.S. mainland— they share the cultural imaginary that prevailed during that period. So, for this specific group of women writers, all pioneers of Puerto Rican female literature in the post-1970s era, the confluence of the patriarchal *muñocista* ideology and the feminist and civil rights movements created a unique situation, which manifested itself in their unwavering critique of the patriarchal foundational myth of *la gran familia puertorriqueña*.

My inquiry into the ties that bind Puerto Rican women's narratives on the island and in its diaspora is not exhaustive and merely represents the tip of the iceberg, but I hope it serves to stimulate more reflection on the topic. In addition to expanding on the writers and works examined here, more investigation using a comparative framework needs to be conducted in all areas of cultural production, including studies that examine additional literary genres as well as works by male authors. For instance, it is well documented that male and female writers of what has been called the *generación del 70* (Generation of 1970), were guided by an ethos of renewal and rupture from the preceding *generación del 50*. Popular discourse (in Spanish) was seen as a weapon against normative language and more traditional aesthetic standards (Acosta-Belén, "En torno" 223). Self-reflexivity, parody, a rejection of the social realism that characterized previous works, and a consciousness of class-, race-, sex-, and gender-based oppression are all characteristics shared—albeit to different extents and degrees—by the narratives of male and female authors who comprise the *generación del 70*. In their effort to debunk those metanarratives that had informed Puerto Rican literary production until then, male authors also challenged the myth of *la gran familia puertorriqueña*, although their works tend to focus on race and class issues, while women's narratives incorporate a robust feminist angle (Gelpí 1993).

While studies on island-based literature by male and female authors could benefit from further examination, including an inquiry into the presence of *la gran familia* in poetry, drama, and the essay, the same could be proposed in relation to U.S. Puerto Rican male authors. As we know, U.S. Puerto Rican literature has been characterized by the predominance of English or a combination of Spanish and English, the focus on the migrants' working-class experience, the conditions of oppression, racism, poverty, and violence faced by this group, the preference and tendency to cultivate poetry and the bildungsroman, and the centrality of literature as a vehicle to validate their cultural heritage (Acosta-Belén 1992). Generally, the works of male and female U.S. Puerto Rican writers tend to share these characteristics to some degree. The most significant difference, as I demonstrate in this study, rests on what Acosta-Belén refers to as the awareness of an additional "dimension of subalterity" brought about by their experiences as women in a patriarchal culture ("Beyond" 990). This same awareness of sex- and gender-based oppression constitutes one of the main continuities between female authors from both sides.

Furthermore, in contrast to post-1970s insular narratives, we can observe a lesser focus on self-reflexivity and the virtual absence of parody—both associated with postmodern literatures—in contemporaneous U.S. Puerto Rican works. More research in these areas could help us illuminate some of the reasons, beyond class and race, that account for these distinctions. As I proposed in chapter 3, the lack of an established diaspora literary corpus can partly explain both the tendency to cultivate the bildungsroman and the scarcity of parody, which entails an original. Given the centrality of *la gran familia* in the island canon it is easy to see why the narratives of male authors would engage in critiques of the myth. In contrast, the works of male U.S. Puerto Rican authors do not seem to share this preoccupation, or at least to the same degree as their island and U.S. Puerto Rican female counterparts. It is not that the metaphor of the family is completely absent from male diaspora narratives—think of Edward Rivera's *Family Installments: Memories of Growing Up Hispanic* (1983), for instance—but overall, they seem to privilege the public realm, street life, as the main site in the construction of a masculine identity. In a sense, the traditional nuclear family is supplanted by friends and peers, who often constitute a virtual "street" family to the male protagonists. Given the wealth of literary works produced by male authors on the island and the mainland, as I have tried to show, it would be interesting to adopt a comparative model to gain a better understanding of the convergences and divergences between their bodies of literature.

The divisions that emerged between *la literatura de aquí* and *la de allá*, and which my book challenges, have become increasingly destabilized over time. The constant migratory flux between island and mainland, and the migration of Puerto Ricans outside the United States, has complicated any easy generalizations regarding language and place of birth and/or residence. Most readers familiar with the work of the island-based author Rosario Ferré are aware that her transition to publishing in English has not been well received by those who hold Spanish as the marker of Puerto Rican identity. The author and academic Carmen Valle, who has been living and working on the East Coast since the late 1970s, publishes her work in Spanish. Víctor Hernández Cruz, who was born in Puerto Rico, grew up in New York, lived in California, relocated to Puerto Rico, and has spent almost a decade shuttling back between Morocco and the island, writes in both English and Spanish. Urayoán Noel, son of a Puerto Rican mother and American father, grew up in Puerto Rico speaking both English and Spanish and now publishes and performs his poetry in both languages. One of the most fascinating and unique aspects of Noel's poetry is that it has been profoundly influenced by Pedro Pierti's work, despite the fact that diaspora literature is not traditionally taught in the academic setting. These are just a few examples of poets and writers whose works not only defy conventional paradigms of classification but also are forcing us to broaden traditional conceptions of insular and diaspora Puerto Rican literature. The application of a transinsular framework would thus acknowledge literature's capacity to reflect the highly transnational character of the Puerto Rican population.

Some may argue that things are changing, and I agree that they have to an extent. Yet, despite the recent interest of island and diaspora-based intellectuals in broadening the understanding that their communities have of each other, bridging the gap between the two sides has proven to be easier in theory than in practice. Today, the literature produced in the diaspora remains relatively invisible on the island and vice versa. The inclusion of a few token diaspora authors in Puerto Rican anthologies may be a significant step, but it is not enough to lift the veil of invisibility that has marginalized this corpus from the one produced on the island. For the most part, critical studies, anthologies, and high school and university courses continue to reflect the paradigm of division that has characterized the understanding and perception of the insular and the diaspora Puerto Rican communities. However, as the present study has shown, a holistic and more profound study of the Puerto Rican experience is not possible without taking into consideration the "other side" of the story. Similar to how a history of Puerto Rico remains incomplete without the treatment of its diaspora, a study of Puerto Rican cultural production must encompass those works produced in and outside the island. Anything less would amount to a partial examination of these topics.

I have proposed the adoption of a *transinsular* model fully aware that this alternative may not be favorably received by those—either on the island or on the mainland—who maintain static notions of identity as a function of language and/or place of birth/residence. Thus far, the Puerto Rican insular canon has successfully functioned as an identity policing mechanism, ensuring that *hispanismo* reigns as the ultimate standard of Puerto Rican identity. As previously discussed, Hispano-philia has played a complex role in the construction of Puerto Rican identity throughout history, and more recently it has been employed to conceal the classism, racism, and prejudice against the other that the diasporan Puerto Rican represents. Awareness of the politicization of the Puerto Rican canon can be a significant first step toward a more profound understanding of how the Puerto Rican experience has been (mis) represented and often manipulated. Rethinking the Puerto Rican canon in terms of its *transinsularity* will transform the traditional standards we have used to define, and thus delimt, the nation-family.

The transinsular paradigm I have proposed here not only can be applied to other areas of cultural production, such as music and the visual arts, but it can also be a model for studies of the cultural dialectics between home country and diaspora populations across the globe. The establishment and growth of Latin American and Latino communities across the United States, and the increasing pace and reach of their cultural production, poses questions similar to those I have explored in the context of Puerto Rican literature. More often than not, studies of

U.S. Latino/a literatures tend to downplay links to the home country's canon, focusing on the migratory experience per se and the subject's adaptation to his or her new environment. It is also typical for Latino/a authors to lack visibility in their home countries, unless they gain international recognition, at which point they are likely to be claimed as national figures. The habitual distinction between the literatures produced at home and in the host society has perpetuated what I see as an artificial division between the cultural productions of both sides. Migration does not imply an immediate transformation; the migrant does not become a tabula rasa the moment he or she steps foot on foreign soil. To varying degrees, and with some exceptions, it is safe to assume that members of the first, second, and third generations continue to be influenced by their cultural and historical roots. The extent to which literature reflects the myths and collective imaginaries that shaped their families in the home country therefore must be critically explored in order to gain a deeper understanding of already established and emergent U.S. Latino/a literatures. Especially in this current era of transnationalisms, the fields of Latino studies and Latin American studies would benefit immensely from a comparative framework that takes into account the dialectics between home and diaspora.

This sort of comparative approach can also prove useful in the fields of women's and feminist studies, not because a similar framework is not already in place, but because more studies are needed that contrast so-called First and Third World feminisms, or even home and diaspora feminisms. In terms of U.S. Latina literature, most of the production displays a highly feminist content across the board. It would be interesting to examine how do the works of, for instance, Cuban Americans, Dominican Americans, Peruvian Americans, Colombian Americans, Nicaraguan Americans, Salvadoran Americans, and others compare to those produced by their counterparts in their countries of origin. Do their works share stylistic and thematic aspects? Do particular national myths emerge in diaspora production, and if so, are they transformed in any way? More important, what experiences link or separate the livelihoods of Latin American and Latina women? Answering these questions might take some time, but finding answers will contribute to a deeper understanding of the ties that unite not only Puerto Rican women, but women across the Americas.

Notes

Introduction

1. El Monumento al Jíbaro Puertorriqueño, sculpted by Tomás Batista and located on Autopista Luis A. Ferré in Puerto Rico, performs a similar function given that it also portrays a Puerto Rican family. Buscaglia's monument, however, proved to be controversial in its depiction of the family for various reasons, including the central position of the male/father figure.

2. For a recent commentary on the Puerto Rican population in Hartford, see Jorge Duany's essay "Jálfol," published in the newspaper *El Nuevo Día*, April 14, 2010.

3. For more details on Pérez's case, see Debra Bogstie's "Eddie Pérez to Serve 3 Years in Prison," *NBC Connecticut*, September 14, 2011; www.nbcconnecticut .com/news/local/WATCH-LIVE-Eddie-Perez-Sentencing-102857264.html) (accessed November 25, 2011). Pérez was succeeded by Pedro E. Segarra, Hartford's second Puerto Rican and first openly homosexual mayor.

4. Here I subscribe to Chandra Talpade Mohanty's definition of *colonization* as a "predominantly *discursive* one, focusing on a certain mode of appropriation and codification of scholarship and knowledge" ("Under Western Eyes" 255). Although she specifically refers to scholarship "about women in the Third World through the use of particular analytic categories employed in specific writings on the subject that take as their referent feminist interests as they have been articulated in the United States and Western Europe," I employ the term to speak about the scholarship and knowledge produced on the island about the Puerto Rican diaspora (255).

5. The terms *First World* and *Third World* have recently been called into question. Talpade Mohanty affirms that the term *Third World* is "inadequate in comprehensively characterizing the economic, political, racial, and cultural differences *within* the borders of Third-World nations" ("Women Workers" 7).

6. The title of José Trías Monge's book, *Puerto Rico: The Trials of the Oldest Colony in the World* (Yale UP, 1997), is reflective of this posture.

7. U.S. Bureau of the Census, "Overview of Race and Hispanic Origin:

2010," 2010 Census Briefs, 2010, p. 3, www.census.gov/prod/cen2010/briefs /c2010br-02.pdf (accessed June 7, 2011).

8. Frances Aparicio points out, "The need to examine the structures of colonialism among U.S. Puerto Ricans, as well as internal colonialism among Chicanos, has awarded Latino studies an important role in the development of the postcolonial. In fact, the gaze toward foreign countries and the so-called Third World that predominates in postcolonial studies has denied or forgotten the existence of colonialism within the countries of the First World, marginalizing these spaces that are so significant" ("Latino" 12).

9. Magnarelli reminds us that this "definition/image of family . . . was brought from the Old World to the New and imposed on the native populations (along with monogamy, property rights, and so on) as part of the Conquest and the European colonization of the New World during the sixteenth, seventeenth, and even eighteenth centuries. It is also a definition/image that continues to be perpetuated today by means of what we might call a global neocolonization that is being effected by mass media and international commerce" (19).

10. Rúa makes a clear distinction between *latinidad*, as she sees it, and Felix Padilla's concept *Latinismo*, which is situational and politically determined. In Rúa's opinion, "By conflating identity and behavior, Padilla's *Latinismo* disconnects the very lived historical experiences of Latinos in Chicago from the process of negotiating a 'Latino identity,'" which is precisely the focus of her own research (122).

11. For instance, this is evident in the inclusion of writers such as Rosario Ferré and Ana Lydia Vega in U.S. Latino/a literary and critical anthologies such as Alvina Quintana's *Reading U.S. Latina Writers: Remapping American Literature* (2003) and Padilla and Rivera's *Writing Off the Hyphen* (2008).

1. The Literary Canon and Puerto Rican Culture

1. In the original: "Hay muchos Puerto Ricos, unidos por una cinta de Moebius que entra y sale de nuestra variada conciencia nacional. El Puerto Rico del que se da testimonio en la literatura producida en la Isla es muy distinto del que se produce en el continente. Ninguno es más o menos auténtico; la combinación de los dos es lo importante, porque da la imagen completa de nuestro pueblo" ("Mientras" 113).

2. In the original: "La búsqueda de la identidad es sin duda el paradigma organizativo del canon literario puertorriqueño" (Ríos Ávila 201).

3. According to the 2010 U.S. Census, there were 4,624,000 Puerto Ricans in the United States (Pew Hispanic Center, http://pewhispanic.org/). In contrast, there were 3,725,789 in Puerto Rico ("Maps: Population Totals," http://2010 .census.gov/news/releases/operations/cb11–cn120.html).

4. Ayala and Bernabé state that the national project was not "a recipe for unanimity, even among authors of a fairly similar social background. Debates immediately ensued . . . not the least on the racial component of the Puerto

Rican identity to be defended. Plus, the promotion of such an identity proved to be compatible with more than one political orientation, from radical nationalism to autonomism and socialism" (91).

5. Here I borrow Barradas's definition of *myth* as "la representación, no científica o racional, muchas veces de carácter estético, a través de la cual un pueblo expresa sus soluciones o interpretaciones de ciertos fenómenos o problemas" (the representation, not scientific or rational, in many instances of an esoteric character, through which a people express its answers and interpretations of certain phenomena or problems) (*Partes* 47). By "patriarchal myths," I am referring to those myths that have contributed to the perpetuation of patriarchy around the world. Like Heather Jones, I view patriarchy as "a general organizing structure apparent in most social, cultural and economic practices world-wide, a structure that is considered to promote and perpetuate, in all facets of human existence, the empowerment of men and the disempowerment of women" (605).

6. In the original: "Fue con el vendaval democratizador iniciado desde 1940, que la sociedad puertorriqueña dio un rápido viraje hacia el matriarcado estilo anglosajón. Los patrones culturales y éticos de una estructura social basada en la tradición del *pater familiae* se deterioraron y sucumbieron con vertiginosidad" (93). In order to more closely reflect the original language used by Marqués, I have added text that was excluded from Bockus Aponte's translation.

7. Marqués's creative writings reflect his patriarchal ideology and, some would argue, his misogynist outlook. Acosta-Belén has examined the negative portrayal of women, paying attention to two particular works, the play *Un niño azul para esa sombra* (1959) and the story "En la popa hay un cuerpo reclinado" (1970) ("Ideology" 132). María Solá, who refers to the latter as his "misogynist story par excellence," also has examined the complex vision of women that permeates his oeuvre (84).

8. For an analysis of the role and portrayal of women in Puerto Rican literature, see Acosta-Belén, "Ideology and Images of Women in Contemporary Puerto Rican Literature."

9. In *Literatura y paternalismo*, Gelpí asserts that the omission of women writers from the island's canon, with the exception of the poet Julia de Burgos, is illustrative of the exclusion generated by the paternalism that characterized Puerto Rican literary history until the 1960s and 1970s (3).

10. For a detailed analysis of the transformations that insular Puerto Rican literature underwent during this period, see Marie Ramos Rosado's *La mujer negra en la literatura puertorriqueña*.

11. The impact of U.S. colonialism on Puerto Rican women became an important research topic, as exemplified by the amount of studies published on birth control experimentation and sterilization campaigns of Puerto Rican women between the 1950s and the 1970s. According to Matos Rodríguez, "Most of this literature demonstrates how Puerto Rico served as a birth control

laboratory for U.S. agencies, companies, and scholars due to the lack of sovereignty the colonial status provided" ("Women's" 16).

12. Angel Rama (1926–1983) was a prestigious Uruguayan scholar and writer recognized for having theorized the concept of transculturation. Marta Traba (1952–1983) was a renowned Argentinian writer and critic of Latin American art who was married to Angel Rama. Both died, along with Jorge Ibargüengoitia and Manuel Scorza, in an airplane accident as they traveled from Paris to Colombia. Their role in the creation of *Zona* represents an understudied link between Puerto Rican and Latin American letters.

13. In the original: "Una meta de *Zona carga y descarga* que se logró plenamente fue el dar a conocer la voz auténtica de la mujer, que hasta aquel momento había sido apabullada en su expresión creativa por la sociedad patriarcal. En *Zona* las mujeres, que fuimos mayoría casi desde un principio, rompimos nuestro silencio y alcanzamos un registro pleno" ("Mientras" 104).

14. In the original: "A propósito, con esto del 'Women's Liberation Movement', ¿cómo quieres que te trate, como Srta., Sra. Mrs. o Ms? Los pobres hombres estamos un tanto confundidos en cuanto a esto. . . . No que yo sea un 'chauvinistic pig'. Acepto cualquier cambio positivo en la sociedad. Pero tienen que ilustrarme. Para saber" ("Carta" 26).

15. Olga Nolla's militant role in the Federación de Mujeres Puertorriqueñas and the creation of her literary journal *Palabra de mujer* is another example of the close links between literature and the struggle for Puerto Rican women's rights on the island (Vélez Camacho 31).

16. Male authors such as Luis Rafael Sánchez, Manuel Ramos Otero, and Edgardo Rodríguez Juliá are also central figures of the *nueva narrativa*. One element that unifies both male and female authors of the island's *nueva narrativa* is the role of popular language and popular music. Regarding the latter, Aparicio affirms that its presence in insular literature "tends to signal social conflict, unveiling race, class, and gender divisions which have been masked by myths of national identity, social harmony, and by a Eurocentric cultural veneer imposed by the structures of colonialism in the island" ("Salsa" 47).

17. Rosario Ferré's rupture with the paternalist canon is explained by Gelpí in his *Literatura y paternalismo en Puerto Rico*.

18. In her essay "Rosario's Tongue," the critic Frances Negrón-Muntaner assures us that "before Ferré's conversion [to English], creating literary works in the language of the current metropolis had been virtually unheard of except by *boricuas* raised in the United States. . . . In this context Ferré represents a significant rupture, as she is a bilingual member of the literary elite—the sector most heavily invested in preserving its considerable power as protector of the cultural patrimony—writing in both English and Spanish, for readers of either language, and with a specific political agenda of integration into selected U.S. public spheres (media, academic institutions, cultural marketplace)" (*Boricua* 183).

19. For a detailed analysis of the debate surrounding Ferré's use of English,

see Frances Aparicio's "Writing Migrations: Readings of Rosario Ferré and Víctor Hernández Cruz," and Negrón-Muntaner's "Rosario's Tongue: Rosario Ferré and the Commodification of Island Literature" in *Boricua Pop*.

20. Some examples of these male-centered narratives are Piri Thomas's foundational novel *Down These Mean Streets* (1967), Nicky Cruz's *Run Baby Run* (1968), and Edwin Torres's *Carlito's Way* (1975).

21. For an analysis of the development of Latina literature during this period, see Eliana Ortega and Nancy Saporta Sternbach's essay "At the Threshold of the Unnamed: Latina Literary Discourse in the Eighties."

22. Pew Hispanic Center, http://pewhispanic.org/ (accessed June 7, 2011). "Maps: Population Totals," http://2010.census.gov/news/releases/operations /cb11–cn120.html (accessed June 7, 2011).

23. In considering the possible implications of the shift in balance between the island and diaspora populations, Acosta-Belén and Santiago point out that "if US Puerto Ricans were to have a political voice in the periodic plebiscites that are conducted on Puerto Rico's future political status and its economic relationship with the United States, their votes could determine the outcome" (84).

24. Of course, this logic cannot be applied to the fate of reggaetón outside (mostly working-class) youth circles, given that a significant percentage of the lyrics are composed in Spanish (Rivera 2003). One must examine how other elements, beyond language—such as class, race, gender, violence, politics—can explain the degree of rejection this musical genre has elicited from older generations and the middle and upper classes.

25. Flores reminds us, "Let's not forget that as late as 1978 salsa was still referred to by some on the Island as 'an offensive, strident, stupefying, intoxicating and frenetic music openly associated with the effects of sex, alcohol and drugs'. . . . It is ironic, though fully consonant with the logic of the music industry and a commodified cultural nationalism, that by the early 1990s salsa had been domesticated and comfortably re-patriated to the Island, to the point that it came to be equated with Puerto Rican identity as such" (*Diaspora* 155).

26. Acosta-Belén and Santiago explain, "The demographic reality and the transnational commuting nature of Puerto Rican migration have helped lessen the sense of separation between Island and US Puerto Ricans, but there has been a propensity to focus on their differences rather than on the issues that might bring both communities closer together. One of the first sectors to point to the separation between these communities was the writers" (186).

27. There is a general lack of comparative studies of insular and diaspora Puerto Rican literatures. Some of the works that have sought to bridge the schism between these two literary corpuses are Margarite Fernández Olmos ("*Growing Up Puertorriqueña*: The Feminist *Bildungsroman* and the Novels of Nicholasa Mohr and Magali García Ramis"), Frances Aparicio ("Writing Migrations: Readings of Rosario Ferré and Victor Hernández Cruz"), and Suzanne Bost ("Transgressing Borders: Puerto Rican and Latina *Mestizaje*").

28. In the original: "la literatura de los puertorriqueños en los Estados Unidos es parte integral, recalco, de la literatura puertorriqueña."

29. In the original: "¿No es acaso esto una forma de colonización, una forma de colonialidad de poder? Si los 'nuyoricans' son ahora parte de la nacionalidad es porque así lo han 'legislado,' en negociación con la elite intelectual puertorriqueña radicada en Estados Unidos, las voces autorizadas de la elite intelectual de la isla" (93). Grosfoguel proposes that the term *coloniality of power,* coined by the Peruvian sociologist Aníbal Quijano, signifies "a crucial structuring process in the modern/colonial/capitalist world-system that articulates peripheral locations in the international division of labor, subaltern group political strategies, and Third World migrants' inscription in the racial/ethnic hierarchy of metropolitan global cities" (4).

30. Asked by Carmen Dolores Hernández about the "confrontation" with Nicholasa Mohr, Ana Lydia Vega replied, "There was no confrontation. At a symposium organized by Manuel Ramos Otero in New York some years ago, Nicholasa broached the subject of the way Nuyoricans were rejected in Puerto Rico and referred to 'Pollito Chicken' as an example. . . . But Nicholasa's reading of the story was not the one I had intended. Susie Bermúdez, the protagonist, is not even a Nuyorican, because she has been in the States for only ten years" ("A Sense of Space" 56).

31. In an interview I conducted with Víctor Hernández Cruz on April 18, 2007, for the Institute for Latino Studies Oral History Project at the University of Notre Dame, he spoke positively about the reception of his work on the island. He said, "On a personal basis, I have met the Puerto Rican poets, those who write in Spanish and have been able to break bread with them and correspond with them. And I've had good relationships, I haven't had directly negative attitudes, nor of rejection."

32. In the original: "La explotación (expropiación del trabajo productivo) era necesaria para el dominio económico del hacendado y para satisfacer las necesidades de consumo de su posición de poder y prestigio. Pero también importante para su posición, para su forma de vivir, era el ser respetado, admirado y querido por los trabajadores de hacienda" (124).

33. In the original: "El modo de producción señorial sobre el cual se basaba esta ideología facilitó la concepción paternalista de la patria como una gran familia: familia estamentada, dirigida por el 'padre de agrego'—el hacendado—, pero familia al fin, constituida por una ciudadanía común" (51).

34. Quintero Rivera clarifies that despite their social hegemony, the colonial condition of the island did not allow *hacendados* to achieve economic hegemony given Puerto Rico's political subordination to the Spanish state (*Conflictos* 20).

35. In the original: "la clase de hacendados había logrado representar sus intereses como los intereses generales del país, a través del concepto de 'la gran familia puertorriqueña' frente al arbitrario y extranjero poder colonial" (35).

36. In November 1897 Spain conceded the "Carta Autonómica" to Puerto

Rico, which among other things granted male universal suffrage. The first elections to take place under the Carta Autonómica resulted in the overwhelming triumph of the *hacendado* party, known at that time as the Partido Autonomista (*Conflictos* 41).

37. Arlene Torres states that the inclusion of blacks and *mulatos* as part of the Puerto Rican family was provisional at best given that they "understood that they were within the geopolitical boundaries of the nation but were not really considered part of that cultural construction" (295).

38. In the original: "Esta segunda generación, nacida cuando la estructura social de haciendas comenzaba a derrumbarse, y nacida políticamente cuando su clase había perdido su hegemonía política y económica, y que por lo tanto estaba en una posición secundaria en la jerarquía social, desarrolló una ideología más radical y orientada al cambio. . . . Con fuertes raíces en sus tradiciones y en su cultura de hacienda, mantuvo, sin embargo, el apoyo de los trabajadores de hacienda y de los agricultures de pequeña tenencia, pero su nueva ideología más radical y su nueva posición social secundaria permitieron una alianza con un importante sector del proletariado" (153).

39. In the original: "a menudo remite a las relaciones familiares, y su metáfora fundamental consiste en equiparar a la nación con una gran familia" (2).

40. Gelpí has observed, "*Insularismo* suele leerse como un ensayo de interpretación de la historia de Puerto Rico, y es, sin duda, uno de los clásicos de la literatura puertorriqueña" (*Insularismo* tends to be read as an essay interpretation of Puerto Rican history, and it is, without a doubt, one of the classics of Puerto Rican literature) (18).

41. In the original: "Para quienes lo leen en las décadas de los cuarenta, cincuenta y sesenta, *Insularismo* es un *logos,* una especie de voz fundadora de la cual emana la verdad acerca de la nacionalidad puertorriqueña" (19).

42. In the original: "En instantes de trascendencia histórica en que afloran en nuestros gestos los ritmos marciales de la sangre europea, somos capaces de las más altas empresas y de los más esforzados heroísmos. Pero cuando el gesto viene empapado de oleadas de sangre africana quedamos indecisos, como embobados ante las cuentas de colores o amedrentados ante la visión cinemática de brujas y fantasmas" (36).

43. In the original: "Su narración histórica articula una identidad en torno a la *figura* del *padre generoso* que defiende la unidad de la familia frente a elementos 'ajenos,' a la vez que reafirma la jerarquía legitimatoria de su autoridad. Es, en muchos sentidos, un discurso patriarcal y paternalista. Construye una historia de bondad paternal, blanca, hispánica, católica, occidental, con la cual anuncia un programa de unidad futura, una vez hayan sido reconocidos y eliminados los elementos 'perturbadores'" (73).

44. In the original: "dificultó la posibilidad de formación de hombres verdaderamente cultos" (106).

45. In the original: "y la desorientación de las masas siguió su curso, pasando

del cándido deslumbramiento al decaimiento y la desorganización, sembrando el titubeo y la duda, dando pábulo a actitudes tan paradójicas y negativas como la resignación inconforme, la desesperación académicamente esperanzada, la jaibería pitiyanqui o patriotera, etcétera" (97). Regarding the term *jaibería*, Grosfoguel et al. state, "The word *jaibería* has its origins in the term *jaiba*, or mountain crab, who in going forward moves sideways. Within the Puerto Rican usage, *jaibería* refers to collective practices of nonconfrontation and evasion. . . . Although it has been mistaken for docility, it is instead an active, low-intensity strategy to obtain the maximum benefits of a situation with the minimum blood spilled" (30, 31).

46. In the original: "cuando se considera al pueblo colonial como inferior, primitivo, atrasado, inmaduro o impreparado" (*Prontuario* 100).

47. In the original: "La génesis de nuestra psicología rural está en la desaparecida hacienda puertorriqueña, la unidad que a un mismo tiempo fué, fortaleza, alcaldía, intendencia, cuarto de cepo, almacén, capilla, cuartel de barraganía, casona de familia, tormentera, atalaya de europeismo, punto de relevo de la guardia civil y de los quincalleros ambulantes. En ella vivió, nuestro hombre blanco europeo, en ella comenzó la estructura de nuestra vida rural, en ella se creó el tipo criollo que hoy se llama puertorriqueño" (40).

48. In the original: "pequeño señor feudal, es árbitro de vida y de hacienda. . . . A él converge en busca de sustento el indio, el negro, el criollo, el mulato y el mestizo que hace vivir en un abigarrado montón" (42).

49. Santiago Segura Munguía's *Diccionario etimológico Latino-Español* defines *dominus* as "dueño [de la casa], señor, propietario" but also "señor, jefe, soberano, árbitro" (227).

50. In the original: "Cada peón se siente 'agregado' a la hacienda como a una mínima patria y adora a su señor mientras el señor dé lo que un hombre de bien necesita: alimento, baile y alcohol" (43).

51. PPD stands for Partido Popular Democrático (Popular Democratic Party), founded in 1938 by Luis Muñoz Marín.

52. Quintero Rivera states how "la clase de 'hijos de antiguos hacendados' va a revivir (con las diferencias de las nuevas estructuras socio-económicas) el paternalismo del viejo sistema de haciendas" [the class of the "old *hacendado* children" will revive (with the difference of the new socioeconomic structures) the paternalism of the old hacienda system] (*Conflictos* 163).

53. In the original: "Desde su surgimiento hasta su avatar más reciente—el populismo desarrollista de los años cuarenta, cincuenta y sesenta—ese discurso ha tenido una metáfora privilegiada: la equiparación de Puerto Rico con una gran familia. Se trata, pues, de un discurso conciliador que está fundamentado en el respeto a la autoridad de una figura paterna simbólica" (22).

54. In his "Prefacio" to *San Juan tras la fachada*, Edwin R. Quiles Rodríguez provides a brief history of *arrabales* (slums) in Puerto Rico.

55. According to Acosta-Belén and Santiago, "The push for population

control was facilitated by the introduction of oral contraceptives to the island. Moreover, U.S. pharmaceutical companies used Puerto Rican women for testing 'the pill' before it was introduced to the U.S. market. . . . Another popular method fostered by the government was the massive sterilization of women through the surgical procedure that became known as *la operación*. These population control practices intensified during the rapid industrialization period of the 1950s, and Puerto Rico currently has one of the highest sterilization rates of women in the world" (50).

56. The concept of internal colonialism, coined by Robert Blauner in *Racial Oppression in America* (1972), has been applied by social scientists to U.S. Latino populations. For some, the concept is too vague and does not adequately reflect the conditions of Latinos. One exception has been its use to describe the condition of Puerto Ricans in the United States. According to Carlos G. Vélez-Ibáñez and Anna Sampaio, "Many Puerto Rican intellectuals and academics in the United States regarded themselves as subject to a type of 'internal colonialism,' especially with regard to language loss, cultural assimilation, and economic exploitation. Internal colonialism was considered an analogue of international colonialism in which territory, population, and material resources were controlled by force and the metropolis was the controlling colonial power. In the case of Puerto Ricans, the island was the colonized entity and most forms of production were in the hands of colonial agents or their surrogates. Puerto Ricans in New York were basically fleeing to the metropolis as the direct consequence of these colonial relations, and these relations were partially duplicated in the city in the sense that Puerto Ricans were concentrated in particular areas such as the Bronx and political and economic control was in the hands of non–Puerto Ricans or their surrogates" (18).

57. In the original: "Estos folletos ayudarán al lector a iniciarse en la lectura de las mejores obras literarias de Puerto Rico y a adquirir conocimientos de la historia, las artes y las ciencias" (*10 Poetas Puertorriqueños*).

58. Catherine Marsh Kennerley has examined the paradoxical situation in which Marqués found himself during his tenure with DIVEDCO. Avidly pro-independence, he was hired by the Commonwealth government (Muñoz Marín)—in the midst of a massive industrialization and modernization campaign—to promote cultural nationalism as a preventive measure. Even though he was extremely critical of *el muñocismo*, he had a prominent position working for one of the most influential programs designed by that same government (77).

59. In the original: "La familia es el grupo o unidad más pequeña de una sociedad. Es la base o fundamento de una nación" (3). In her bibliography, Marsh Kennerley gives 1967 as the year of publication for *La familia*, but this date corresponds to the second edition. I have not been able to locate a first edition, but according to my calculations, as the ninth book in the series, it must have been published around 1955. I would like to thank Thomas F. Anderson for pointing out this discrepancy.

60. In the original: "Lo que sean los individuos, será la familia de que forman parte. Lo que sean las familias, será la patria de que forman parte. Lo que sea Puerto Rico, dependerá de los individuos puertorriqueños y de sus relaciones dentro de la familia puertorriquena. Lo que seamos como pueblo, como nación, depende en gran medida de cómo sea usted y cómo sea su familia" (69).

61. In the original: "Y el puertorriqueño que decide formar parte de una comunidad americana debe saber que es parte de esa comunidad y que es responsable del mejoramiento y bienestar colectivo" (47). Again, Marsh Kennerley gives 1966 as the date of publication of *Emigración*, when in fact this corresponds to its second edition. As the eighth book in the series, it was probably first published in 1954.

62. In the original: "Para los que se quedan aquí, es distinto. Los que aquí se quedan deben afirmar y engrandecer su modo de ser puertorriqueños. Deben conservar sus costumbres y hábitos cuando estos sean buenos y deseables. Deben conservar su idioma y su cultura. Deben sentir orgullo de su historia y de su tradición. . . . Los que aquí se queden tienen, pues, la responsabilidad de ayudar al engrandecimiento de Puerto Rico" (47).

63. The *jíbaro* was already a central component of the PPD's iconography since the party's inception in 1938, when his profile appeared as its main emblem, accompanied by the motto, "Pan, Tierra y Libertad" (Bread, Land and Freedom).

64. One telling example is Duchesne-Winter's political shift from a *neo-independentista* (*lite*) posture to his present defense of *radical statehood* (Vivoni 82).

65. In the original: "Para este autor [Pabón] el puertorriqueñismo es un discurso reduccionista y esencialista debido a que reduce la nacionalidad puertorriqueña a una esencia étnica-lingüística centrada en la hispanidad y el idioma español. Pabón no niega la existencia de la nacionalidad puertorriqueña, sino que critica el carácter excluyente y homogeneizante del neonacionalismo. . . . Las definiciones de 'lo puertorriqueño' centradas en el idioma español y la hispanidad, sostiene Pabón, excluyen a poblaciones que se consideran puertorriqueños, pero no cumplen con estos requisitos, por ejemplo, los que viven en Estados Unidos y no hablan español o que residen en P.R., pero no se adscriben a la categoría étnica hispana" (87–88).

66. Ortíz Márquez has examined Banco Popular de Puerto Rico's appropriation of the narrative of *la gran familia* in its videos. As she states, "Whereas [the video] *Somos un solo pueblo* represents the Puerto Rican diaspora as an unwanted member of the Puerto Rican "family," *Raíces* goes beyond the bank's original promotional intent to present a more complex version of the history of the diaspora," which ironically responds to the bank's "growth as a corporate power in Latino communities in the United States" (101).

67. In the original: "El afán de custodiar la 'puertorriqueñidad' se manifiesta con particular intensidad en el asunto de la lengua y la literatura" (Pabón 93).

68. Linguistic prejudice continues to be an obstacle to the acceptance of

U.S. Puerto Rican literature on the island, according to Duany, who claims that "even today many local scholars and creative writers deride Puerto Ricans in the diaspora because they cannot speak Spanish well or conduct themselves in a proper Puerto Rican fashion" (*Puerto Rican* 29).

69. Regarding Manrique Cabrera's posture in *Historia* vis-à-vis diaspora literature, Barradas explains, "Por ello en sus palabras se puede entrever una concepción de la literatura nacional que no daría cabida dentro del canon a una literatura puertorriqueña que no fuera la de la Isla. Para él la *Historia . . .* es para los puertorriqueños que están fuera de la Isla un recurso para curar la nostalgia por la patria perdida y sólo eso. Pero lo creado fuera de la Isla—productos que todavía no existían en números considerables, pero sí existía—no tendrá entrada al canon" (Therefore in his words one can begin to see a notion of national literature that would not allow for the inclusion of any other literature besides that from the island. In his opinion, for Puerto Ricans outside the island his *Historia* is only a resource to heal the nostalgia for their lost homeland, and only that. But works created outside the island—which existed, although not in great quantities—will not fit into the canon) ("Los silencios" 30).

70. This point is illustrated by the fact that no U.S. Puerto Rican authors writing in English appear in anthologies published after Manrique Cabrera's, including René Márqués's *Cuentos puertorriqueños de hoy* (1958); Efraín Barradas's *Apalabramiento: Diez cuentistas puertorriqueños de hoy* (1984); José Luis Vega's *Reunión de espejos* (1984); José Ángel Rosado's *El rostro y la máscara* (1995); Mayra Santos Febres's *Mal(h)ab(l)ar* (1997) and *Cuentos de oficio: Antología de cuentistas emergentes en Puerto Rico* (2005); Mario Cancel and Alberto Mártinez Márquez's *El límite volcado* (2000); Reynaldo Marcos Padua's *Relatos en espiga: Cuentos del Grupo Guajana* (2007); Carmen Dolores Hernández's *Convocados: Nueva narrativa puertorriqueña* (2009).

71. Duany points out that the marginal status occupied by U.S. Puerto Rican literature on the island is evident in the fact that "no Puerto Rican writer currently living in the United States and writing in English is now included in the Island's official curriculum at the elementary and high school levels. Very few are taught in elective courses at local universities. Neither Spanish nor English departments have made these authors required reading, largely because of their hybrid, bilingual writings" (*Puerto Rican* 30).

72. Pedro Pietri and Tato Laviera appeared in the *Heath Anthology of American Literature* (Aparicio, "Writing" 81), and Judith Ortíz Cofer has been anthologized in *Norton and Oxford* (Kevane and Heredia 115).

73. In his introduction, Víctor Federico Torres justifies the choice of authors as follows: "En el caso de los autores de la diáspora, cuya cantidad por sí sola constituiría un volumen aparte, se incluyen únicamente aquellos nombres cuya obra se ha incorporado al estudio de nuestras letras tal y como lo evidencian las antologías que se utilizan en el currículo de escuelas y universidades del país" (In the case of diaspora authors, who given their numbers would comprise a volume

of their own, we include only those whose works have been incorporated to the study of our literature based on their inclusion in anthologies that are part of the school and university curriculum) (18). While this observation signals relative progress regarding the inclusion of diaspora studies in the island's academic curricula, the small number of diaspora authors included is indicative of the lesser significance ascribed to these on the island.

74. Of course, it is possible that the inclusion of a study on Ferré's *The House on the Lagoon* responds to the ambiguity that has been generated by Ferré's strategic and commercial self-identification as a Latina writer in recent years.

75. To date, Bost's essay remains one of the few studies to link and compare the literature of Puerto Rican women authors from the island and the U.S. mainland. As previously noted, most critical and scholarly research has traditionally focused on either literary corpus and has seldom delved into the continuities that exist between them.

2. Our Family, Our Nation

1. In the original: "Es que frente a cada casa campesina nuestra, por humilde que sea, hay un batey señorial, una reminiscencia del batey de la hacienda puertorriqueña" (44).

2. In the original: "A mi juicio el gran problema del momento en Puerto Rico es que estamos en un período de franco desorden, motivado principalmente por el hecho de que aún estamos en un período de segregación de un ancho plasma étnico, religioso, idiomático, creado por la españolidad homogénea que formó el esplendoroso Imperio de las Indias" (24).

3. In the original: "la retórica de la nación como una gran familia se sustenta en unas jerarquías sociales, raciales y genéricas que garantizan la hegemonía del sector criollo" (Santiago-Díaz 218).

4. In the original: "a los afropuertorriqueños la discusión del racismo comúnmente se les presenta como una trampa incómoda, porque entienden que hacer reclamaciones desde su condición de negros significa poner en entredicho la ciudadanía y el lugar que 'tan generosamente' se les ha abierto en el seno de 'la gran familia puertorriqueña'" (59).

5. Regarding the lack of an Afro–Puerto Rican consciousness movement, Santiago-Díaz explains, "Si bien la evidencia empírica tiende a validar el argumento de que los puertorriqueños negros no se han movilizado políticamente ni han articulado sus demandas sobre las bases de afirmación racial sino dentro de proyectos nacionalistas o de clase, cuando se examinan cuidadosamente las incidencias de los miembros de este grupo en la política y la cultura, uno se da cuenta de que en la configuración del pensamiento afropuertorriqueño no siempre es fácil determinar cuáles son las instancias de lo racial dentro de dichos proyectos y de que, a veces, han sido los propios críticos sociales quienes han reducido propuestas predominantemente raciales a discursos de clase, de nación, o de otra índole" (Even if empiric evidence tends to validate

the argument that black Puerto Ricans have not mobilized politically nor have they articulated their demands upon the basis of racial affirmation, but rather within nationalist or class projects, when the political and cultural impact of the members of this group is carefully examined, one realizes that, in the configuration of Afro–Puerto Rican thought, it isn't always easy to determine the racial aspects of such projects, and that sometimes, it's been the social critics who have reduced predominantly racial proposals to class, nation and other types of discourses) (45).

6. In the original: "En Puerto Rico no sabemos todavía muy bien lo que es el prejuicio racial" (105).

7. In the original: "La iniciación, el desarrollo y triunfo del sentimiento abolicionista en nuestro país es la página más clara de la historia de la isla" (71).

8. Blanco states, "Sin embargo, durante este breve y agitado período se alcanzaron fundamentales reformas para la isla, muy principalmente la abolición de la esclavitud" (Nevertheless, during this brief period of unrest fundamental reforms were achieved for the island, principally the abolition of slavery) (*Prontuario* 66).

9. In the original: "nuestra cultura general es blanca, occidental, con muy pocas y ligerísimas influencias no españolas" (*El prejuicio* 133); "el elemento africano ha influido sólo muy ligeramente sobre los rasgos culturales" (*El prejuicio* 138).

10. In the original: "somos españoles hasta la médula, y en nuestro contenido nacional hay una cantidad respetable de españolismo vital" (55).

11. In the original: "El negro de Puerto Rico, es sin embargo, el negro más blanco de toda América" (56).

12. In the original: "Yo espero una profunda desilución [sic] para el turista que nos visite. No tenemos ni negro, ni gaucho, ni bandolero, ni indio" (70).

13. Regarding the influx of African-descent people from the French and English Caribbean, see A. Torres (292). For European migration to Puerto Rico, see Torres 1998; Scarano 1989; and González 1989.

14. Namely, the "reverse flow . . . resulting from massive circular and return migration and the ongoing remittance of cultural values and practices through friends, relatives, and the media" (Flores, *Diaspora* 4).

15. For more information on the links established between the U.S. Puerto Rican and the African American communities during the civil rights era, see Roberto Rodríguez-Morazzani's "Political Cultures of the Puerto Rican Left in the United States" and James Early's "An African American-Puerto Rican Connection," in *The Puerto Rican Movement: Voices From the Diaspora* (Ed. Andrés Torres and José E. Velázquez, Temple UP, 1998) and Juan González's *Harvest of Empire: A History of Latinos in America* (2000).

16. In the original: "la metáfora del intelectual como 'legislador' se encuentra en crisis hoy" (151).

17. Figures obtained from the Pew Hispanic Center's web page: http://

pewhispanic.org/reports/report.php?ReportID=143 (accessed November 21, 2011).

18. In the original: "La metáfora de la nación como casa u hogar—una metáfora de familia, el escenario del *primal scene* de la nación—suele ir de la mano con las metáforas orgánicas de la 'identidad'" (344).

19. Some texts by U.S. Puerto Rican authors that also dismantle the house as a symbol of patriarchal order are Judith Ortíz Cofer's *The Line of the Sun* (1991) and Esmeralda Santiago's *When I Was Puerto Rican* (1993).

20. While *Maldito amor* has been described as both a short novel and a long story, *Silent Dancing* is technically considered a hybrid of genres that include story, essay, poetry, fiction and autobiography.

21. In the original: "la unión de la familia puertorriqueña había comenzado a quebrarse" (*Conflictos* 43).

22. In the original: "*Maldito amor* intenta, de alguna manera, parodiar esa visión de la historia y de la vida señorial de la hacienda, arrebatarle al mito su poder de conferir autoridad e identidad, ya que la tierra (y la sociedad que generó entre nosotros) constituyó siempre en nuestro caso una realidad conflictiva e insuficiente" (10). All translations are from *Sweet Diamond Dust*, translated by the author herself in 1988. Discrepancies between the original Spanish text and its English translation have fueled the debate surrounding this controversial translation, which, interestingly, is longer than the "original." See Negrón-Muntaner's "Rosario's Tongue" for an analysis of Ferré's use of English.

23. In the original: "Doña Elvira, educada en París entre algodones de seda, se había enamorado de un *negro*. Era por eso, entonces me di cuenta, que mientras en la casa abundaban los retratos de Doña Elvira no había un solo óleo, silueta o daguerrotipo del pobre Don Julio Font" (75; my emphasis).

24. In the original: "Al llegar a esta casa de recién casada, me di cuenta de que aquella familia era muy extraña. La única pasión de las tías, que Ubaldino también compartía, consistía en investigar, en enormes libros de polvorienta piel de chivo, las intricadas ramas del árbol genealógico de los De la Valle. Que si la abuela mengana era hija de la condesa zutana, que si el abuelo perencejo era bisnieto del marqués perengano, y por lo tanto ellas eran tataranietas de las hijas del Cid" (71).

25. In the original: "aquel afán desesperado y clandestino de aparentar, no sólo ante los espejos biselados del Casino sino ante su propio espejo privado, una pureza de sangre que no tenía por qué buscar" (76).

26. *Maldito amor*, therefore, works as an allegory of the whitening campaign launched by Puerto Rican intellectuals in the 1930s to define the nation. The novel not only provides an alternative black/African paternal figure but also emphasizes the racist politics that underlie the discourse of intellectuals such as Tomás Blanco (*El prejuicio racial en Puerto Rico*, 1948) and Antonio S. Pedreira (*Insularismo*, 1934), who claimed their authority as paternal figures of the nation.

27. In the original: "al enterarse de nuestro noviazgo Doña Emilia y Doña Estéfana se opusieron terminantemente a nuestro matrimonio, porque según ellas mis apellidos no eran lo suficientemente encumbrados para casarme con un De la Valle" (71).

28. In the original: "El delirio de grandeza de las tías era tan grande que, aun siendo angustiosamente pobres (la Central no dejaba dividendos aún y ellas se ganaban la vida por aquellos tiempos tejiendo mantillas y rebozos de encaje para las señoras adineradas del pueblo), no podían vivir sin soñarse servidas por muchedumbres de obsequiosos sirvientes" (72).

29. In the original: "Un día mi curiosidad ante aquella fea costumbre pudo más que yo y, deteniéndome junto a ellas, les pregunté riendo que si no exageraban un tanto, ya que la profusión de malhadados matrimonios era tal, que para aquella fecha no debería de quedar ni una sola familia blanca en todo Guamaní" (72).

30. The connection between blackness and sexuality is a widespread phenomenon according to Ania Loomba: "The sexuality of black men and especially that of black women 'becomes an icon for deviant sexuality in general.' Thus black women are constructed in terms of animals, lesbians and prostitutes; conversely the deviant sexuality of white women is understood by analogies with blackness" (160). Frances Aparicio explores the representation of these images in Puerto Rican music, where "the African-derived sensuality, dangerous promiscuity, and voluptuosity will characterize the discourse about the plena, about Afro-Puerto Rican music in general, and analogously, about the mulatta and black woman" (*Listening* 10).

31. In the original: "El Niño Ubaldino fue siempre un hombre digno, que se hubiese dejado cortar una mano antes de venderle una pulgada de tierra a los extranjeros. El Destino Manifiesto, la política del 'garrote grande,' el '*American Army Mule*,' y hasta el jabón Palmolive y el cepillo de dientes, pasaron a formar parte del vocabulario de odio con que él imprecaba al cielo todas las mañanas" (33).

32. In the original: "Cuando las señoritas de la casa comenzaron a crecer y a casarse con los hijos de los dueños de la Central Ejemplo . . . el Niño [Ubaldino] estuvo durante un mes postrado de gravedad en cama" (33).

33. Also known as Malintzin, Doña Marina, and la Chingada, the historical figure of La Malinche (c. 1500–c. 1527) was said to be Hernán Cortés's "translator and consort," and "has been blamed in the Mexican popular imagination for the Spanish conquest of the Aztecs" (Allatson 148). She is the symbolic mother of the first *mestizo*. "*Mestizo* illegitimacy underwrites *malinchismo*, by which Mexican women are always open to the accusation of treachery. . . . Thus, la Malinche potentially gives her name to all traitors, to all Mexicans who have been contaminated or seduced by foreign people, cultures, and values . . . , especially those emanating from the USA" (Allatson 149).

34. In the original: "Si no puedes devolverle a ese hombre su brazo, al menos

haz que por el resto de su vida se le pague una renta. —Y añadió que el accidente había sido culpa suya, por dejar a Don Casildo, que era un hombre mayor, a cargo del funcionamiento de las masas" (24).

35. In the original: "En esta casa las mujeres hablan cuando las gallinas mean, y te prohíbo que en adelante vuelvas a meter las narices en lo que no te importa. —Y mientras seguía golpeándola a diestra y siniestra, aseguraba que tan negreros habían sido los De la Valle como el resto de los hacendados de la comarca" (25).

36. In the original: "Nos preparábamos ya Ubaldino y yo a enfrentarnos a una vejez relativamente serena, premio de una vida ordenada y sin sobresaltos, cuando hice un descubrimiento aterrador. En sus correrías políticas por la Capital, Ubaldino había contraído sífilis y yo, aterrada de que la espina dorsal se me desintegrara o el cuerpo se me brotara de pústulas, me negué a tener más relaciones sexuales con él" (74).

37. In the original: "Por un lado defendía la independencia y bordaba, con su pico de oro, las glorias de nuestra patria mística, esa patria tan sentidamente cantada por nuestro gran Gautier . . . mientras que por otro lado se oponía violentamente a la ley de las quinientas cuerdas, al salario mínimo y a la jornada de ocho horas de trabajo, medidas que hundían a Guamaní cada vez más en el hambre y en la desesperación" (83).

38. In the original: "Y cuando, además de eso, se hizo evidente que el nuevo régimen económico—o sea la suplantación de la economía de haciendas por una economía de plantaciones—significaba la ruina de la clase hacendada insular y el comienzo de la participación independiente de la clase trabajadora en la vida política del país, la retórica 'patriótica' de los hacendados alcanzó tal nivel de demagogia que incluso el sector liberal de los profesionales no vaciló en ridiculizarla y condenarla" ("El país" 30).

39. In the original: "Y juré entonces a pleno pulmón, para que todo Guamaní me oyera, que ya que el apellido De la Valle era una farsa, y que nadie en aquella casa tenía derecho a él, yo, a la hora de mi muerte, los desheredaría a todos, y le dejaría la Central Justicia a Gloria Camprubí y a su hijo" (80).

40. In the original: "Escucha el restallar de las cañas encendidas como quien oye el chasquido de esos látigos de azúcar que ya no han de caer más sobre las espaldas indefensas de los peones; regocíjate porque la Central Justicia va por fin a desaparecer, consumida por el fuego de un amor maldito" (82).

41. While the central role of autobiography in U.S. Puerto Rican literature is beyond the scope of the present study, it is important to underscore its prevalence in the narratives of female authors. The preference for this genre signals a desire to assert their protagonists' Puerto Rican identity by cementing their experiences both on the island and in the diaspora.

42. In the original: "sitiales de cuero labrado que diz que pertenecieron en un tiempo a los doce pares de Francia"; or "la Catedral, el lecho centenario de los

De la Valle . . . [construído] con la quilla del galeón en que Juan Ponce de León había arribado a la isla hacía cuatro siglos" (69, 68).

43.   See "'More Room': Space, Woman, and Nation in Judith Ortíz Cofer's *Silent Dancing*," *Hispanic Journal* 22.2 (Fall 2001): 437–446.

44.   In addition to the grandfather, the narrator-protagonist's father represents an alternative depiction of the dominant father figure. Although his career in the U.S. Navy reinforces the stereotypes of the authoritarian and dominant patriarch, his extended journeys during navy duty ultimately render him an absent father figure. The physical and symbolic absence of the father, similar to the displacement of the grandfather, challenges traditional views of the dominant father figure by undermining his influence over his family.

45.   Two versions of the tale of María Sabida appear in *Folklore Portorriqueño: Cuentos y adivinanzas recogidos de la tradición oral* (1926), by Rafael Ramírez de Arellano, an island intellectual who compiled volumes of Puerto Rican folktales, riddles, and songs in an effort to preserve the island's tradition. A more recent version of the story emerged in the summer of 2001, when the New York–based Pregones Touring Puerto Rican Theatre performed the *Ballad of María Sabida*, an adaptation based on Ortíz Cofer's version of the tale. Although the implications of the tale's translocation from the literary to the theatrical realm have yet to be explored, the revival of this island-based myth among communities in the diaspora forces us to rethink the role that U.S. Puerto Ricans are playing in the recuperation and perpetuation of insular folklore.

46.   In *Silent Dancing*, the mother's acceptance by her husband's Spanish family is partly explained by the fact that she married at an early age, while she was still "an unspotted lamb," and her innocence (i.e., virginity) was valued above her race.

3. Retrieving the Past

1.   Felix Matos Rodríguez explains how "[*la nueva historia*] rejected the foundational paradigms of Puerto Rico's first generation of professional historians. . . . The younger generation introduced several innovations: a concern with documenting the life of oppressed and marginalized peoples in Puerto Rico; reliance on economics and material conditions as central explanatory phenomena and on the social sciences for theoretical and methodological insights; exploration of new and often untapped sources for research; and a desire to make the results of historical research available to audiences outside the academic community" ("New Currents" 194). While *la nueva historia* marked a period of significant progress and transformation in Puerto Rico's historiography, it has been critiqued by various sectors. See Matos Rodríguez's article for a more detailed analysis.

2.   In the original: "La emigración ha sido la otra gran ausente. En la historiografía puertorriqueña—tanto la 'vieja' historia como la 'nueva'—el estudio de la emigración *ha brillado por su ausencia*" (46).

3. Coincidentally, Ferré and García Ramis revolutionized Puerto Rican insular letters when they irrupted on the insular literary scene in 1976, the year they published their first short story collections, *Papeles de Pandora* and *La familia de todos nosotros*, respectively.

4. A closer look at these texts reveals a number of significant connections between them, which range from their references to Morel Campos's *danzas* in their titles to the image of the ruined house as symbolic of the disintegration of the dominant and totalizing metaphor of *la gran familia*.

5. Pérez Torres explains that her reservations about considering *Falsas crónicas* a bona fide example of "historiographic metafiction" is problematized by the correlation between this model and postmodernism. Given the overt pro-independence ideology that underlies some of the collection's texts, and the so-called incompatibility between postmodernism and neonationalist discourses, she questions the application of the postmodernist label to *Falsas crónicas del sur*.

6. In the original: "Como lo sugiere su metaficcional y satírico título, el texto intenta parodiar el género de la novela romántica. . . . El status ontológico del relato se complica entonces al estar constituido por una novela romántica escrita en forma de diario, enmarcada en otra narración que es un cuento (¿o una novela corta?)" (573).

7. In the original: "Me interné entonces en el denso universo de las bibliotecas públicas y los archivos privados para confirmar la proteica multiplicidad de 'los hechos' y la desconcertante ambigüedad de las perspectivas. Sobre las siempre cambiantes versiones de sucesos vividos o escuchados, construí éstas que ahora someto a la imaginación de ustedes" (*Falsas* 1).

8. In the original: "*El baúl de Miss Florence*, relato al que acabo de aludir, enfoca muy directamente la ideología esclavista y decididamente anti-abolicionista del ilustre inventor y su familia. El relato, además, le echa sal y vinagre a la llaga, insistiendo bastante sobre las fechorías del yerno de Morse, Edward Lind, en la famosa y muy opulenta Hacienda Enriqueta, antaño situada en la carretera de Arroyo a Patillas. Algunos lectores de Arroyo, que es un pueblo de fuertísima presencia negra, al enterarse de que su venerado héroe era nada menos que un racista negrero de siete suelas, pusieron el grito en el cielo. De inmediato surgieron propuestas para bajar del trono a Don Sami y poner en su lugar a algún héroe arroyano" ("Nosotros" 109).

9. In the original: "Pero estos desgraciados sucesos es mejor perdonarlos," he admits, "eclipsarlos con las relaciones edificantes de aquellos gestos de los que nuestros próceres también han sido capaces" (36).

10. In the original: "La llamada 'crisis de la agricultura' del decenio 1865–1875—la mayor de las crisis económicas del XIX—fue, en cambio, una de carácter *estructural* en la que se manifestó decisivamente la imposibilidad de prolongar la vida de la hacienda tradicional, fundamentada en el trabajo coaccionado (esclavo o de otro tipo) y en el uso de técnicas y métodos arcaicos de

transformación industrial. Esta crisis marcó el inicio de la desintegración de la hacienda tradicional, incapaz ya de generar suficiente plusvalía y sustentar la hegemonía social de sus propietarios" (Scarano 32). (The so-called agricultural crisis of the decade 1865–1875—the biggest economic crisis of the nineteenth century—was, in contrast, one of a *structural* character which clearly manifested the impossibility of extending the life-span of the traditional hacienda and was based on forced labor (slavery and others) and the use of archaic techniques and methods of industrial transformation. This crisis signaled the beginning of the disintegration of the traditional hacienda, incapable of producing enough capital gains and maintain the social hegemony of its owners).

11. In the original: "Al alcanzar el recodo del camino, entre la maleza espesa que oscurecía lo que una vez había sido el diseño perfecto de los jardines, divisé de pronto el perfil espectral de la casa. El sol de la media tarde lo encendía todo, revelándome la visión desoladora que en vano rechazaban mis ojos incrédulos. Con el techo hundido y las barandas desplomadas, mutilada su real escalera y condenadas por enormes tablas sus puertas y ventanas, la mansión señorial de *La Enriqueta* yacía, pasada su agonía, contra el verdor de los árboles como un cuerpo sin alma" (67). All translations of *El baúl* are from Andrew Hurley's translation, *Miss Florence's Trunk*.

12. In the original: "ese otro fuego parejo al nuestro [de ella y de Nicolás], que ha comenzado ya a crepitar al fondo de la casa" (81).

13. In the original: "los ríos de becina azul que derramamos ahora" (81).

14. In the original: "nos quedará la satisfacción de saber que ya nunca podrá escribir la apología de un hombre que él creía un líder y un prócer, y que estaba desde hacía tiempo tan corrupto" (81).

15. Edna Acosta-Belén and Santiago identify the 1970s as a pivotal point in Puerto Rican scholarship given that since that time "Puerto Rican scholars at North American universities and colleges have concentrated their efforts in recovering and documenting the historical roots and evolution of the Puerto Rican presence in the United States, especially the different ways in which Puerto Ricans construct and reaffirm a collective sense of identity within the various communities of the diaspora" (186).

16. In the original: "Otros se han mantenido en la marginalidad militando en las filas del desempleo y aferrados a las ayudas gubernamentales. Muchos de ellos terminaron como desertores escolares, adictos y asociados de la criminalidad. Lamentablemente, durante mucho tiempo se ha proyectado, tanto en los Estados Unidos como en Puerto Rico, una imagen negativa de los puertorriqueños que residen en ese país" (375).

17. See Martin Japtok's *Growing Up Ethnic: Nationalism and the Bildungsroman in African American and Jewish American Fiction* for a detailed analysis of this topic.

18. I draw on Fentress and Wickham's concept of *social memory* as opposed to the more widely used *collective memory* because I recognize the latter's

limitations. As the authors explain, "An important problem facing anyone who wants to follow Halbwachs in this field is how to elaborate a conception of memory which, while doing full justice to the collective side of one's conscious life, does not render the individual a sort of automaton, passively obeying the interiorized collective will. It is for this reason (as well as to avoid the image of a Jungian collective unconscious) that we shall normally use the term 'social memory' rather than 'collective memory', despite the greater recognizability of the latter phrase" (ix).

19. In the original: "que lucha por construir la nación a la manera de una familia, es 'ilegal' decir 'yo', tanto en el interior de los textos como en su presentación. Esa prohibición repercute, por supuesto, en los géneros que autoriza y fomenta esa literatura: de ahí que se haya marginado la poesía lírica o que se hayan cultivado muy poco los textos autobiográficos" (138).

20. In the original: "Yo te diría que en mi caso, el no sentirme puertorriqueña se debía a la influencia cultural de mi familia [española] y la escuela católica americana, la cual me hacía estar tan avergonzada de ser puertorriqueña. Yo no quería saber de Puerto Rico, yo quería ser americana. Cuando me gradué, solamente hablaba inglés" (90).

21. In the original: "yo, mis hermanos y primos éramos parte de una primera generación de puertorriqueños, en mi familia, porque nuestros padres eran hijos de españoles o dominicanos o cubanos" ("El deber" 78).

22. Quiles Rodríguez states, "Entre ambos lugares, el barrio y la ciudad, se desataron procesos complejos de interacción. . . . Atraídos por el progreso de San Juan, debido al desarrollo industrial y comercial, y empujados por la pobreza, resultado en parte del descalabro de la industria agrícola, una ola de migrantes del interior del país inundó la ciudad. Unos se alojaron en casas de vecindad y ranchones en la ciudad colonial y los barrios urbanos cercanos. Otros ocuparon el tremendal, los terrenos 'de nadie', los lugares de las márgenes para construir su propia versión de lo urbano" (*San Juan* 2–3).

23. García Ramis has stated that the genesis of the novel lies in her search for the roots of that generation that grew up in the 1950s ("El deber" 77).

24. While the myth's ideals of familial unity and uncontested patriarchal authority are also woven into the fabrics of the novels, my present focus is on how these novels question and rewrite alternative versions of the past.

25. In the original: "Eran los tiempos de esperanzas que todavía olían a nuevo. Eran años de cercenar montes de barro rojo para construir urbanizaciones, de abrir caminos de bitumul en cada monte verde, de florecer el cemento y los hoteles, de inaugurar represas y estaciones de electricidad . . . " (6). All translations of *Felices días* are from Carmen Esteves's *Happy Days, Uncle Sergio*.

26. Some examples of studies that focus on sexuality and political consciousness include Alvin Joaquín Figueroa's "Feminismo, homosexualidad e identidad política: el lenguaje del otro en *Felices días, Tío Sergio*" (*La Torre* 5.20 [1991]: 499–505); Luis Felipe Díaz's "Ideología y sexualidad en *Felices días, Tío*

Sergio de Magali García Ramis" (*Revista de Estudios Hispánicos* 21 [1994]: 325–341); Susana Matos Freire's "El sujeto femenino y la escritura: *Felices días, Tío Sergio* de Magali García Ramis" (*Revista de Estudios Hispánicos* 20 [1993]: 327–333); and Lawrence La Fountain-Stokes's "Tomboy Tantrums and Queer Infatuations: Reading Lesbianism in Magali García Ramis's *Felices días, Tío Sergio*" (in *Tortilleras: Hispanic and U.S. Latina Lesbian Expression,* ed. Lourdes Torres and Inmaculada Pertusa [Philadelphia: Temple UP, 2003]).

27. In the original: "En nuestra calle, casi todas las casas eran de madera, de dos o tres pisos, con salientes y torres de adorno y laterales de buhardilla, y todas las casas, desde la más pequeña, la de los Rojas, hasta la casi mansión de los Soto Morales, llevaban un nombre escrito al pie del portón de entrada o en una plaquita incrustada en la pared que daba a la calle: Villa Mercedes, Villa Sol, Villa Margarita. La nuestra era Villa Aurora" (39).

28. A significant amount of scholarship has been produced recently on the function of modern gated communities in the San Juan area. As Carlos Suárez-Carrasquillo puts it, "Industrialization has facilitated the emergence of these communities, in particular, its tendency of privatizing spaces in order to deal with social differences" (6). These social differences are also recognized by Ivelisse Rivera-Bonilla: "Only residents of elite residential areas can afford the costs of installing gateways, a practice that in turn increases their residence value and, thus, secures their privileged class status. It is in that sense, that gating serves to reasserts [*sic*] both a particular class position and social difference" (237). She proposes that one "of the unexpected consequences of the simultaneous proliferation of these three types of closed-off housing models is the material and symbolic hardening of class differences" (262).

29. Quiles Rodríguez describes the role of the balcony in urban Puerto Rico as follows: "El balcón constituye una metáfora de la vivienda y de la presencia de los moradores en la comunidad. Establece un diálogo con la casa y la calle. Es el lugar donde la casa, como espacio privado se protege de la calle, el lugar donde la casa como objeto público se convierte en parte de la calle. El balcón es un espacio de transición, un mediador entre el afuera y el adentro" (The balcony constitutes a sort of metaphor for the dwelling itself and the presence of its inhabitants within the community. It establishes a dialogue between the house and the street. It is the place where the house, as private space, protects itself from the street, the place where the house as a public object becomes an extension of the street. The balcony is a space of transition, a mediator between the outside and the inside") (*La ciudad* 109).

30. In the original: "pasábamos la vida en el balcón, mirando pasar a la gente que se aventuraba a caminar bajo el sol terrible, oyendo a lo lejos a los niños de la calle jugar todos los juegos peligrosos del mundo—calle, niños y mundo vedado para nosotros—y velando a la Margara" (7).

31. In the original: "El balcón establecía el límite del entorno cotidiano y hacía presentes en el espacio público a los que permanecían mucho tiempo en

las casas: las mujeres, los niños y los ancianos. Para los niños era un espacio educativo, su primera exposición a la vida de la ciudad. El balcón, frontera de la intimidad, era un lugar de estar donde la actividad cotidiana fluía continuamente" (*La ciudad* 111).

32. In the original: "'Mi abuelo se embarcó por unos años,' 'y nunca volvió a ver la tierra de sus padres,' decía Sara F. y aquí el tono era dramático. 'Entonces conoció a Mamá.' '¿Verdad que ella es francesa?,' decía Andrés. 'No, no, su mamá era de las islas francesas, su papá era canario, de Islas Canarias, Don Manuel Villegas y Castro, y su mamá era Marie Dubois'" (40).

33. In the original: "Setenta años más allá de haber vivido en España, con tres generaciones de por medio, la legitimidad de los aspirantes al trono no dejaba de ser discutida en mi familia" (86).

34. Casa de España was designed by the architect Pedro de Castro and was built in 1932 to provide a meeting place for an organization of Spanish citizens living in Puerto Rico.

35. In the original: "Juntos, separados, haciendo muecas, mostrando nuestros disfraces, poniéndonos cuernos por detrás de las cabezas, parados derechitos, españolizados en aquel ambiente, eternizados como españolitos para futuras generaciones de Solís, blancos, gente y miembros de la Casa de España" (128).

36. In the original: "Y así fui llevada en peregrinaje a la tierra de los ancestros, pues se suponía que todas nuestras raíces venían de Europa. Algunos primos españoles me parecieron más oscuros de la cuenta, pero cuando volví y se lo conté a Andrés me dijo que recordara que los moros estuvieron en España 800 años, pero que no molestara a la familia con eso, y yo tan civilizada y señorita, ni se lo comenté" (148).

37. This topic has recently been explored by the U.S. Puerto Rican poet Víctor Hernández Cruz in his latest collection, *The Mountain in the Sea* (2006), where he writes about the connections between the Caribbean and the Maghreb. As he reminds us in one interview, "The European culture that came to the Spanish-speaking Americas was the Spanish culture of the Mediterranean coasts, and this culture had been under Islamic Moroccan influence for many centuries" (*Poet's Truth* 56).

38. In the original: "Era un hombre. Y nosotros, por todo lo que podíamos recordar de nuestras vidas, habíamos vivido siempre entre mujeres. . . . en la cotidianeidad de nuestro mundo, todo era organizado, ideado y llevado a cabo por mujeres" (13).

39. In the original: "Y sobre todas ellas, y sobre nosotros, estaba Mamá Sara. Mamá Sara tenía una silla alta, como de reina, que ponía a la cabecera de la mesa del comedor e insistía en que la del otro lado se dejara vacía para que allí se sentara el Hombre, que podía ser, según quien estuviera de visita, el tío Roberto, el monseñor Serrano o aún el Primo Germánico" (15).

40. In the original: "dominaba en espíritu el hogar sin hombre de nuestra familia" (15).

41. In the original: "se parecía a nosotros pero era un extraño" (12).

42. In the original: "el Tío Sergio se sentaba a leer junto a nosotros, o a buscar en los anaqueles, libreros y tablillas que forraban el cuarto, entre los libros y papeles viejos de Papá, todas las cosas sin ningún valor que son las que las familias más valoran: fotos de viajes, tarjetas de cumpleaños, lentes viejos, todo lo que había ido quedando por espacio de cuarenta años en las esquinas del estudio" (41).

43. In the original: "Entonces quiso ver las fotos. Pidió que todos buscáramos las fotos de la familia y quiso verlas y repasarlas todas. . . . Y Tío Sergio se dispuso a organizarlas, a sacar copias de las que estaban muy gastadas, a mandar a hacer ampliaciones de las que más le gustaban, a escribirles los nombres y fechas aproximados de cuando se tomaron. . . . —Hay que tomar unas de la casa, por si la tumban, decía.—Hay que hacer un árbol genealógico—nos dijo" (133).

44. In the original: "No tenías que haber ido allá, no te metas en problemas" (57).

45. In the original: "No es bueno que uno visite las casas de los nacionalistas. . . . Uno no debe mezclarse con gente así porque entonces van a creer que uno es como ellos" (58).

46. In the original: "ellos existían como algo prohibido, y [nosotros] queríamos verlos" (77).

47. In the original: "Era cierto que no sabíamos casi nada de nuestro país, porque ni ellos ni nadie nos lo había enseñado. Vivimos tantos años encerrados tras el cerco agridulce de la casa donde todo lo heredado era europeo y todo lo porvenir era norteamericano, que no podíamos saber quiénes éramos" (157).

48. In the original: "Años después cuando les cuestionamos, mi familia negó que hubiesen condicionado la relación de Tío Sergio con nosotros a que no nos hablara nunca de cosas de Puerto Rico, pero creemos que sí, porque no volvió a hablarnos jamás de ningún prócer, ni nosotros a preguntarle" (64).

49. In the original: "Los adultos no sospechan jamás, o quieren imaginar que no existen, lazos íntimos y fuertísimos entre sus niños y la gente prohibida" (84).

50. In the original: "toda esa música que mi familia rechazaba porque preferían escuchar pasodobles españoles y canciones de películas americanas" (154).

51. In the original: "para que [se] fuera con [su] música a otra parte" (154).

52. In the original: "Del lado del Bien estaban la religion Católica, Apostólica y Romana, el Papa, Estados Unidos, los americanos, Eisenhower, Europa, sobre todo los europeos finos, Grace Kelly, la gente preferiblemente blanca, todos los militares, Franco, Evita Perón, la ópera, la zarzuela, todos los productos de España. . . . Del lado del Mal estaban los comunistas, los ateos, los masones, los protestantes, los nazis, las naciones recién formadas por negros en Africa (porque derramaban sangre europea y mataban hermanitas de la caridad), los nacionalistas e independentistas puertorriqueños, el mambo, Trujillo, Batista y María Felix, pájara mala culpable de que Jorge Negrete estuviera en el Infierno" (33).

53. Although homosexuality does not appear on this list, there are examples of the Solís homophobia throughout the text (35).

54. In the original: "él como que no encajaba en ningún lugar" (121); "un paria, un inconforme y, probablemente, un homosexual" (160).

55. For example, Sandra Cisneros's *House on Mango Street*, Cristina García's *Dreaming in Cuban*, Julia Álvarez's *How the García Girls Lost Their Accents*, Esmeralda Santiago's *When I Was Puerto Rican*, Denise Chávez's *Face of an Angel*, and Helena María Viramontes's *Under the Feet of Jesus*, to name a few.

56. I know for a fact, through conversations with colleagues who teach at the high school level in Puerto Rico, that they have taught this book in their history classes. Although this is an isolated example, it speaks to the advantages of teaching the work in Puerto Rican history courses.

57. It is important to stress, as Flores points out in *The Diaspora Strikes Back*, that my argument applies to the literature of first-generation U.S. Puerto Rican women. The second and third generations do not tend to exhibit the same degree of attachment to the island. Torres-Padilla stresses that "with every passing generation firmly rooted in the United States, the [island] metaphor loses relevance and currency," to the point that it is possible that these writers "view Puerto Rico from a widening distance that foments weary recognition of—if not disinterest in—island culture, politics, and current events" (as the case of Abraham Rodríguez illustrates) (88).

58. "Several crucial elements were required to achieve the increases in per capita income that the massive industrialization process of Operation Bootstrap was intended to produce. First, population growth had to be reduced. . . . Family planning and population control initiatives to reduce births on the island and accelerated migration to the United States were given high priority" (Acosta Belén and Santiago 76).

59. Commenting on the importance of the traditional setting of the *círculo democrático*, Marsh Kennerley observes, "En la mayoría de las ocasiones [el círculo] estaba enmarcado en un paisaje rural. Éste era el círculo que Muñoz había inaugurado en sus primeras campañas electorales, la conversación al aire libre, fuera del gabinete letrado, en el batey" (181). (In most cases the rural landscape formed the [circle's] backdrop. This was the circle that Muñoz had inaugurated during his first electoral campaigns, the open-air conversation, outside government offices, in the batey).

60. According to Irwin-Zarecka, "To construct a sense of community, one almost inevitably needs the presence of the Other; the oppressor serves this role very well indeed" (60).

61. These distinctions are further emphasized by the divergent class experiences that these two protagonists have: as a middle-class girl, Lidia is trapped inside her urban home, whereas Negi, as a lower-class girl, enjoys more freedom to roam outside, particularly in Macún.

62. According to Guerra, in the 1930s "the majority of the rural families

lived in small one-room huts elevated on poles and made of boards, thatch, palm bark, and occasionally galvanized metal roofing. . . . Most Puerto Ricans' dwellings were barren of any but the most basic material possessions, yet inevitably they were overcrowded. As such, they could easily become sources for the spreading of disease due to a lack of sanitation facilities and limited access to water" (33).

63. The image of el Mangle (i.e., Caño Martín Peña)—a shantytown established in a swampy area of the Santurce–Hato Rey vicinity as a result of rural migration to urban areas—is also a central component in Alba Ambert's *A Perfect Silence,* another (semi)autobiographical coming-of-age narrative that traces the protagonist's journey back and forth between Puerto Rico and New York during the Great Migration.

4. Patriarchal Foundations

1. The threat that women pose to the nation is primarily seen as a function of female sexuality, as Ania Loomba explains: "The fear of cultural and racial pollution prompts the most hysterical dogmas about racial difference and sexual behaviours because it suggests the instability of 'race' as a category. Sexuality is thus a means for the maintenance or erosion of racial difference. Women on both sides of the colonial divide demarcate both the innermost sanctums of race, culture and nation, as well as the porous frontiers through which these are penetrated. Their relationship to colonial discourses is mediated through this double positioning" (159).

2. *Heteropatriarchy* is a term used to refer to the intersection and workings of heterosexuality and patriarchy. The father figure at the center of the heteropatriarchal family model must always be a heterosexual male who enjoys a privileged position within the gender hierarchy (Craske 201).

3. The parallels between woman and colony have been the subject of recent scholarship in the field of postcolonial feminism, as exemplified by the title of Maria Mies and Veronika Bennholdt-Thomsen's study, *Women: The Last Colony.* As the authors see it, women and colonies are both relegated to the "realm of nature" and are therefore treated "as if they did not belong to society proper" under any kind of exploitative system (5).

4. According to Mies, "Not only is this concept [the family] used and universalized in a rather Eurocentric way, presenting the nuclear family as the basic and timeless structure of all institutionalization of men-women relations, it also hides the fact that this institution's structure is hierarchical and unegalitarian" (69).

5. *Machismo,* according to Nikki Craske, "endorses aggressive behaviour including heavy drinking and violent behaviour when protecting 'honour,' stresses fecundity, and assumes a male breadwinning role" (215).

6. Rafael Ramírez cautions the reader against viewing *machismo* as synonymous with sexism: "Sexism is an ideology that is of great specificity and lacks

the contradictions and ambiguities of the term 'machismo.' Sexism is based on
biological differences between men and women and, in turn, maintains that
these differences are expressed by or are translated into cultural characteristics
or behaviors. Sexism argues a specificity about each sex, an inherent inequality
that attributes to one sex superiority over the other" (19). He concludes that
machismo cannot be easily defined due to its complexity; there are simply too
many variations and subtleties, "according to the conceptualizations or pur-
poses of those who write about the subject" (11). What he does assure us is that
machismo has been misunderstood and has led to reductionism by presenting
men as homogeneous and disregarding the complexities of masculinity (23).

7. Acosta-Belén explains that "throughout the first three and a half centuries
of Spanish colonial rule in Puerto Rico there was an absence of a feminist consciousness or a feminist movement, in contrast to other more developed regions
of the world where these movements develop in the early nineteenth century.
This situation was evidently the result of the low educational and employment
levels of the vast majority of the female population" ("Puerto Rican Women" 3).
She adds that the backwardness of the island had a profound influence on the
lack of educational opportunities for women, because "in spite of these achievements by a handful of women, for three centuries of colonial rule, Puerto Rico
remained one of Spain's most backward colonies. Education for women was
practically unknown and reserved for the privileged class. Illiteracy, particularly among the peasant population, was rampant" ("Puerto Rican Women" 5).

8. Paradoxically, Marqués's fierce defense of patriarchy and his "existential-
ist machismo"—as Efraín Barradas has proposed—does not appear to correspond, or reflect, his homosexuality. In a way, the contrast between his misog-
yny and his homosexuality is a reminder that gender and sexuality are distinct
categories.

9. Craske observes, "If Western conceptions of men's sexuality stress the
active, women's sexuality has been dichotomized around the virgin/whore complex. In the former, women are seen as pure and non-carnal, more associated
with mothering than female sexuality. . . . In the latter women are temptresses
and anything but passive. This representation fits the Eve paradigm where she
tempts Adam away from good behaviour and into sin" (203).

10. According to Carmen Teresa Whalen, "As Puerto Rican women arrived
in the continental United States, policy makers and social service workers constructed a 'culture of poverty' narrative to interpret their experiences. The culture of poverty was a national discourse, with important local and gendered
dimensions, that attributed Puerto Ricans' perceived problems to their culture"
(217). Among these problems was the fact that "women were portrayed as fail-
ures in their reproductive roles. They were 'submissive wives' who had too many
children, and inadequate mothers" (218).

11. Ana Lydia Vega has traced the transformation of Puerto Rican literature
to the publication of Ferré's *Papeles de Pandora*: "La expropiación femenina

de la narrativa puertorriqueña es bastante reciente. Data, en mi opinión, de la publicación del importantísimo *Papeles de Pandora* en 1976" (The feminine expropiation of Puerto Rican narrative is quite recent. It dates, in my opinion, to the publication of the very important *Papeles de Pandora* in 1976) ("De bípeda" 94).

12. In the original: "Aparentemente, son ellos—*los* escritores—los únicos que en la sociedad puertorriqueña han reaccionado con agresividad y rebeldía ante la desaparición del último baluarte cultural desde donde podía aún combatirse, en parte, la docilidad colectiva: el *machismo*, versión criolla de la fusión y adaptación de dos conceptos seculares, la *honra* española y el *pater familiae* romano" ("El puertorriqueño" 175; my emphasis).

13. Margarita Ostolaza Bey's observations on the connection between patriarchy and the island's pro-independence movement, which traces its roots to the nationalist party, can also illuminate the conflict that exists between nationalism and feminism in Puerto Rican culture. According to her, "La prédica independentista, tal como se ha planteado en Puerto Rico, aparece amenazante para la mujer. . . . El independentismo tradicional, nacionalista . . . se ha escandalizado ante las reformas feministas tales como el derecho de la mujer sobre el propio cuerpo o el control de la natalidad y el divorcio. . . . Recordemos una vez más: para la mujer, todo tiempo pasado siempre fue peor" (The pro-independence discourse, as it has emerged in Puerto Rico, appears threatening to women. . . . The traditional nationalist pro-independence movement . . . has been scandalized by feminist reforms such as women's rights over their bodies or birth control, and divorce. . . . We have to keep in mind that for women, the past was always worse) (126).

14. In the original: "Escritora y puertorriqueña, tremendo cruce de cables. Leves contradicciones asoman entre una y otra misión evangélica"(93).

15. Fernández Olmos has observed, "Los escritos de las autoras puertorriqueñas en la actualidad contrastan con las viejas imágenes de las mujeres creadas por los escritores durante la fecunda producción narrativa de los años 40 y 50" (The writings of contemporary Puerto Rican women authors contrast with the old-fashioned images of women created by male writers during the prolific narrative production of the 1940s and 1950s) ("Desde una" 304).

16. In her essay, "De bípeda desplumada a escritora puertorriqueña," Ana Lydia Vega comments about the repercussions that the publishing of her novel had for Nolla: "Cuenta otra [Nolla] que sus amigos más fieles y respetuosos han comenzado súbitamente a intentar seducirla tras la publicación de su libro, quien alguien clasificó XXX. Esta recatada madre de familia se ha convertido en 'mujer fácil' en virtud (valga la expresioncita) de una supuesta ninfomanía literaria" (Another friend [Nolla] has talked about how her most faithful and respectful friends have suddenly tried to seduce her following the publication of her book, which someone rated as XXX. This modest mother has become a 'loose woman' by virtue (pardon the pun) of an alleged literary nymphomania)

(97). Vega's observation regarding her female colleague, who by all indications is Nolla, is illustrative of how the discourse of sexuality remains a masculine terrain, threatening any woman who reappropriates this discourse to be judged as *Eva*, even when her actual behavior is in alignment with the *Ave* side of the dichotomy.

17. In the original: "El viejo Ríos nunca la perdonó. Hizo todas las trampas del mundo para dejarla sin un centavo. Se murió maldiciendo su nombre y el de su esposa por haberle dado una hija semejante" (31). Hintz has argued that "the primary voice of the novel is a homodiegetic witness to the events of the protagonist's life" and that in the end this homodiegetic witness "becomes an autodiegetic, proleptic narrator of what might happen to her life in the future" (409). Because I do not completely agree on the reason for the transformation of the homodiegetic witness into an autodiegetic narrator—which Hintz bases on one single utterance—I believe that in following Gennette's model, a better classification would be a homodiegetic-extradiegetic narrator, given that this voice is part of the narrative while also it seems to have virtually complete knowledge of the story she narrates.

18. In the original: "los hombres quieren a las mujeres obedientes nada más: por eso insisten tanto, cuando somos chiquitas, en que seamos obedientes. Cuando las mujeres hacen lo que quieren, los hombres dejan de quererlas; las castigan, eso es. Abuela pensaba como los hombres, eso creo" (25).

19. In the original: "Cuando se fue mi madre, los primeros días no nos hizo falta" (24).

20. In the original: "Los habitantes de una casa organizan la vida alrededor de [los niños]: hay que vestirlos y bañarlos, alimentarlos y distraerlos y quererlos mucho. Son los dioses: tan caprichosos como ellos; tan exigentes. Yo sabía estas cosas porque siempre viví en una casa llena de niños y de familiares. Pero no me había dado cuenta, porque yo era dios. Ahora, al crecer, he pasado a ser servidora. A mucha gente no le gusta que sea así y por eso no les gustan los niños. Yo entiendo que así es la vida, que así tiene que ser: como Abuela, eso es. Esmeralda nunca ha entendido. Tal vez por eso es diferente y tal vez por eso la odio" (77).

21. In the original: "un experto jugador de los juegos eróticos oficinescos, un campeón. Ella no lo sabía porque acababa de llegar de Worcester y su temprana infancia transcurrió en Jayuya. Se enamoró perdidamente" (53).

22. In the original: "Ella vivió durante años esa vida de mujer soltera que aterra a muchas mujeres. No se trata de la mujer divorciada que creía dos o tres niños y trabaja en una oficina y tiene que ir a corte porque la pensión alimenticia no llega; el exmarido volvió a casarse y no quiere pagar. Se trata de la soltera de treinta años que siente la presión familiar para casarse y si no lo hace piensa que su vida es un fracaso" (89).

23. In the original: "Se casará con un hombre rico diez años mayor que ella"; "aplicará sus conocimientos universitarios y su experiencia profesional a la administración de la casa"; "dará a luz un hijo. . . . Se sentirá realizada y

volverá a pensar que la vida tiene sentido"; "será un factor positivo en la carrera profesional de su marido" (91–92).

24. In the original: "ella se convertirá en la mujer que él siempre soñó tener. Ella será idéntica a su ideal" (93).

25. This same predicament was also faced by other U.S. Latina women in the post–civil rights movement era and became a key issue in the politics of academia at the time. As Acosta-Belén and Bose explain, "Out of the subordination of Latinas and their initial exclusion from both a male dominated ethnic studies movement and a white-dominated women's movement, Chicanas, puertorriqueñas, and women from other disenfranchised U.S. ethnoracial minorities began to forge and articulate a feminist consciousness and a collective sense of struggle based on their experiences as members of diverse individual nationalities, as well as on their collective panethnic and cross-border identities as Latinas and women of color" ("U.S. Latina and Latin American Feminisms" 1114).

26. Margarita Ostolaza Bey's *Política sexual en Puerto Rico* addresses the dynamics through which Puerto Rican men's subordination under colonialism works to strengthen their domination at home as a way to cope with their own feelings of oppression as colonial subjects (44). M. Jacqui Alexander echoes this claim when she states, "Violence within the domestic sphere, then, did not originate there but drew strength from, and at times was legitimated by, larger organized state and economic violence, which was itself responsible for the increase of sexual violence within the home" (*Pedagogies* 72).

27. Regarding the effects of masculine domination on sexuality, Bourdieu says, "If the sexual relation appears as a social relation of domination, this is because it is constructed through the fundamental principle of division between the active male and the passive female and because this principle creates, organizes, expresses and directs desire—male desire as the desire for possession, eroticized domination, and female desire as the desire for masculine domination, as eroticized subordination or even, in the limiting case, as the eroticized recognition of domination" (21).

28. It is important to call attention to the irony behind Casto's name. Literally translated as "chaste," the husband's name seems to mock precisely the essence of manhood in *machista* cultures, which stresses masculine sexuality.

29. Casto's sense of failure as a man is based on the correlation between masculinity and a man's capacity to sexually satisfy a woman. As Ramírez suggests, "Satisfying a woman or believing that he has satisfied her is very important for the man. The need to bring her to orgasm or many orgasms, in addition to giving her pleasure, is due to the male's presentation as a powerful individual. In addition, this need is in keeping with the belief that a sexually unsatisfied woman is a potential adulteress because she may find, or look for, another man *que se lo haga mejor* (who will do it better for her)" (48). This notion is also echoed by Bourdieu, who states, "Male pleasure is, in part, enjoyment of female pleasure, of the power to give pleasure" (20).

30. Regarding the latter, Maria Mies states, "The aim of the witch-hunt was not only to effect direct disciplinary control over women's sexual and reproductive behaviour but also to establish the superiority of male over female productivity. . . . The ideologues of the witch-hunt were indefatigable in denouncing female nature as sinful ('sin' is synonymous with 'nature'), as sexually uncontrollable, insatiable and ever ready to seduce the virtuous male. . . . [T]heir sexual activity was seen as a threat to the virtuous man, that is the man who wants to control the purity of his offspring, the heirs to his property" (90). Mies's observation draws a connection between women's sexuality and reproductive capabilities and men's anxiety over the legitimacy of their offspring. The fact that paternity can be questionable, as opposed to the indisputability of maternity, leads men to "secure" their paternity by strictly controlling female sexuality.

31. Reminding us of the limits of the weapons of the weak, Bourdieu states, "These strategies, which are not strong enough really to subvert the relation of domination, at least have the effect of confirming the dominant representation of women as maleficent beings, whose purely negative identity is made up essentially of taboos each of which presents a possibility of transgression" (32).

32. María Jesús Pola Z. supports this position: "Durante mucho tiempo, el reducto familiar fue intocable y protegido por la creencia de una privacidad que había que mantener a toda costa, invisibilizó grandes crímenes contra las mujeres, las/os niñas/os y las/os envejecientes" (For a long time, the family redoubt was untouchable and protected by the belief in a privacy that had to be kept by any means, it rendered invisible awful crimes against women, children, and the elderly) (125). The silence surrounding the issue of domestic violence was broken in 1989 with the passage of Puerto Rico's Domestic Violence Prevention and Intervention Law (better known as Ley 54, or Law 54). According to Jenny Rivera, Law 54 was "considered a model internationally because of its ambitious and comprehensive approach to domestic violence, its recognition of the seriousness of violence against women, and its criminalization components" (348).

Epilogue

1. In the original: "La mujer, triunfante ya en la lucha, ha sabido en el mundo de hoy beneficiarse sabiamente de los derechos legales. Pero, más sabiamente aún, no ha permitido que el goce de esos derechos de igualdad ante la ley la priven de las dos misiones primordiales para las cuales Dios la puso en el mundo: el amor y la maternidad" (viii).

2. In the original: "Es asombroso cómo, la mujer en el Puerto Rico de hoy, sin descuidar sus sagrados deberes de esposa y madre, ha podido llegar a ser tan útil y activa en sus deberes de ciudadana" (63).

3. In the original: "Para que la madre pueda dedicarse a la noble tarea de la maternidad, el hombre asume la responsabilidad de librarla a ella de la carga

económica. Es decir, en el matrimonio el hombre es responsable de sostener el hogar. Él provee bienestar económico a la mujer" (7).

4. In the original: "[La mujer] [e]s un ser humano con voz y voto en las elecciones políticas, en decisiones comunales, en el manejo de los problemas del hogar, en las relaciones matrimoniales" (23).

5. In the original: "promover, divulgar y rescatar las manifestaciones culturales de Puerto Rico" (copyright page).

6. In the original: "una puesta al día del *Libro del Pueblo* (sic) sobre los derechos de las mujeres" (back cover).

7. In the original: "Para ese entonces, era una creencia prevaleciente que a las mujeres no se les debía educar, no se les debía enseñar a leer, pues la cultura machista sostenía que la educación las echaría a perder y no seguirían siendo esposas sumisas y madres abnegadas" (14).

8. In the original: "Sin embargo, todavía las mujeres no reciben igual paga por igual trabajo. . . . Siguen siendo objeto sexual descarnado y burdo de los anuncios publicitarios y de los medios de comunicación en general" (38).

9. In the original: "Para resumir, todavía hay un déficit de democracia en la vida de las mujeres, aún cuando ellas han resistido y luchado por su igualdad" (39).

Bibliography

Acosta-Belén, Edna. "Beyond Island Boundaries: Ethnicity, Gender, and Cultural Revitalization in Nuyorican Literature." *Callaloo* 15.4 (1992): 979–998. Online.

——. "Ideology and Images of Women in Contemporary Puerto Rican Literature." *The Puerto Rican Woman: Perspectives on Culture, History, and Society.* Ed. Edna Acosta-Belén. New York: Praeger, 1986. 120–146. Print.

——. "Puerto Rican Women in Culture, History, and Society." *The Puerto Rican Woman: Perspectives on Culture, History, and Society.* Ed. Edna Acosta-Belén. New York: Praeger, 1986. 1–29. Print.

Acosta-Belén, Edna, and Christine Bose. "U.S. Latina and Latin American Feminisms: Hemispheric Encounters." *Signs* 25.4 (Summer 2000): 1113–1119. Online.

Acosta-Belén, Edna, and Carlos E. Santiago. *Puerto Ricans in the United States: A Contemporary Portrait.* Boulder: Lynne Rienner, 2006. Print.

Acuña, Rodolfo. *Occupied America: The Chicano's Struggle toward Liberation.* New York: Canfield P, 1972. Print.

Alexander, M. Jacqui. *Pedagogies of Crossing: Meditations on Feminism, Sexual Politics, Memory, and the Sacred.* Durham: Duke UP, 2005. Print.

Alexander, M. Jacqui, and Chandra Talpade Mohanty. "Introduction: Genealogies, Legacies, Movements." *Feminist Genealogies, Colonial Legacies, Democratic Futures.* Ed. M. Jacqui Alexander and Chandra Talpade Mohanty. New York: Routledge, 1997. xiii–xlii. Print.

Allatson, Paul. *Key Terms in Latino/a Cultural and Literary Studies.* Malden, MA: Blackwell Publishing, 2007. Print.

Ambert, Alba. *A Perfect Silence.* Houston: Arte Público P, 1995. Print.

Anderson, Benedict. *Imagined Communities: Reflections on the Origin and Spread of Nationalism.* London: Verso, 1983. Print.

Aparicio, Frances. "Jennifer as Selena: Rethinking Latinidad in Media and Popular Culture." *Latino Studies* 1.1 (March 2003): 90–105. Print.

——. "Latino Cultural Studies: Frances Aparicio Interviewed by Juan

Zevallos Aguilar." *Critical Latin American and Latino Studies.* Ed. Juan Poblete. Minneapolis: U of Minnesota P, 2003. 3–31. Print.

———. *Listening to Salsa: Gender, Latin Popular Music, and Puerto Rican Cultures.* Hanover, NH: Wesleyan UP, 1998. Print.

———. "*Salsa, Maracas,* and *Baile*: Latin Popular Music in the Poetry of Víctor Hernández Cruz." *MELUS* 16.1 (Spring 1989–1990): 43–58. Print.

———. "Writing Migrations: Transnational Readings of Rosario Ferré and Víctor Hernández Cruz." *Latino Studies* 4.1–2 (2006): 79–95. Online.

Arroyo, Jossianna. "'Roots' or the Virtualities of Racial Imaginaries in Puerto Rico and the Diaspora." *Latino Studies* 8.2 (2010): 195–219. Online.

Ayala, César, and Rafael Bernabé. *Puerto Rico in the American Century: A History since 1898.* Chapel Hill: U of North Carolina P, 2007. Print.

Azize-Vargas, Yamila. "The Emergence of Feminism in Puerto Rico, 1870–1930." *Latino/a Thought: Culture, Politics, and Society.* Ed. Francisco H. Vázquez and Rodolfo D. Torres. Lanham, MD: Rowman & Littlefield, 2003. 175–184. Print.

Barradas, Efraín. "Los silencios del canónigo: Francisco Manrique Cabrera y su *Historia de la literatura puertorriqueña.*" *Revista de Estudios Hispánicos* 30.1 (2003): 23–36. Print.

———. *Partes de un todo: Ensayos y notas sobre literatura puertorriqueña en los Estados Unidos.* San Juan: Editorial UPR, 1998. Print.

Belaval, Emilio. *Los problemas de la cultura puertorriqueña.* Río Piedras: Cultural, 1977. Print.

Blanco, Tomás. *El prejuicio racial en Puerto Rico.* Río Piedras: Huracán, 1985. (1942). Print.

———. *Prontuario histórico de Puerto Rico.* Río Piedras: Huracán, 1983. (1935). Print.

Bose, Christine, and Edna Acosta-Belén. *Women in the Latin American Development Process.* Philadelphia: Temple UP, 1995. Print.

Bost, Suzanne. "Transgressing Borders: Puerto Rican and Latina *Mestizaje.*" *MELUS* 25.2 (2000): 187–211. Online.

Bourdieu, Pierre. *Masculine Domination.* Trans. Richard Nice. Stanford: Stanford UP, 2001. Print.

Brison, Susan J. "Trauma Narratives and the Remaking of the Self." *Acts of Memory: Cultural Recall in the Present.* Ed. Mieke Bal, Jonathan Crewe, Leo Spitzer. Hanover, NH: Darthmouth College, UP of New England, 1999. 39–54. Print.

Bustos Fernández, María José. "Subversión de la autoridad narrativa en *Maldito amor* de Rosario Ferré." *Chasqui* 23.2 (1994): 22–29. Print.

Caminero-Santangelo, Marta. *The Madwoman Can't Speak: Or Why Insanity Is Not Subversive.* Ithaca: Cornell UP, 1998. Print.

Cancel, Mario. *Literatura y narrativa puertorriqueña: La escritura de entre siglos.* San Juan: Editorial Pasadizo, 2007. Print.

Cancel, Mario, and Héctor Feliciano Ramos. *Puerto Rico: Su transformación en el tiempo*. San Juan: Editorial Cordillera, 2008. Print.

Celani, David P. *The Illusion of Love: Why the Battered Woman Returns to Her Abuser*. New York: Columbia UP, 1994. Print.

Coss, Luis Fernando. *La nación en la orilla (respuesta a los posmodernos pesimistas)*. San Juan: Punto de Encuentro, 1996. Print.

Craske, Nikki. "Gender and Sexuality in Latin America." *The Companion to Latin American Studies*. Ed. Philip Swanson. London: Arnold, 2003. 200–221. Print.

Cruz-Malavé, Arnaldo. "Toward an Art of Transvestism: Colonialism and Homosexuality in Puerto Rican Literature." *¿Entiendes? Queer Readings, Hispanic Writings*. Ed. Emilie L. Bergmann and Paul Julian Smith. Durham: Duke UP, 1995. 137–167. Print.

Dávila, Arlene. *Latinos, Inc.: The Marketing and Making of a People*. Berkeley: U of California P, 2001. Print.

———. *Latino Spin: Public Image and the Whitewashing of Race*. New York: New York UP, 2008. Print.

———. *Sponsored Identities: Cultural Politics in Puerto Rico*. Philadelphia: Temple UP, 1997. Print.

Dentith, Simon, and Philip Dodd. "The Uses of Autobiography." *Literature and History* 14 (1988): 4–22. Print.

Díaz Quiñones, Arcadio. "Tomás Blanco: Racismo, Historia, Esclavitud." Introduction. *El prejuicio racial en Puerto Rico*. By Tomás Blanco. Río Piedras: Huracán, 1985. 13–91. Print.

———. *La memoria rota: Ensayos sobre cultura y política*. 2nd ed. San Juan: Ediciones Huracán, 1996. Print.

División de Educación de la Comunidad. *10 Poetas Puertorriqueños*. Ed. René Marqués. San Juan: Departamento de Instrucción Pública, n.d. Print.

———. *Emigración*. Ed. René Marqués. San Juan: Departamento de Instrucción Pública, c. 1954. Print.

———. *La familia*. Ed. René Marqués. San Juan: Departamento de Instrucción Pública, c. 1955. Print.

———. *La mujer y sus derechos*. Ed. René Marqués. San Juan: Departamento de Instrucción Pública, 1957. Print.

———. *Los derechos del hombre*. Ed. René Marqués. San Juan: Departamento de Instrucción Pública, 1957. Print.

Duany, Jorge. "Popular Music in Puerto Rico: Toward an Anthropology of 'Salsa.'" *Latin American Music Review/Revista de música latinoamericana* 5.2 (Autumn–Winter 1984): 186–216. Online.

———. *The Puerto Rican Nation on the Move: Identities on the Island and in the United States*. Chapel Hill: U of North Carolina P, 2002. Print.

Duncan, Karen A. *Healing from the Trauma of Childhood Sexual Abuse: The Journey for Women*. Westport, CT: Praeger, 2004. Print.

Eakin, Paul John. *Living Autobiographically: How We Create Identity in Narrative*. Ithaca: Cornell UP, 2008. Print.

———. *Touching the World: Reference in Autobiography*. Princeton: Princeton UP, 1992. Print.

Fentress, James, and Chris Wickham. *Social Memory*. Oxford: Blackwell, 1992. Print.

Fernández Olmos, Margarite. "Desde una perspectiva femenina: La cuentística de Rosario Ferré y Ana Lydia Vega." *Homines* 8.2 (1984): 303–311. Print.

———. "*Growing Up Puertorriqueña*: The Feminist *Bildungsroman* and the Novels of Nicholasa Mohr and Magali García Ramis." *Centro* 2.7 (Winter 1989–1990): 56–73. Online.

———. "Survival, Growth, and Change in the Prose Fiction of Contemporary Puerto Rican Women Writers." *Images and Identities: The Puerto Rican in Two World Contexts*. Ed. Asela Rodríguez de Laguna. New Brunswick: Transaction Books, 1987. 76–88. Print.

Ferré, Rosario. *Maldito amor*. 3rd ed. Río Piedras: Huracán, 1994. Print.

———. "Mientras estoy escribiendo, soy: Rosario Ferré." *A viva voz: Entrevistas a escritores puertorriqueños*. Ed. Carmen Dolores Hernández. Bogotá: Editorial Norma, 2007. 92–117. Print.

———. *Sweet Diamond Dust and Other Stories*. Trans. Rosario Ferré. New York: Plume, 1996. Print.

Flores, Juan. *From Bomba to Hip Hop: Puerto Rican Culture and Latino Identity*. New York: Columbia UP, 2000. Print.

———. *The Diaspora Strikes Back:* Caribeño *Tales of Learning and Turning*. New York: Routledge, 2009. Print.

García Ramis, Magali. "El deber, la historia y la ficción." *Horizontes: Revista de la Universidad Católica de Puerto Rico* 47.93 (Oct. 2005): 75–87. Print.

———. *Felices días, Tío Sergio*. Río Piedras: Cultural, 1986. Print.

———. *Happy Days, Uncle Sergio*. Trans. Carmen C. Esteves. Fredonia, NY: White Pine P, 1995. Print.

Gelpí, Juan. *Literatura y paternalismo en Puerto Rico*. San Juan: Editorial UPR, 1993. Print.

Glasser, Ruth. "From 'Rich Port' to Bridgeport: Puerto Ricans in Connecticut." *The Puerto Rican Diaspora: Historical Perspectives*. Ed. Carmen Teresa Whalen and Víctor Vázquez-Hernández. Philadelphia: Temple UP, 2005. 174–199. Print.

Glick Schiller, Nina, Linda Basch, and Cristina Blanc-Szanton. "Transnationalism: A New Analytic Framework for Understanding Migration." *Towards a Transnational Perspective on Migration: Race, Class, Ethnicity, and Nationalism Reconsidered*. Ed. Nina Glick Schiller et al. New York: New York Academy of Sciences, 1998. 1–24. Print.

Goldstein, Alyosha. "The Attributes of Sovereignty: The Cold War, Colonialism, and Community Education in Puerto Rico." *Imagining Our Americas:*

Toward a Transnational Frame. Ed. Sandhya Shukla and Heidi Tinsman. Durham: Duke UP, 2007. 313–337. Print.

González, José Luis. "El país de cuatro pisos." *El país de cuatro pisos y otros ensayos*. Río Piedras: Huracán, 1989. 11–42. Print.

Grosfoguel, Ramón. *Colonial Subjects: Puerto Ricans in a Global Perspective*. Berkeley: U of California P, 2003. Print.

———. "The Divorce of Nationalist Discourses from the Puerto Rican People: A Sociohistorical Perspective." *Puerto Rican Jam: Essays on Culture and Politics*. Ed. Frances Negrón-Muntaner and Ramón Grosfoguel. Minneapolis: U of Minnesota P, 1997. 57–76. Print.

Grosfoguel, Ramón, et al. Introduction. *Puerto Rican Jam: Essays on Culture and Politics*. Ed. Frances Negrón-Muntaner and Ramón Grosfoguel. Minneapolis: U of Minnesota P, 1997. 1–36. Print.

Guerra, Lillian. *Popular Expression and National Identity in Puerto Rico: The Struggle for Self, Community, and Nation*. Gainesville: UP of Florida, 1998. Print.

Heredia, Juanita. *Transnational Latina Narratives in the Twenty-First Century*. New York: Palgrave Macmillan, 2009. Print.

Hernández, Carmen Dolores. "A Sense of Space, A Sense of Speech: A Conversation with Ana Lydia Vega." *Hopscotch: A Cultural Review* 2.2 (2000): 52–59. Online.

———. *A viva voz: Entrevistas a escritores puertorriqueños*. Bogotá: Editorial Norma, 2007. Print.

———. "On Language, Writing, and Exile: An Interview with Alba Ambert." *MultiCultural Review* 6.2 (1997): 34–60. Print.

———. *Puerto Rican Voices in English: Interviews with Writers*. Westport, CT: Praeger, 1997. Print.

Hernández Cruz, Víctor. Interview. *A Poet's Truth: Conversations with Latino/Latina Poets*. By Bruce Allen Dick. Tucson: U of Arizona P, 2003. 55–64. Print.

———. Interview with Marisel Moreno. University of Notre Dame, 18 April 2007. (Unpublished.)

Hintz, Suzanne. "Olga Nolla's *La segunda hija*: The Real, the Imaginary, the Physical, and the Emotional." *Monographic Review/Revista Monográfica* 12 (1996): 406–415. Print.

Hutcheon, Linda. "Historiographic Metafiction: Parody and the Intertextuality of History." *Intertextuality and Contemporary American Fiction*. Ed. Patrick O'Donell and Robert Con Davis. Baltimore: Johns Hopkins UP, 1989. 3–34. Print.

Instituto de Cultura Puertorriqueña. *Las mujeres en Puerto Rico*. Ed. Norma Valle Ferrer. San Juan, 2006. Print.

Irwin-Zarecka, Iwona. *Frames of Remembrance: The Dynamics of Collective Memory*. New Brunswick: Transaction Publishers, 1994. Print.

Japtok, Martin. *Growing Up Ethnic: Nationalism and the Bildungsroman in African American and Jewish American Fiction.* Iowa City: U of Iowa P, 2005. Print.

Jiménez-Muñoz, Gladys. "'So We Decided to Come and Ask You Ourselves': The 1928 U.S. Congressional Hearings on Women's Suffrage in Puerto Rico." *Puerto Rican Jam: Essays on Culture and Politics.* Ed. Frances Negrón-Muntaner and Ramón Grosfoguel. Minneapolis: U of Minnesota P, 1997.140–165. Print.

Jones, Heather. "Patriarchy." *Encyclopedia of Contemporary Literary Theory: Approaches, Scholars, Terms.* Comp. and ed. Irena Makaryk. Toronto: U of Toronto P, 1997. 605–606. Print.

Jusdanis, Gregory. *Belated Modernity and Aesthetic Culture: Inventing National Literature.* Minneapolis: U of Minnesota P, 1991. Print.

Kadir, Djelal. *Questing Fictions: Latin America's Family Romance.* Minneapolis: U of Minnesota P, 1986. Print. Theory and History of Literature 32.

Kanellos, Nicolás. *The Hispanic Literary Companion.* Detroit: Visible Ink, 1997. Print.

Kaser-Boyd, Nancy. "Battered Woman Syndrome: Clinical Features, Evaluation, and Expert Testimony." *Sexualized Violence against Women and Children: A Psychology and Law Perspective.* Ed. B. J. Cling. New York: Guilford Press, 1995. 41–70. Print.

Kevane, Bridget, and Juanita Heredia. *Latina Self-Portraits: Interviews with Contemporary Women Writers.* Albuquerque: U of New Mexico P, 2000. Print.

Laviera, Tato. "nuyorican." *AmeRícan.* Houston: Arte Público P, 1985. Print.

Lionnet, Françoise. "Geographies of Pain: Captive Bodies and Violent Acts in the Fictions of Gayl Jones, Bessie Head, and Myriam Warner-Vieyra." *The Politics of (M)Othering: Womanhood, Identity, and Resistance in African Literature.* Ed. Obioma Nnaemeka. London: Routledge, 1997. 205–227. Print.

Loomba, Ania. *Colonialism/Postcolonialism.* London: Routledge, 1998. Print.

Magnarelli, Sharon. *Home Is Where the (He)art Is: The Family Romance in Late Twentieth-Century Mexican and Argentine Theatre.* Lewisburg: Bucknell UP, 2008. Print.

Maldonado, A. W. *Luis Muñoz Marín: Puerto Rico s Democratic Revolution.* San Juan: Editorial UPR, 2006. Print.

Manrique Cabrera, Francisco. *Historia de la literatura puertorriqueña.* Río Piedras: Editorial Cultural, 1986. (1956) Print.

Marqués, René. "Carta." *Zona Carga y Descarga.* San Juan 3.8 (January 1975): 26. Print.

———. "El puertorriqueño dócil." *El puertorriqueña dócil y otros ensayos: 1953–1971.* Puerto Rico: Editorial Antillana, 1993. 151–215. Print.

———. *The Docile Puerto Rican.* Trans. Barbara Bockus Aponte. Philadelphia: Temple UP, 1976. Print.

Marsh Kennerley, Catherine. *Negociaciones culturales: Los intelectuales y el proyecto pedagógico del estado muñocista.* San Juan: Ediciones Callejón, 2009. Print.

Martínez-San Miguel, Yolanda. *Caribe Two Ways: Cultura de la migración en el Caribe insular hispánico.* San Juan: Ediciones Callejón, 2003. Print.

Matos Rodríguez, Felix. "New Currents in Puerto Rican History: Legacy, Continuity, and Challenges of the 'Nueva Historia.'" *Latin American Research Review* 32.3 (1997): 193–208. Print.

———. "Women's History in Puerto Rican Historiography: The Last Thirty Years." *Puerto Rican Women's History: New Perspectives.* Ed. Felix Matos Rodríguez and Linda C. Delgado. Armonk, NY: M. E. Sharpe, 1998. 9–37. Print.

McClintock, Anne. *Imperial Leather: Race, Gender and Sexuality in the Colonial Contest.* New York: Routledge, 1995. Print.

McCracken, Ellen. *New Latina Narrative: The Feminine Space of Postmodern Ethnicity.* Tucson: U of Arizona P, 1999. Print.

McKay, Nellie Y. "Race, Gender, and Cultural Context in Zora Neale Hurston's *Dust Tracks on a Road.*" *Life/Lines: Theorizing Women's Autobiography.* Ed. Bella Brodzki and Celeste Schenck. Ithaca: Cornell UP, 1988. 175–188. Print.

Mies, Maria, Veronika Bennholdt-Thomsen, and Claudia von Werlhof. *Women: The Last Colony.* London: Zed Books Ltd., 1988. Print.

Mohanty, Chandra Talpade. "Under Western Eyes: Feminist Scholarship and Colonial Discourses." *Dangerous Liaisons: Gender, Nation, and Postcolonial Perspectives.* Ed. Anne McClintock et al. Minneapolis: U of Minessota P, 1997. 255–277. Print.

Mohr, Nicholasa. "Aunt Rosana's Rocker." *Rituals of Survival: A Woman's Portfolio.* Houston: Arte Público P, 1985. Print.

———. "Puerto Rican Writers in the U.S., Puerto Rican Writers in Puerto Rico: A Separation beyond Language." *Breaking Boundaries: Latina Writing and Critical Readings.* Ed. Asunción Horno-Delgado et al. Amherst: U of Massachusetts P, 1989. 111–116. Print.

———. "The Journey toward a Common Ground: Struggle and Identity of Hispanics in the U.S.A." *The Americas Review* 18.1 (1990): 81–85. Print.

Morris, Nancy. *Puerto Rico: Culture, Politics, and Identity.* Westport, CT: Praeger, 1995. Print.

Negrón-Muntaner, Frances. "English Only Jamás but Spanish Only Cuidado: Language and Nationalism in Contemporary Puerto Rico." *Puerto Rican Jam: Essays on Culture and Politics.* Ed. Frances Negrón-Muntaner and Ramón Grosfoguel. Minneapolis: U of Minnesota P, 1997. 257–285. Print.

———. "Rosario's Tongue: Rosario Ferré and the Commodification of Island Literature." *Boricua Pop: Puerto Ricans and the Latinization of American Culture.* New York: New York UP, 2004. 179–205. Print.

Nolla, Olga. *La segunda hija*. San Juan: Editorial UPR, 1992. Print.

Oboler, Suzanne. *Ethnic Labels, Latino Lives: Identity and the Politics of (Re) Presentation in the United States*. Minneapolis: U of Minnesota P, 1995. Print.

Ortega, Eliana and Nancy Saporta Sternbach. "At the Threshold of the Unnamed: Latina Literary Discourse in the Eighties." *Breaking Boundaries: Latina Writing and Critical Readings*. Ed. Asunción Horno-Delgado et al. Amherst: U of Massachusetts P, 1989. 2–23. Print.

Ortíz Cofer, Judith. *Silent Dancing: A Partial Remembrance of a Puerto Rican Childhood*. Houston: Arte Público P, 1990. Print.

———. *Woman in Front of the Sun: On Becoming a Writer*. Athens: U of Georgia P, 2000. Print.

Ortíz Márquez, Maribel. "*Somos un solo pueblo* y la construcción de la migración en el Banco Popular." *Centro Journal* 16.1 (Spring 2004): 100–119. Online.

Ostolaza Bey, Margarita. *Política sexual en Puerto Rico*. Río Piedras: Edición Huracán, 1989. Print.

Pabón, Carlos. *Nación postmortem: Ensayos sobre los tiempos de insoportable ambigüedad*. San Juan: Callejón, 2003. Print.

Pedreira, Antonio S. *Insularismo*. Río Piedras: Edil, 1969. Print.

Pérez, Gina M. *The Near Northwest Side Story: Migration, Displacement, and Puerto Rican Families*. Berkeley: U of California P, 2004. Print.

Pérez Ortíz, Melanie. *Palabras encontradas: Antología personal de escritores puertorriqueños de los últimos 20 años (Conversaciones)*. San Juan: Callejón, 2008. Print.

Pérez Torres, Yazmín. "*Falsas crónicas del sur* y la escritura de la historia." *Romance Languages Annual* 6 (1994): 570–576. Print.

Pérez y González, María. *Puerto Ricans in the United States*. New Americans Series. Westport, CT: Greenwood P, 2000. Print.

Pola Z., María Jesús. "El sistema de derecho dominicano y la violencia de pareja." *Miradas desencadenantes: Los estudios de género en la República Dominicana al inicio del tercer milenio*. Santo Domingo: Centro de Estudios de Género, INTEC, 2005. 123–137. Print.

Pratt, Mary Louise. *Imperial Eyes: Travel Writing and Transculturation*. London: Routledge, 1992. Print.

Quiles Rodríguez, Edwin R. *La ciudad de los balcones*. San Juan: Editorial UPR, 2009. Print.

———. *San Juan tras la fachada: Una mirada desde sus espacios ocultos (1508–1900)*. San Juan: Editorial Instituto de Cultura Puertorriqueña, 2003. Print.

Quintana, Alvina. *Reading U.S. Latina Writers: Remapping American Literature*. New York: Palgrave Macmillan, 2003. Print.

Quintero Rivera, Ángel. *Conflictos de clase y política en Puerto Rico*. Río Piedras: Huracán, 1986 (1977). Print.

————. *Ponce: La Capital Alterna.* Ponce: Centro de Investigaciones Sociales de la U de PR, 2003. Print.

Ramírez, Rafael L. *What It Means to Be a Man: Reflections on Puerto Rican Masculinity.* Trans. Rosa E. Casper. New Brunswick: Rutgers UP, 1999. Print.

Ramos Rosado, Marie. *La mujer negra en la literatura puertorriqueña: Cuentística de los setenta.* San Juan: Cultural, 1999. Print.

Ríos Ávila, Rubén. *La raza cómica: Del sujeto en Puerto Rico.* San Juan: Callejón, 2002. Print.

Rivera, Carmen S. *Kissing the Mango Tree: Puerto Rican Women Rewriting American Literature.* Houston: Arte Público P, 2002. Print.

Rivera, Jenny. "Puerto Rico's Domestic Violence Prevention and Intervention Law: The Limitations of Legislative Responses." *Global Critical Race Feminism: An International Reader.* Ed. Adrien Katherine Wing. New York: New York UP, 2000. 347–361. Print.

Rivera, Raquel. *New York Ricans from the Hip Hop Zone.* New York: Palgrave, 2003. Print.

————. "Rapping Two Versions of the Same Requiem." *Puerto Rican Jam: Essays on Culture and Politics.* Ed. Frances Negrón-Muntaner and Ramón Grosfoguel. Minneapolis: U of Minnesota P, 1997. 243–256. Print.

————. *Reggaeton.* Durham: Duke UP, 2009. Print.

Rivera-Bonilla, Ivelisse. "Divided City: The Proliferation of Gated Communities in San Juan." Ph.D. diss., University of Califormia, Santa Cruz, 2003. Online.

Rivero, Yeidy M. *Tuning Out Blackness: Race and Nation in the History of Puerto Rican Television.* Durham: Duke UP, 2005. Print.

Rogers, Mary F. *Novels, Novelists, and Readers: Toward a Phenomenological Sociology of Literature.* Albany: State University of New York P, 1991. Print.

Rúa, Mérida. "*Colao* Subjectivities: PortoMex and MexiRican Perspectives on Language and Identity." *CENTRO Journal* 13.2 (Fall 2011): 116–133. Online.

Ruíz, Vicki L. Introduction. *Memories and Migrations: Mapping Boricua and Chicana Histories.* Ed. Vicki L. Ruíz and John R. Chávez. Urbana: U of Illinois P, 2008. 1–12. Print.

Sánchez González, Lisa. *Boricua Literature: A Literary History of the Puerto Rican Diaspora.* New York: New York UP, 2001. Print.

Sánchez Korrol, Virginia. *From Colonia to Community: The History of Puerto Ricans in New York City.* Berkeley: U of California P, 1994. (1983) Print.

————. "The Star in My Compass: Claiming Intellectual Space in the American Landscape." *Memories and Migrations: Mapping Boricua and Chicana Histories.* Ed. Vicki L. Ruíz and John R. Chávez. Urbana: U of Illinois P, 2008. 196–214. Print.

Santiago-Díaz, Eleuterio. *Escritura afropuertorriqueña y modernidad.* Pittsburgh: Instituto Internacional de Literatura Iberoamericana, 2007. Print.

Santiago, Esmeralda. *When I Was Puerto Rican*. Reading, MA: Addison-Wesley, 1993. Print.

Scarano, Francisco. "Inmigración y estructura de clases: Los hacendados de Ponce, 1815–1845." *Inmigración y clases sociales en el Puerto Rico del siglo XIX*. Ed. Francisco Scarano. Río Piedras: Huracán, 1989. 21–66. Print.

Segura Munguía, Santiago. *Diccionario etimológico Latino-Español*. Madrid: Ediciones Generales Anaya, 1985. Print.

Solá, María. "René Marqués ¿escritor misógino?" *Sin Nombre* 10.3 (Octubre–Noviembre 1979): 83–97. Print.

Sommer, Doris. *Foundational Fictions: The National Romances of Latin America*. Berkeley: U of California P, 1993. Print.

Stanchich, Maritza. "Towards a Post-Nuyorican Literature." *Sargasso* 2 (2005–2006): 113–124. Print.

Suárez Carrasquillo, Carlos. "City Marketing and Gated Communities: A Case Study of Guaynabo, Puerto Rico." (2009). Open Access Dissertations. Paper 139. http://scholarworks.umass.edu/open_access_dissertations/139.

———. "Women Workers and Capitalist Scripts: Ideologies of Domination, Common Interests, and the Politics of Solidarity." *Feminist Genealogies, Colonial Legacies, Democratic Futures*. Ed. M. Jacqui Alexander and Chandra Talpade Mohanty. New York: Routledge, 1997. 3–29. Print.

Torrecilla, Arturo. *El espectro posmoderno: Ecología, neoproletario, intelligentsia*. San Juan: Publicaciones Puertorriqueñas, 1995. Print.

Torres, Arlene. "La gran familia puertorriqueña 'ej prieta de beldá' (The Great Puerto Rican Family Is Really Really Black)." *Blackness in Latin America and the Caribbean: Social Dynamics and Cultural Transformations*. Vol 2. Ed. Arlene Torres and Norman E. Whitten Jr. Bloomington: Indiana UP, 1998. 285–306. Print.

Torres, Víctor Federico. *Narradores puertorriqueños del 70: Guía bibliográfica*. San Juan: Plaza Mayor, 2001. Print.

———. *Diccionario de autores puertorriqueños contemporáneos*. San Juan: Plaza Mayor, 2009. Print.

Torres-Padilla, José L. "When 'I' Became Ethnic: Ethnogenesis and Three Early Puerto Rican Diaspora Writers." *Writing Off the Hyphen: New Perspectives on the Literature of the Puerto Rican Diaspora*. Ed. José L. Torres-Padilla and Carmen Haydeé Rivera. Seattle: U of Washington P, 2008. 81–104. Print.

Torres-Padilla, José L., and Carmen Haydée Rivera. "The Literature of the Puerto Rican Diaspora and Its Critical Practice." Introduction. *Writing Off the Hyphen: New Perspectives on the Literature of the Puerto Rican Diaspora*. Ed. José L. Torres-Padilla and Carmen Haydée Rivera. Seattle: U of Washington P, 2008. 1–28. Print.

Vega, Ana Lydia. *El baúl de Miss Florence: Fragmentos para un novelón romántico. Falsas crónicas del sur*. San Juan: Editorial UPR, 1991. Print.

———. "De bípeda desplumada a Escritora Puertorriqueña." *Esperando a Loló y otros delirios generacionales.* San Juan: Editorial UPR, 1994. 91–100. Print.

———. *Miss Florence's Trunk.* Trans. Andrew Hurley. *True and False Romances.* London: Serpent's Tail, 1994. 163–261. Print.

———. "Nosotros los historicidas." *Esperando a Loló y otros delirios generacionales.* San Juan: Editorial UPR, 1994. 101–111. Print.

Vélez Camacho, Myrna. *Grupos feministas en Puerto Rico: Luchas y logros en busca de la equidad del género (1971 2006).* Hato Rey, Puerto Rico: Publicaciones Puertorriqueñas, 2008. Print.

Vélez-Ibáñez, Carlos, and Anna Sampaio. "Processes, New Prospects, and Approaches" (introd.). *Transnational Latina/o Communities: Politics, Processes, and Cultures.* Ed. Carlos Vélez-Ibáñez and Anna Sampaio. Lanham, MD: Rowman & Littlefield, 2002. 1–37. Print.

Vivoni, Francisco. "Postmodernidad, globalización e identidad nacional en P.R." *Globalización, nación, postmodernidad.* Ed. Luis Felipe Díaz and Marc Zimmerman. San Juan: Ediciones LACASA, 2001. 71–105. Print.

Whalen, Carmen Teresa. "Colonialism, Citizenship, and the Making of the Puerto Rican Diaspora: An Introduction." *The Puerto Rican Diaspora: Historical Perspectives.* Ed. Carmen Teresa Whalen and Víctor Vázquez-Hernández. Philadelphia: Temple UP, 2005. 1–42. Print.

———. "Labor Migrants or Submissive Wives: Competing Narratives of Puerto Rican Women in the Post–World War II Era." *Puerto Rican Women's History: New Perspectives.* Ed. Felix Matos Rodríguez and Linda C. Delgado. Armonk, NY: M. E. Sharpe, 1998. 206–226. Print.

Index

Acosta-Belén, Edna, 18, 23, 27, 135, 137, 150–151, 154, 181n7, 204n7, 207n25. See also *Puerto Ricans in the United States* (Acosta-Belén and Santiago)

Afra-jíbara experience, 121–122

Afro–Puerto Ricans (*afropuertorriqueños*), 10, 53, 190–191n5

afuera (outside the island), 3

Albizu Campos, Pedro, 16, 35–36

Alexander, M. Jacqui, 6, 130, 131, 136–137, 155, 207n26

Ambert, Alba: context of writing, 24; feminist project of, 166–167; *la gran familia* metaphor of, 4; self-identification of, 73; work: *A Perfect Silence*, 101, 137, 160–167, 203n63

Americanization: components highlighted in *Felices días*, 115–116; education as means of, 18, 30, 31; *la gran familia* deployed against, 29–31, 39–43; in *Maldito amor*, 66–67; paternalist rhetoric against, 33–35; Spanish language as resistance to, 48, 188–189n68; violence of, 122–124. *See also* colonialism; English language; U.S.–Puerto Rican colonial relations

Anderson, Benedict, 57, 106

Aparicio, Frances, 25, 26, 48, 50, 82, 117, 180n8, 182n16, 183n27, 193n30

autobiography, 99–104, 117, 197–198n18. *See also* bildungsroman

Ave/Eva paradigm. *See* virgin/whore trope

Ayala, César. See *Puerto Rico in the American Century* (Ayala and Bernabé)

Azize-Vargas, Yamila, 18

el balcón (the front porch or balcony) symbol, 106–107, 199n29

Barradas, Efraín, 27, 43, 181n5, 189n69, 204n8

barrios and *arrabales* (slums), 23, 37, 126–129, 203n63

Belaval, Emilio S., 32, 33–35, 51, 54–55

Belpré, Pura, 161

Bernabé, Rafael. See *Puerto Rico in the American Century* (Ayala and Bernabé)

bildungsroman (coming-of-age narrative): *Felices días* as urban version of, 105–116; of island and diaspora, compared, 101–104; *La segunda hija* as, 142; *When I Was Puerto Rican* as rural version of, 118–128. *See also* autobiography

blackness, 19, 32, 62–65, 82–83, 193n30

blacks: incorporated into "nation," 30–31, 185n37; migration to island, 56–58; self-censorship of, 53, 190–191n5

Blanco, Tomás, 32–33, 53–55

blanqueamiento, desire for, 52–53, 54, 63, 64. *See also* whiteness

Bose, Christine, 23, 137, 207n25

boundaries, paradox of, 106–107. See also *frontera intranacional*

Bourdieu, Pierre, 130–133, 149, 153, 156, 157, 158, 207n27, 208n31

Burgos, Julia de, 181n9

Buscaglia, José, 1–2, 179n1

campesina, 121–122. See also *jíbaro*; rural communities

Capetillo, Luisa, 18, 161

Caribbean region, contact zones in, 11,
56–58, 200n37
Casa de España (Puerto Rico), 107–108,
113, 200n34
la casa/house: cultural meanings of, 87–
89; demythification of, 152; displaced
version of, 125–129; *la gran familia*
parallel to, 111–113; resignification of,
74–79; as totalizing metaphor, 105–108
la casa patriarcal: Felices días and
fall of, 108–116; *insularismo* of, 79;
Maldito amor as challenge to, 61–67;
matriarchal home substituted for,
88–89; of nation, 59–60. *See also* father
figure; hacienda system; patriarchy
Chicanos, as colonized group, 38, 180.
See also U.S. Latinos/as
child abuse, 160–167
citizenship status, 31, 37–38
civil rights movement, 19–20, 57–58,
117, 151, 207n25. *See also* social justice
movements
colonialism: concept of, 179n4; conditions
for patriarchal violence in, 134–135;
contact zones in, 10–11; definition/
image of family imposed in, 180n9;
heteropatriarchal family fostered
in, 131–135, 203n2; internal, 7,
37–38, 180n8, 187n56; literary canon
formation under, 16–17; masculine
domination strengthened under,
207n26; monument to *la familia* and
resistance to, 1–2, 179n1; woman and
colony analogy under, 135–136, 203n3.
See also Americanization; U.S.–Puerto
Rican colonial relations
coloniality of power concept, 27, 184n29
contact zones concept, 10–11. *See also*
literary contact zones
Coss, Luis Fernando, 45
criollo elite, 29–32, 65–67

Dávila, Arlene, 47, 72, 121
decolonization, 135–139, 150–152
diaspora community: alternative family
models of, 9; depiction of difficulties
of, 128; as doubly marginalized,
11, 49–50, 166; *la gran familia*
metaphor deployed against, 52; insular
stereotypes of, 3, 47–48, 98, 114,
122–123; internal colonialism felt

by, 7; island's place in imaginary of,
119; island writer's depiction of, 142;
mending memory by narrating story
of, 117–129; national imaginary's
exclusion of, 46–48; "nation" redefined
to include, 24, 27–28; official rhetoric
on, 41–42; popular music of, 25;
postmodernos (intellectuals) in, 10,
27, 43–45; racialization of, 57–58;
self-identification of, 73. *See also* island
community; migrants and migration;
returnees
diaspora literature: favored genres of,
101; further questions about, 174–176;
insular acceptance of music and painting
but not, 25; island-centered perspective
in, 74; migration explored in, 84–86;
Puerto Rican past rescued in, 106–108,
110–116; self-life-writing mode of,
98–99; virgin/whore trope in, 23
diaspora women writers: autobiography's
centrality for, 194n41; decolonization
and, 135, 150–152; differences between
first vs. later generations of, 202n57;
on female agency, sexuality, and desire,
153–160; folklore and national history
utilized by, 79–80, 195n45; *la gran
familia* challenged by, 72–73, 119–121;
myth of American Dream reinforced
by, 161; new awareness as historical
subjects, 117; prejudice experienced
in Puerto Rico by (*see* returnees); as
recuperating women's history, 23;
scholarship's focus on 1990s for, 6;
social status of, 138–139; timing of high
point for, 24; as writing against the
void, 97–104. *See also* Ambert, Alba;
Mohr, Nicholasa; Ortíz Cofer, Judith;
Santiago, Esmeralda
Díaz Quiñones, Arcadio, 27, 33, 90
División de Educación de la
Comunidad (DIVEDCO): challenge
to ideal underlying, 123–124; *círculo
democrático* of, 118, 123, 127, 202n59;
family/nation rhetoric of, 9–10; *la gran
familia* deployed in booklet series of,
39–42, 169–170, 171–172, 173; slums
as outside of focus, 127–128. *See also*
Marqués, René
domestic abuse, 160–167, 208n32. *See
also* violence

Eduardo González, *Cuba and the Fall: Christian Text and Queer Narrative in the Fiction of José Lezama Lima and Reinaldo Arenas*

Jeff Karem, *The Purloined Islands: Caribbean-U.S. Crosscurrents in Literature and Culture, 1880–1959*

Faith Smith, *Sex and the Citizen: Interrogating the Caribbean*

Mark Anderson, *Disaster Writing: The Cultural Politics of Catastrophe in Latin America*

Raphael Dalleo, *Caribbean Literature and the Public Sphere: From the Plantation to the Postcolonial*

Maite Conde, *Consuming Visions: Cinema, Writing, and Modernity in Rio de Janeiro*

Monika Kaup, *Neobaroque in the Americas: Alternative Modernities in Literature, Visual Art, and Film*

Marisel C. Moreno, *Family Matters: Puerto Rican Women Authors on the Island and the Mainland*